SADDAM'S BOMBMAKER

THE TERRIFYING INSIDE STORY OF THE IRAQI
NUCLEAR AND BIOLOGICAL WEAPONS AGENDA

KHIDHIR HAMZA

with Jeff Stein

A LISA DREW BOOK

SCRIBNER
New York   London   Toronto   Sydney   Singapore

SCRIBNER
1230 Avenue of the Americas
New York, NY 10020

SCRIBNER and design are trademarks of Macmillan Library Reference USA, Inc.,
used under license by Simon & Schuster, the publisher of this work.

DESIGNED BY ERICH HOBBING

Set in Sabon

Manufactured in the United States of America

1   3   5   7   9   10   8   6   4   2

Library of Congress Cataloging-in-Publication Data

Hamza, Khidr'Abd al-'Abbas.
Saddam's bombmaker: the terrifying inside story of the Iraqi nuclear
and biological weapons agenda/Khidhir Hamza with Jeff Stein.
p. cm.
"A Lisa Drew book."
Includes index.
(alk. paper)
1. Nuclear weapons—Iraq. 2. Iraq—Military policy.
3. òamzah, Khiòr °'bd al-°'bbås. 4. Hussein, Saddam, 1937– .
5. Persian Gulf War, 1991. 6. Nuclear arms control—Iraq.
7. United Nations. Special Commission on Iraq. I. Stein, Jeff. II. Title.

UA 853.I72 H35 2000
355.02'1 7'09567—dc21   00-055609

ISBN 0-684-87386-9

I dedicate this book
to the suffering Iraqi people,
who have not had a decent break
for eight hundred years.

CONTENTS

SADDAM'S
BOMBMAKER

Don't tell me about the law. The law is anything I write on a scrap of paper.

SADDAM HUSSEIN

INTRODUCTION

I've been wanting to write this story since the day I fled Iraq to warn the West about Saddam Hussein's nuclear bomb. It's taken me five years and a lifetime's worth of narrow escapes. Now, finally, I am putting the words on paper.

I am lucky to be alive. No one who has worked closely with Saddam has lived to tell the whole inside story—not just of his clandestine programs to build nuclear, chemical, and biological weapons, but of the horrible man himself and his terrifying palace intrigues.

I was there. From 1972, shortly after the regime forced me to return from America, where I had gotten my degrees in theoretical nuclear physics, until my escape in 1994, I worked to build Saddam's bomb. As this frightening story will show, we came all too close to succeeding—and *he may well yet*. It wasn't the West who stopped him, moreover, it was Saddam's own mistakes. His obsession with acquiring weapons of mass destruction marks him as a man who will accept nothing less than total domination of the Arab world, which he thinks is rightfully his.

This is the first inside look at Iraq's weapons programs from their inception in the early 1970s. Hopefully, it will shed new light on Saddam's personal demons and his singularly ruthless style of governing.

I have tried to write this book for both general readers and experts. Through the telling of my own personal story, I hope all readers will have a better understanding of the terrors of living inside a totalitarian regime, greater sympathy for the ordinary Iraqis who are forced to endure it, and a renewed appreciation for simple freedoms. Science-minded readers, I hope, will be fascinated by my recounting of how we made the bomb and the role of Iraq's Atomic Energy Commission in the biological weapons program. (See Appendix.)

For those interested in, or responsible for, U.S. policy toward Iraq, I hope this book will generate better alternatives for dealing with Saddam than have been used to date. The lesson in this book is that U.N. inspectors should pay as much attention to the human factor as they do to finding and destroying hidden weapons. Behind every closed door in Baghdad is a scientist or official who would like to leave. Saddam can get everything he needs to rejuvenate his chemical, biological, and nuclear weapons—except the people who design them. Help them get out, and Saddam's days as a global threat will expire.

This book owes its existence to my literary agent, Gail Ross. She nurtured it through three false starts until it gelled in a form that made it acceptable to publishers. We were thrilled, of course, that it found a home at Scribner's with Lisa Drew, whose constant enthusiasm and close ministrations carried us through a book's inevitably difficult stages. We also want to thank her assistant, Jake Klisivitch, whose cheerful attention to the progress of pages kept us on track.

But it was Washington writer Jeff Stein who breathed new life into this project by seeing the human drama at the core of my story. In his hands, what might have been a rather technical accounting of my role in the regime and how I built the bomb became an Everyman's story of the will to survive.

Several hands guide a book successfully from raw idea to finished manuscript, but in particular we want to thank Louis Toscano, a former editor for United Press International, whose special insights contributed to every page. Lorraine Gray, the documentary filmmaker, also provided valuable tips on narrative flow and character. The Fund for Constitutional Government in Washington, D.C., gave timely, early support for this project. Susan Fox cheered on this project when it was only an idea, and her support and sacrifice during that crucial early stage are fully appreciated.

Many thanks are also due to David Albright, president of the Institute for Science and International Security. A former inspector himself, David provided guidance and support in my first years here, introduced me to the U.S. nonproliferation community, and helped me understand the problems the arms inspectors faced in Iraq.

But the greatest thanks of all must go to my family. The steely nerves and steadfast loyalty of my eldest son, Firas, is the main reason we are all alive today. To my younger boys, Sami and Zayd, goes the thanks of a proud father for enduring such hardship.

But it is my wife, Souham, who above all deserves praise. Her support during the writing of this book was crucial. She suffered through multiple proposal drafts and more than a year of ups and downs. I thank her from the deepest place in my heart.

KHIDHIR HAMZA
WASHINGTON, D.C.
MARCH 2000

___

CHAPTER ONE

ESCAPE

The moon was fading from the purple sky over Baghdad, a sign that the time had finally come. This was the day in August 1994 that I was leaving my family, slipping out of the country over the mountains in the north, and heading for the United States, where I could tell the West about Iraq's nuclear bomb.

My wife, Souham, was weeping softly in the kitchen as she cooked breakfast. For weeks she had kept up a brave front, assuring me I was doing the right thing. But now that the moment had come, I knew what she was thinking: If my plan failed, she faced a future alone, a terrifying prospect for any woman in Iraq, but especially for one who had grown up an orphan. I struggled to control my guilt about leaving her behind, even temporarily.

We both knew, however, that we were out of options. Emigration was out of the question. For the last decade, no senior official had been permitted to leave. Blacklists at the borders had all of our names. Iraqi Airways had been grounded since the invasion of Kuwait in 1990. Escaping together through the underground was next to impossible as well. A family racing toward the Kurdish frontier was sure to attract the suspicions of the guards at the roadblocks along the way.

As I dressed, I went through a mental checklist, wondering what I might have overlooked. I checked my pockets again for incriminating documents. Even a slip of paper could give me away. And if I were found out, I would quickly disappear into the dungeons, followed by my wife and three sons, all of us facing such inventive tortures that we would beg for our deaths.

17

The terror of Saddam's regime knew no bounds. Two colleagues had been imprisoned for simply expressing doubts about the nuclear program. One was hung daily by his thumbs and beaten every day for ten years. The other, in a way, fared worse. He also was thrown into the dungeon and beaten, then other people were brought to his cell to be tortured in front of him.

Those who escaped were tracked down. Just the year before, Muayed Naji, an employee at our Atomic Energy Commission, managed to get to Jordan. After visiting the American embassy, he was gunned down on the street by two Iraqi operatives.

As I packed, my hands were clammy and my mouth went dry. Certainly Saddam would design a special regimen of suffering for me if I were caught trying to flee. I was his nuclear bombmaker. I held secrets no one outside Iraq, and only a handful of people inside the country, could know. I could tell the world about our secret work developing the device, our hidden research facilities, the technical equipment we obtained from Germany and other countries, about the twelve thousand nuclear workers we had successfully hidden by scattering them around the country. Not even the aggressive U.N. inspectors, now crawling all over Baghdad, knew what we still had or how dangerous the situation was. None of them knew that Saddam had been within a few months of completing the bomb when he invaded Kuwait. None knew of Saddam's crash program to bypass a test and drop one on the Israelis if his survival were threatened—no matter that it guaranteed Iraq's own incineration. Saddam couldn't care less for anybody else. He planned to take all of us down with him.

This was the story I had to tell.

I finished dressing and made my way downstairs to the kitchen, where the Iraqi army officer who had arranged my escape was finishing breakfast. Adnan, in his thirties, was a Kurd, one of the famously independent people of the mountainous north, where smuggling was a way of life. With his sandy hair and blue eyes, however, he wouldn't have looked out of place in a Left Bank cafe. As a Kurd, of course, his loathing for Saddam was almost genetically wired, but somehow he'd managed to keep his true allegiances under wraps while successfully operating an underground railway. Today I was his cargo to the frontier.

Sitting at the table was my friend Ali, who'd suffered the murders of both his father and a brother by the regime. For months, security agents had been harassing him for information on the whereabouts of another brother, who had gone underground and joined the Iraqi opposition in the north. In exchange for my paying his way, Ali would serve as my guide among the treacherous Iraqi exiles.

I looked around the kitchen. My eldest son, Firas, twenty-two, barely a man, was fighting off the jitters, smoking incessantly. His face was deathly pale. From the beginning, he had been a key part of the escape plan. He had contacted a go-between to get me out, and before that helped me concoct a cover story to explain my absence from the city: With windfall profits I'd earned from Baghdad's stock market, I was starting a small business on the side in my hometown.

I'd actually earned a reputation as a savvy trader among the regime's senior officials. Some of the stocks I'd bought multiplied ten and twenty times within months. There wasn't any mystery about making a killing: I started with inside information, then invested in companies that imported food and essential goods like auto parts, figuring that Saddam would never relinquish his weapons of mass destruction, that confrontations with U.N. inspectors would continue, and so would the sanctions. The price of essential goods would stay high, along with the profits of the importers whose stock I bought. To me it was only common sense, but most Iraqis shied away from such investments, expecting that sanctions would be removed soon and the bottom would drop out of the import market. I made a small fortune—and, as it turned out, manufactured a credible cover story along the way.

Now Firas would take on his greatest responsibility, accompanying me partway to the north to make sure I was safely handed off to the next smuggler. When I saw him zip shut his bag and stand up, I knew he was ready.

We ran through the arrangements with my wife one last time. I would carry half of a torn Iraqi dinar note with me. The other half of the bill would remain with Firas. There would be a code word written on his half, known only by the two of us. Only when I arrived safely across the border would I write the matching code word on my half and hand it to the smuggler to take back. When my son got that, he would know I had landed all right.

Finally, at four A.M., there was nothing left to be done. I picked up my bags, set them by the door, turned and embraced my wife. As I held her in my arms, I could feel her tears flooding my cheek.

"Now, please, don't worry," I whispered.

She looked at me through puffy, reddened eyes and nodded uncertainly.

"Next year in Washington," I joked feebly. "We made a good plan."

And then it was time to go. As I walked down to the car, I could hear my thirteen-year-old boy Zayd crying just inside the door. "Is Daddy really going away?" he said.

I couldn't turn around.

Outside, in the tropical heat, the street was deathly quiet. On the eastern horizon, a thin red line hinted at the baking desert ahead. If we had left earlier the ride would have been more comfortable, but traveling at night also invited closer inspection at the roadblocks. The night guards are more wary, tending to inspect cars more closely, looking for army deserters or insurgents.

But first we had to get out of my neighborhood safely. We scanned the quiet street. No patrols. A sentry box was just out of sight, at the corner of the main boulevard, near the houses of Saddam and the deputy prime minister. We piled into the car, drove quietly in the opposite direction, and with a few turns through the palm-laced streets, we were out of the neighborhood. By the time the sun splintered over the horizon, we were clearing the outskirts of Baghdad, safely on the road, we hoped, to freedom.

Behind us was the most prominent symbol of Saddam's long and hideous rule: two huge, cast-iron forearms rising from the ground with crossed swords in their hands. Beneath them, in ghastly piles, were the helmets of thousands of Iranian soldiers killed in the Iran-Iraq war. As we drove off, the tips of the swords were visible above the rooftops, reminding us all of the death and destruction of so many years.

It never should have happened. I was happily becoming an American. Then the order came: Come back to Iraq, or else.

I'd enjoyed the dream of many Iraqi students in the 1960s by coming to America for college, in this case a master's degree at MIT, followed by a Ph.D. in theoretical nuclear physics at Florida State University (which had just acquired an accelerator and was attracting a lot of students). In those halcyon years before Saddam came to power, Iraq and the United States were on fairly friendly terms. I was teaching at a small college in Georgia, perfectly acclimated to the land of hamburgers and wide highways, weekend dates and barbecues.

Then the roof fell in. Baghdad wanted something back for the scholarship money it had advanced. They wanted it in trade, by my taking a post at Atomic Energy (AE), and they hinted none too lightly that my father, who had cosigned the loan, would be held responsible until I came back.

When I returned in 1970, I was resigned to my predicament. I actually began bubbling with ideas and enthusiasm for the peaceful development of nuclear energy. In 1971, I was made chairman of the physics department at Atomic Energy, leapfrogging over many more senior colleagues. Later, I was put in charge of the computer committee, and purchased Iraq's first mainframe from IBM. I also established a popular newsletter about the AEC, and then took charge of all its reports and publications. I was also on the board of the Iraqi Physics and Math Society, participating in panels on the introduction of modern math in the school curricula, and teaching graduate courses at a couple of universities. All in all, much to my surprise, I was having fun, making a good living, and along the way becoming perhaps Iraq's best-known scientist.

Then they tightened the vise. Two senior appointees of Saddam, then Iraq's fast-rising vice president, came to me with his instructions to lay the groundwork for an atomic bomb. Even though they framed their request in the most innocuous terms, my shock must have registered.

"We understand it can't be done overnight," one said soothingly. "In fact, we don't have any completion date for an actual bomb in mind. We just want you to begin laying down the scientific and technological foundation for a project sometime in the future."

The two officials offered other reasons to go forward with the program. First, Saddam wanted it. That alone was a sufficient reason to end the conversation right there. But the officials also warned that without Saddam's backing, funds for all atomic energy programs would dry up, from research to nuclear medicine. I had to play along, they said, to keep the money flowing. Besides, they reassured me, making an atomic bomb would take twenty, thirty years. By the time we had a testable device, the entire situation could have changed. Who could predict that Saddam would still be around?

So we began. We dragged our feet from day one, taking more than a month alone just to craft our proposal. It promised only the creation of an infrastructure for a broad atomic energy program that could not conceivably develop a bomb for at least twenty years.

But we had underestimated Saddam. Armed with our blueprint, he quickly took over the atomic program, making himself chairman and replacing the top officials. Once in control, he stepped back and began pouring money into the effort.

For a time, however, it still didn't seem too bad. The only unsettling facet of his control was the introduction of heavy security at AE, and even then he went to great lengths to rationalize it to us. After all the money he had poured into the program, we were in a forgiving mood.

But after Saddam became president in 1979, things changed. No longer satisfied with our leisurely pace, he began demanding concrete results. It was only later that we learned the reason: Saddam was planning to attack Iran, a country with four times the population of Iraq. If things went badly, he wanted the ultimate equalizer, a bomb that could vaporize an invading army or obliterate Teheran. And in the larger picture, he yearned for the same respect Israel got from its nuclear bombs.

Saddam reacted poorly to delay. Some of my colleagues were sent to jail to refresh their enthusiasm for the bomb. I was spared, probably because there was no one to replace me as head of the nuclear fuel division, where we planned to manufacture plutonium. But I nearly felt the ax. When I saw problems in our contract for the French-supplied reactor and refused to sign off on it, Saddam seethed with rage. Interpreting my action as an attempt to distance myself from responsibility, he immediately promoted to the position of personal adviser two scientists who did approve the contract.

They would soon enough regret it. In December 1979, the bespectacled Dr. Hussein al-Shahristani, an expert in neutron activation, made the mistake of challenging the bomb program to Saddam's face. He was immediately jailed and savagely tortured.

Saddam's other science adviser, a willowy genius named Jaffar Dhia Jaffar, beseeched the president to relent on his gifted colleague. He, too, was arrested. To give him a taste of what could come, Jaffar was strapped to a dungeon wall and forced to watch as other men were tortured. He recanted and returned to work.

I became his assistant. Needless to say, I was frightened. And my fear grew when Saddam named me his personal nuclear adviser and ordered me to design and build the bomb—and fast. What an ironic reward, I often thought, for someone who had balked at dissecting a laboratory frog, who had shied away from hunting trips with my father.

Now I knew I had to get out. My application for a routine exit visa for my family was turned down, and for a time the security services placed me under tight surveillance. Eventually, I convinced the regime I was loyal, but when the intense scrutiny eased I began to think about an escape.

In 1990, I persuaded Saddam's erratic son-in-law Hussein Kamel to let me teach again and back off from the program into a role as a consultant. With Desert Storm looming, the crash program to build the bomb had been shelved, so I had little reason to fear the dungeons. I was still, moreover, the regime's ace in the hole. I knew how far the program had progressed. I knew where all the secret components of the program were. The calamity in Kuwait had forced the bomb program underground, but it was still creeping forward. Perhaps Saddam thought he could wait things out and then order me back into the program. Or maybe he didn't have any better ideas. But it was time for me to run.

We were headed north, the first step in a journey to freedom for those who couldn't get permission to travel—virtually anyone of consequence. Under the so-called Operation Provide Comfort, the Allies had established a protected zone in the Kurdish area of northern Iraq, flying constant air patrols to ward off Saddam's helicopters and troops. Meanwhile, exile opposition groups, under the umbrella of the Iraqi National Congress, took advantage of the situation to establish a frontline headquarters. It was headed by Dr. Ahmad al-Chalabi, whom I'd known when we were students at MIT in the 1960s. I was counting on al-Chalabi remembering me.

The road to Mosul, capital of the Arabic north, was dusty and crumbling. For such a major thruway to be in such disrepair was a sign of the regime's twisted priorities. With billions spent on weapons, there was no money to maintain such basic services as roads. Nor were there any trees along the blistering hot highway: Most of them had been chopped down to eliminate the chance of an ambush on Saddam's motorcade. In 1982, at Dujail, fifty miles north of Baghdad, gunmen were foolish enough to fire on Saddam and miss. The town was subsequently bulldozed, every male executed, and every woman and child thrown in jail.

All things considered, we were in a pretty jovial mood as we sped up the highway. Adnan was telling tall tales about Saddam and his family, most of which I knew were untrue. But I let him ramble, not wanting to provoke a man who held my life in his hands. Conversely, I thought, he was watching me for any hint that I was losing my nerve. I knew he'd drop me in a second if I jeopardized his safety.

It had been difficult enough to convince Adnan of my bona fides. Since Firas had introduced us three months earlier, Adnan had been studying me carefully, coming to our house for food and drink, talking about everything under the sun without committing himself to an escape, much less a departure date. He could not comprehend why a man of my position and affluence would want to leave Iraq. The people he took out were usually hardship cases, people in imminent danger or serious distress. A comfortable senior official like me spelled trouble. What finally tipped the scales in my favor was my relationship with Ali. Adnan knew him well and our close friendship ultimately convinced Adnan to help me.

I was heartened by Adnan's extraordinary caution. Betrayal by close friends and colleagues was routine in Iraq. People sometimes turned in friends out of fear they were being tested. Everyone knew the story of Amal al-Mudarris, probably the best-known personality on Baghdad radio, a woman who had covered the news in an especially clear and cultured voice that endeared her to the educated elite. Her insistence on presenting the news objectively won her a wide following, especially among those of us who were aware of the depth of Saddam's lies and repression.

Her demise was instructive. Saddam's wife, Sajida, began calling

her with complaints that she wasn't covering newsworthy events—
mostly those extolling her husband, of course. The calls became
more frequent, annoying, even crude. One day al-Mudarris, talking
with some longtime friends at the station, remarked that Sajida was
unfit to be Iraq's first lady. One of her colleagues slipped away from
the table and called her husband at the Ministry of Information. A
few minutes later the station was surrounded, and security officers
hauled al-Mudarris away. After a round of torture, she confessed to
what she had said and was sentenced to death. After she was
hanged, her tongue was cut out and delivered to her family.

Even a wife could not be trusted, a point Saddam himself made
on television one day. A woman had reported that her husband had
become so angry at the sight of Saddam's face on TV that he had
cursed the image and tossed something through the screen. Saddam
praised the woman for informing on her husband, and reminded his
viewers that insulting the presidency, even in the privacy of one's
own home, was a crime punishable by death.

When he failed to announce a draconian sentence, many people
were impressed by his restraint. But a friend later told me what
happened. The husband was arrested on Saddam's orders and
beaten within an inch of his life. Since he was no longer of any use
to his wife, they cut off his genitals and watched him bleed to death.
A few days later his body and severed genitals were delivered to his
brothers.

I thoroughly understood, therefore, Adnan's caution.

So far the trip was uneventful. A carload of men heading to Mosul,
a popular resort, was commonplace and we were waved through
the checkpoints routinely. After we passed the exit for Tikrit, Saddam's birthplace, the condition of the highway deteriorated sharply.
We might as well have been driving through Afghanistan. The evidence of deprivation was everywhere.

Wedged into a Volkswagen Passat for over four hours, we all
sighed with relief when we finally reached Mosul as the sun was
beginning to burn. With its famous minarets and expansive houses,
Mosul was once the major trading city in the north, a hub between
Iraq and its neighbors Turkey and Syria. But Saddam, years of war,
and Mosul's proximity to the troubled Kurdish north had turned it

into a seedy Iraqi Casablanca, home to smugglers and spies, a magnet for Saddam's security forces and army.

It was time for a second breakfast. Because of the ubiquity of Saddam's agents, we decided to avoid the better restaurants, where they hung out. Instead, we went to a student cafe and managed to find a table in the smoky dining room. The waiter was unshaven and indifferent, dropping a handful of pita bread on the table and asking what we wanted. We all ordered kabob, Mosul's famous dish, which I'd enjoyed on previous visits. This time, though, the food had little appeal. In the back of all our minds were the three remaining highway checkpoints ahead. If we were picked up, this would be one of our last meals.

There was also the question of the smuggler to whom we'd be handed over shortly. By reputation, smugglers were treacherous. Stories about them killing their charges and taking their money were common. But our safety was linked to Adnan's, and his to ours. He knew his own life depended on making sure he left me in reliable hands. Simply put, if I were betrayed, he knew that my family would make sure he paid with his life. It was a code a Kurd understood.

My son and Ali registered for a cabin on the outskirts of town and then slipped me in later. Then we waited while Adnan located his man. For two days, we talked, read, paced, and played cards. Firas was getting nervous, worried the smugglers would find out who I was and refuse to help, or worse. But Adnan would not be rushed. Finally, early on the morning of August 18, we were told to get ready.

I turned to my son. "There is nothing more you can do now. Not for me," I said. "But you are your mother's and your two brothers' protector now. You are the man of the family. Until I arrange to bring you out."

Firas nodded, but he was very tense. He now faced the immense reach of Saddam's police state alone if the security service ever suspected something was wrong. Once inside Saddam's torture centers, he would tell the truth. The only question would be how long he could hold out. But we'd known this for a long time. With a brief embrace and pat on the back, I left.

The smuggler kept Adnan, Ali, and me waiting in an auto repair shop until noon, then sent us a message to move to another location. We did, and waited again. After a flurry of telephone calls from Adnan, the smuggler then ordered another change of location. Finally, late in the day, he came to fetch us.

Our man was in his early twenties, with a filthy face and ragged clothes that made him look like a Baghdad street beggar. I looked at his truck, a battered old white Toyota pickup. My heart sank.

He apologized for the delay. The dreaded Special Security Organization, the SSO, Saddam's elite security force, had been swarming the checkpoints all day looking for Kurdish infiltrators. He'd waited for the normal patrols to take over before picking us up.

He sounded shrewd, I decided. His appearance was probably a good idea, too, but now I was concerned about going into the mountains in such a wreck.

"Don't worry," he said with a laugh, patting the Toyota's fender. "It's very good, a very good truck." So we drove off, on the final and most dangerous leg of our journey.

The road to Kurdistan was a two-lane obstacle course of cracked cement, packed dirt, potholes, and random rocks. As we climbed slowly through the timeworn hills, our young guide went over the rules. The Kurdish region was a lucrative source of hard currency for Saddam's family. His son Uday received kickbacks from the black market in food and merchandise coming down from Turkey and oil and gas going out—all of it busting the U.N. embargo. The traffic in political refugees was less official. The border guards shook down the smugglers and gave a cut to their commanders, who were rumored to be making ten thousand dollars or more a month from the trade.

The real problem was the intermittent presence of the SSO, he said. If we were stopped by them we were doomed. Mostly, however, they were scouting for rogue corruption. If we looked nervous, the regular guards might be spooked into thinking we were part of an SSO sting. It was the worst possible mistake, our smuggler warned. It would tip the guards that something was awry, presenting us with three alternatives, all of them bad: They'd either demand all of our money, or arrest us, or both.

My stomach tightened as we approached our first checkpoint, a wooden booth where the guards raised their hands for us to stop.

As they approached, we sat silently. It turned out to be a false alarm. Our man knew the guards, and quickly produced a portable radio as a gift. "Does it work?" one of them asked, laughing. Assuring them that it did, we were quickly waved through.

The second checkpoint also went smoothly. But instead of a radio, the smuggler handed over a paper bag—"Lunch," he said. The guard looked inside and then smiled. There was also a wad of cash. With a friendly wave, we were through.

That left the most dangerous part of the journey, the last checkpoint before the border, a stretch of highway often patrolled by the SSO. Our man visibly tensed. Special precautions were demanded. As we chugged up the mountain, creeping slowly around the hairpin curves, we were met twice by other trucks whose drivers waved us forward. If the SSO had been on patrol, they would have told us to turn back.

About an hour later, we reached the frontier. The roadblock with the Iraqi tricolor flag flying on a pole was ahead. It was an army post. Soldiers were everywhere. I took a deep breath.

As we pulled to a stop, a sergeant and two soldiers approached us. After months on top of a windblown, inhospitable mountain, they looked irritable and bored, and my heart began to pound. But their only interest, as at the other stops, was in whether we had any supplies for them. Our driver pointed to the back of the truck and the soldiers unloaded some boxes. Then he got out of the truck, took the sergeant aside, and discreetly handed him two hundred dollars' worth of Iraqi dinars.

The camp went about its business as if we weren't even there. I glanced out the window at the landscape around me. Something strange had happened to the mountains. As a young man, I had vacationed here and remembered the forested hills. But now the mountainsides were barren and scorched black. Every tree and shrub of these once verdant and beautiful peaks was gone.

Saddam's army had done this—dumped chemical weapons on the hills, not just to erase any cover for Kurdish guerrillas, but to snuff out any potential whatsoever for life. They'd burned down the entire mountain range. The heartlessness of the whole operation, and the deprivation it caused the local Kurds, was a story I would hear again in the coming weeks.

Finally, we pulled out of the camp and started over the crest of the hill. I grew excited, but our smuggler cautioned me to stay alert. The SSO was known to lurk on the other side of the mountain, he said, and the word going around was that they were under pressure because of the recent defection of Wafiq al-Samarrai, Saddam's close confidant and chief of military intelligence. Apparently, it had come as a huge shock to the regime. So we crept forward, our nerves jangling, perhaps even more so now that our freedom was so near.

Then, suddenly, the goal line was in sight. A huge valley spread out below us. Far below was a wide, shallow stream. On the other side, men were loading and unloading trucks. We drove down the mountain, and in a short while we were finally there. The driver pulled to a stop at the water's edge and turned off the engine.

The silence was eerie after the long drive. The dust blew by us. The only sounds were the bubble of the stream and the soft chatter of the Kurds, unloading cans of gasoline. Armed men stood on the hillside above.

I opened the Toyota's creaky door and stepped slowly from the rusty cab. I walked forward to the water's edge, fell to my knees, and scooped up handfuls of water from the rippling stream. I splashed my face, neck, and arms. Never had water felt so fresh.

I'd made it.

"Are you all right?" Ali asked me, grinning at my obvious elation.

"Yes, I'm all right!" I smiled. "Fine. Excellent. Absolutely excellent."

We forded the stream together. On the other side, I started to offer my thanks to our guide.

"The dinar," he said.

The half bill, of course! The signal for Firas. I reached for my wallet, found the precious note, and signed the code word on the back. I handed it to the smuggler.

"I'll make sure it gets there," he said. We shook hands and he was gone.

Ali and I rested that night in a small village a few miles into the Kurdish mountains. Adnan had given me the name of the local sheik, who welcomed us warmly into his hut. I lay back on a pillow and smiled. The cool mountain air was a welcome change after our long, hot day. It was hard to believe I was out of Saddam's control.

Dinner was simple fare—rice, bread, and vegetables cooked with bits of lamb—but it seemed like a feast. As we ate, some of the stress I'd carried with me all day began to dissolve. But I could not really relax with my family left behind. As long as they were trapped in Baghdad, they were in danger. If my whereabouts became known, they would die. With Saddam's spies infesting this part of the world, from now on I had to be extremely careful of what I said and to whom.

Meanwhile, the tribal sheik and his villagers were full of surprises. After dinner they began complaining about their Kurdish leaders, who were hoarding aid from the Allies, they said. And they expressed a grudging admiration for Saddam. Any man who could do so much damage must be unusual, very brave, they said.

"After all," the sheik asked me with a mischievous smile, "aren't you yourself running away from him?" The villagers laughed.

Saddam had bombed and strafed the Kurds, burned their villages, and dumped chemical weapons on them. And they admired him!

But it was classic Kurdish thinking. The tribes had always ruled through a system of sheiks and their enforcers. They admired men who ruled by steel. That was their history. Why wouldn't they admire a man who was the toughest sheik of all?

Somehow we managed to avoid a confrontation. The next day, the sheik arranged for a car, driver, and security passes to get us through the next Kurdish checkpoints—for a fee, of course. By the end of the day we'd arrived in Arbil, the capital of the Kurdish north.

Iraqis often call Arbil the world's oldest city, although Jericho probably deserves the distinction. But Arbil is indeed ancient. In 300 B.C., Alexander the Great defeated the Persians there, and a hill in the center of the city still shows some of the old ruins. Unfortunately, the rest of the city hardly looks much newer.

In the mountains outside Arbil is the "new" town of Salahiddin, which was the base of the Iraqi opposition. We found our way to a modest yellow-brick building that served as headquarters for the Iraqi National Accord, founded by two disaffected members of Saddam's ruling Baathist Party. It was where Ali's brother Tariq worked.

Tariq invited us to dinner that evening with the local head of the

Accord and other officials. It was a frustrating evening. From conversation around the table, I concluded that nobody did any real work. The exiles spent most of their time gossiping about who was up and who was down and who did what to whom. Many seemed homesick and had given up on the possibility of toppling Saddam. Worse, many had concluded that they had been tricked and abandoned by the Allies, especially the United States.

Three years after the Gulf War ended, Saddam seemed as entrenched as ever. At best, it was a stalemate, with thousands of Iraqis stranded among the Kurds and spending their days bitching among themselves. At worst, Saddam was preparing a new arsenal of weapons—chemical, biological, and nuclear—right under the noses of the hapless United Nations. And here in Salahiddin, the Allies seemed little interested in what the exiles had to say. Where were the Americans?

I got the impression that far from being real political forces, the two main opposition groups—the Accord and the Iraqi National Congress—were principally engaged as employment agencies. A refugee registered and was put on a pay plan. But fresh cash arrived only sporadically from the United States, and some people never got paid. Everyone worried about what they would do when the Americans got bored and stopped paying altogether. Everyone was searching for a way out. A lucky few got visas, while others arranged to be smuggled into Europe, where they registered as political refugees. But most, it seemed to me, were just sitting and rotting.

The local administrator of the Iraqi National Accord was an amiable man in his late fifties, who had been a leader of the Shiite uprising in the Iraqi south at the end of Desert Storm. When the revolt was crushed, he drove his family to the Saudi border, ditched the car, and joined the thousands of other Iraqis herded into refugee camps by U.S. forces. After several months he reached the United States, but quickly found life in the suburbs lonely and boring. Even his sons were too busy to talk to him. After much hand-wringing, he contacted the opposition groups and managed to land a job back in the sand-blown mountains of northern Iraq. He was happier than ever, he said, with a new young wife and a new baby. But he was also one of the lucky few, I thought. He had a home in the United States if things didn't go well.

To my dismay, I quickly learned that attracting the attention of U.S. officials was next to impossible. There were private U.S. relief workers everywhere, but they were useless to me. I didn't need food; I needed a discreet contact, someone who could instantly recognize and understand the urgency and significance of what I had to say: the CIA.

There was an Allied military intelligence unit near the Turkish border, Ali told me, but to talk to them you had to stand in a long line and first speak with a bored clerk who was unlikely to do much more than thank you for stopping by. The only likely way to reach the Americans was through the Iraqi National Congress. My old MIT classmate Ahmad al-Chalabi, I learned, was the CIA's man up here.

The fact was, I did not know if al-Chalabi would remember me from our student days at MIT. Thirty years had passed, and we hadn't known each other all that well to begin with. I pondered what to say, especially since the cover story I'd been using was that I was just a lowly university professor trying to get out of Iraq. But I drove over there and took a chance.

Al-Chalabi's headquarters was a sprawling pair of large adjacent houses connected by jerry-built corridors. Antennae sprouted from one roof. The reception rooms seemed to function like coffee shops, with people sitting around gossiping. On the first floor of one of the houses were offices busy with computers and the production of INC publications, as well as al-Chalabi's personal administrative office.

I took a deep breath, walked in, introduced myself, and told the assistant that I wanted to see the boss. I had worked for the security services under Saddam's son-in-law, I said. At the presidential palace, I added for good measure. Mr. al-Chalabi and I had gone to college together in America.

The aide cautiously took my measure, then stood up and asked me to follow him.

At another office, we passed through a reception area crowded with more men sitting around drinking tea, smoking, and talking. The aide told me to wait and strode right past a protesting secretary, shutting the door behind him. A few minutes later he reappeared, and summoned me into the office.

Al-Chalabi greeted me cordially and motioned me to a chair.

Portly now, with the jowls of middle age, we wouldn't have recognized each other on the street after all these years. Yes, he said, he was the same man who had studied mathematics at MIT in the early 1960s. He smiled. But he was very sorry, he did not remember me.

I started reminding him of our chats back then, about student life for a young Iraqi in Cambridge, and I could see him search his memory. He started to nod.

"Ah, yes," he finally said, "now I remember you."

His interest quickened. What did I do after I left MIT? he asked. After I mentioned my Ph.D. in nuclear physics at Florida State, his eyes narrowed. When I told him about being forced to return to Iraq and work at Atomic Energy in 1970, I hesitated. Sensing that I wanted to talk to him privately, he turned to his aides, clapped his hands, and pointed to the door, a signal for everybody to leave. When the door closed, he turned back to me, his eyes now somber.

Thirty years ago, few people would have predicted that al-Chalabi would have ended up in this forlorn city. His family had been one of the richest in Iraq, his father finance minister to the king. Then came the colonels' coup in 1958 that overthrew the monarchy. His father fled to Lebanon, where he opened a bank and prospered. Ahmed, his youngest son, was sent to MIT, and then on to the University of Chicago, where he earned his Ph.D. in mathematics.

He returned to the Middle East to join the family business and by 1977 had opened his own bank in Jordan. In 1989, however, a change in the Jordanian government brought a pro-Saddam prime minister to power, and the new regime moved to take control of his business. Al-Chalabi fled the country in a hail of charges that he'd looted the bank, but he insisted he'd left with only the family funds.

Then came Saddam's defeat in Kuwait. The fractured Iraqi opposition had a new lease on life and al-Chalabi stepped in to help lead it. It wasn't long before he had dealt himself to the top of the deck. The CIA made him their main man in the north.

Al-Chalabi's eyes widened noticeably when I offered a brief résumé of my role in the nuclear program. He understood that something valuable had just walked in his door, someone the Americans would want. He invited me to have dinner at his house.

Nobody knows how to put on a show of power like an Arab leader. When we stepped outside, a line of sport utility vehicles was waiting for us, engines running. An aide sprang forward to open a door, and we slipped inside. Then we sped off like a presidential motorcade, with cars of armed bodyguards bracketing our way. Outside his house it was the same. Armed guards filled the grounds.

But when we walked inside, all pretense disappeared. There seemed to be but one servant, who soon faded away.

Al-Chalabi said he ate only one meal a day, and from the looks of the dishes on the table, the cook wasn't taking any chances. It was the strangest combination of food I'd ever seen. There was a breakfast-style offering of honey, heavy cream, cheese, and eggs. But there were also plates of roasted turkey, chicken, lamb, and stews. Bowls of fruit were delivered, and sweets were placed strategically around the room.

Al-Chalabi wasn't hungry, so as I heaped food on my plate he dug for more details on the Iraqi bomb. It turned out that he knew my two former associates in the program—al-Shahristani, who'd escaped to Iran during Desert Storm, and Jaffar, through family connections. It was obvious he wanted to make sure I knew what I was talking about. One of his responsibilities, he told me, was to screen defectors for the CIA. If I were an impostor, he'd be humiliated. But if I were the real thing, his stature with the Agency would soar, and in the cutthroat exile world, that was money in the bank.

What I didn't know was that he was already on shaky ground with the CIA.

After dinner, al-Chalabi excused himself and went upstairs. When he returned, he told me he had called the CIA on a satellite phone. He expected a return call shortly.

The servant brought tea, and we talked for a while about our lives and families, the latest Baghdad gossip, the deteriorating Iraqi economy. The uncertain future we both faced drifted like a bubble over the table. Then Ahmad crossed his arms on his ample chest and gave me some advice.

"You know," he said, "if they get what they want from you easily, they won't help you out with your family."

I looked at him evenly. He meant the CIA. But I could tell from the way he spoke that he was holding something back. And for my part, I knew this moment was a time to be careful. I could afford no missteps. If al-Chalabi was the Agency's man in Arbil, he could make me or break me. And I had to be made, because there was no going back. So I stalled with a sip of my tea, and then leaned forward attentively.

"They won't help you get out," he advised, "unless you hold back something good. You have to find a way to persuade them that they have to bring you into the country. Either that, or prepare to spend the rest of your days here. Because if you tell them everything on the phone, they'll wring you dry and leave you here. You can trust me on that."

Just make yourself a good deal, his eyes told me.

Then the satellite telephone rang, and Ahmad disappeared upstairs.

The moment I'd been planning for many years was finally at hand. In the next few minutes I could achieve the dream of getting myself and my family safely into the United States. An odd jumble of thoughts cascaded through my mind—of my naïve thinking that we could fend off Saddam's drive for a bomb, of the horrible fate of my colleagues who had resisted him.

Now, thank God, all that was behind me.

Ahmad called from the top of the stairway, summoning me to the phone.

I rose from my chair, and began to make my way up the stairs.

CHAPTER TWO

——

ROOTS IN THE SAND

ABOUT FIFTY YEARS AGO, when I was just a little boy and Saddam was decades away from turning our lives inside out, I remember touching an electrical wire for the very first time. The jolt threw me halfway across the room.

This was Iraq in the late 1940s. Electrical power had just come to Diwaniyah, the small city on the Euphrates where I grew up. For centuries life had gone on unchanged in this area, a flat, dirt-packed plain of palms, date trees, and rice fields where, eons earlier, written history began. Centuries passed, and darkness ensued. But with the coming of electricity the shops suddenly filled with lightbulbs, fans, radios, refrigerators, coolers, even ice makers. People began wiring their homes as fast as they could, tacking the lines right to the walls. The market was suddenly lit with strings of bare bulbs.

Right away, I began tinkering with the wires and appliances in our house. It was direct current, 220 volts—very powerful stuff. Instead of American-style alternating current, which flows through your body as if you were just another loop in the wire, direct current rejects you like a bad piece of meat. *Bam!* You're spat out and put flat on your back. Which is exactly what happened to me when I was about ten. The hair on my head seemed to sizzle.

But something, something deep in my genes, perhaps, drew me back. I continued to fiddle with the wires and appliances in our modest home, an ordinary two-story dwelling built from hard mud brick—southern Iraq has no stones—around an interior courtyard. Such magic in those wires! I had to see for myself how it worked. So I'd peel back the thin sheath from the copper, or poke at bulbs and appliances, to try to figure out what made them work, even if I got the occasional shock. In time, I began to learn how things moved, and I found that there was a name for my research: science.

Not that I was a nerd. I wasn't awkward, or clumsy, or near-sighted, or an introvert. On the contrary, I was scrappy. I had my pals. I ran. I played basketball, and soccer on a hard dirt field (and still have the scratches and pains to prove it). But early on what really captured my imagination was the flow of nature's unrevealed forces, and in particular, the intersection of electricity and mechanical power—physics.

Not for me cutting up frogs, pulling wings off flies, slicing open fish, or cataloging butterflies. Biology held no interest for me whatsoever. It was the practical inventors who captured my attention. I must have gotten this from my father, who had some interest in this himself and brought home boxes of magazines and books, which I tore through like a lion's little cub. I wanted to read everything, but especially stories and biographies of scientific tinkerers and thinkers like Alexander Graham Bell, Thomas Edison, and, eventually, Albert Einstein.

I was born in January 1939. The corner of Iraq where I grew up in the 1940s was pretty much at peace, a quasi-colonial backwater of Arab farmers, herders, and merchants. But there were deep resentments and spasms of violence. Power was in the hands of our regional sheiks, the big landowners who held sway throughout the country, who were often squabbling with each other under the benign neglect of a popular monarch—and direct descendant of the prophet Muhammad—whom the British had imported from Syria to rule in 1923. We had no experience with democracy, having passed from Turkish into British hands as a prize of war. But there was also little yearning for it. With rising oil revenues, Iraqis cared little about democracy, or even the Great Depression that mired the West. We escaped the next war as well, which set fire to Europe and most of Asia in 1939–1945. The closest the war came to us was North Africa, a thousand miles to the west, where Nazi tanks were crushed at the hands of the Allies in 1943. Sleepy Iraq, on the eastern edge of the "Arab Island," sold its grain and oil to any side. The guns were far over the horizon. With the end of the war, prosperity expanded, although rarely down to small farmers like my father, and his father, who were caught between two sets of thieves—desperate, hungry peasants on the bottom, and the sheiks at the top.

Iraq had always been a rough-and-tumble society, the Wild East. My father, Abbas, like his father, started out as a farmer. He was a husky, no-nonsense kind of guy, as you had to be in that business, but like most fathers he had a soft spot for his children. One of our favorite games with him was "Toe." He'd challenge us to bend back the big toe on his foot, with a reward of ten fils, about a dime, to any of us who could do it. I've sometimes wondered, thinking back through the years, how many Iraqi farmers and their children were so fortunate. We were never really poor, but there had to have been many fathers who thought, if I let my toe bend, I won't have enough money for seeds. Or food.

We always had rice. Fields full of rice so sweet its fragrance wafted over Diwaniyah. Rice piled in mounds in the fields, in the city streets at harvesttime, waiting for shipment to Basra, piles of rice in our courtyard, or stored in five-foot-high ceramic jugs in the house. It was called amber rice and had a bouquet as sweet as jasmine.

The rice was pulled from the vast marshlands quilting the plains of southern Iraq, broken only by the occasional stand of palm trees or orchards near the Euphrates. It was said that the rice farmers stood so long in the water that their legs rotted and their wives had to stand guard at night lest the dogs start gnawing on their skin. This, in the Garden of Eden, the valley of the Tigris and Euphrates, where civilization was born a hundred centuries ago. What had happened in those thousands of years to bring us so low?

The sheiks, my father might well have muttered. The sheiks, and the mullahs—the Islamic clergy—who took advantage. When electricity came to Diwaniyah, we were still living in the Middle Ages compared with the West. Nine of my brothers and sisters died at birth or before they reached their first birthday, from easily preventable complications or respiratory diseases. Only five of the fourteen children survived, and the last one killed my mother in childbirth.

The sheiks never paid their tenant farmers fairly, and thieves were a constant nuisance. My grandfather Hamza could usually scare them off with a shot over their heads, but one night it turned unexpectedly bloody. The thieves fired back, and a gun battle ensued. My father, only thirteen but a good shot, stood loyally at his father's side, trading fire with the intruders. But that was enough for them. They moved into town. My father took up trading grain, and my grandfather Hamza went to work for the government as a guard.

By my father's lights, my grandfather had a storied life. In the First World War he'd been press-ganged into the Turkish army but deserted and was hidden by Kurdish Shiites. Then a sheik gave him a daughter to marry, and he brought her down to Diwaniyah, where she gave birth to my father. Then she ran away. He killed his second wife when she got between him and a brother with whom he was feuding—an accident, I was told.

His legacy to me was a shelf crammed with books such as *A Thousand and One Nights,* the head-spinning tales of Scheherazade, Sinbad, and Ali Baba and the Forty Thieves. I spent hours on the floor flipping through the pictures. My mother, Fatima, listened to the Koran on the radio. We nagged father to tell us stories, which he did with the aid of a few cups of arak, the local brew. With a charcoal fire in full blast, and the teakettle steaming, he'd spin the yarns until his eyelids drooped shut. Then mother would call it a night and send us all to bed.

Although my father was a Shiite by birth, he was indifferent, if not hostile, to organized religion. His one concession to Ramadan, the annual fast, was not to drink.

"Ramadan," he'd mutter. "They fast all day and eat all night."

As it happened, I became friends with a boy in An Najaf, Shiite Islam's holiest city, whose father was a mullah and ran a religious school. At night he rented out the classroom floors to pilgrims, most of whom traveled long distances at great sacrifice, as a place to sleep. He also turned a covetous eye on their daughters.

"Don't you want her to marry a direct descendant of Muhammad?" he'd ask an anxious mother. Of course she did, but he was just a sexual predator. After the girls became pregnant, he'd toss them out on the street, where they became recruits for the brothels. Likewise, little of the money that merchants tithed to the mullahs for the poor actually got to them. One time my friend took me down into the imam's cellar and showed me bags upon bags of cash. Whatever regard I might have held for the Islamic clergy forever disappeared right there.

Books, in any event, were my religion. By high school, I'd cut a wide swath through Diwaniyah's modest library—toting home biographies of Einstein, Newton, and Jean-Jacques Rousseau. I read *War and Peace,* Agatha Christie, the *Iliad,* books about the great explorers and the discovery of America. But I have to confess that the biggest impact on my imagination came from the Arabic-language *Reader's Digest,* whose well-thumbed copies could be picked up by the boxful in the market. Everything was in those pages, from funny stories to political articles to news of scientific advances. From that time forward I vowed I would one day visit America.

Meanwhile, I was burrowing deeper into science, and had made up my mind to attend Baghdad University. My high school physics texts were written by an Iraqi educated at MIT, Abdul-Jabbar Abdullah, a recognized expert on wave theory, who had also translated a book on nuclear physics. One day after my senior year, Dr. Abdullah summoned me for the interview that would determine what I would study next.

When I entered his disheveled university office, he was still reading through my transcripts. I sat patiently and waited. Then he pushed the papers forward and looked up.

"What do you wish to study?" he asked.

I shifted in my seat. Math, I ventured. My best grades were in math.

He assessed me for what seemed forever.

"No," he finally said. "You will study physics." And that was that.

By some accounts, Saddam Hussein arrived in Baghdad at about the same time I did, in the fall of 1956. Rudimentarily schooled, precociously violent, a product of a notoriously crude Tikriti clan, Saddam quickly plunged into the street politics roiling the capital, eventually joining up with the Baath ("renewal") Party, a collection of socialist-minded Arab nationalists. Their immediate protest target was Iraq's enlistment in the pro-U.S. Baghdad Pact two years earlier, but their real quarry was the monarchy itself, the last vestige of colonialism in the Middle East. King Faisal II had nearly been overthrown in World War Two by a cabal of pro-Hitler military officers that included Saddam's uncle. Now, in the fall of my freshman year, 1956, the invasion of Egypt by a combined force of British, French, and Israeli troops only threw more sticks on the fire.

Outside Baghdad University's palm-fringed campus, demonstrators and police battled back and forth. Saddam, most likely, was among them, no doubt packing a pistol. I stuck to my classes. Frankly, I was more interested in girls. American-style dating was unheard of, but for the first time I was able to just sit and talk with a young woman, usually over tea in the cafeteria.

My mentor, Dr. Abdullah, had turned out to be a spellbinding lecturer. Even as revolutionary fervor swirled over the campus, my enthusiasm for pure learning soared, and I began to foresee a lifetime of teaching and research. Unfortunately, however, Abdullah taught only classical physics, the science of matter and energy; the most beguiling developments were in nuclear energy, including the atom bomb.

On July 14, 1958, meanwhile, the monarchy was finally toppled in a military coup. The young king and his hated regent were overthrown and executed. The prime minister, fleeing in women's clothes, was stopped on a Baghdad street and killed. According to a story that later made the rounds, he had been fingered by a clever young high school student, Jaffar D. Jaffar.

The colonels' pan-Arabism, meanwhile, was quickly felt on campus. The American professors left, replaced by Egyptians. The other foreign professors, such as Indians, were pitifully behind the times. There was no one at the university who could teach the newer physics of nuclear fission. I busied myself with other courses, but got a sinking feeling that Iraq was drifting in a bad direction.

In my senior year Dr. Abdullah urged me to follow in his footsteps to MIT. One route led through an organization called American Friends of the Middle East, which had an office in Baghdad. The only thing I cared about was that it gave the English-language exam and waived the application fee.

When the results came back, I'd scored 98 percent on the English proficiency test. My grades were top drawer and I had the backing of Dr. Abdullah, a distinguished MIT alumnus. But in a harbinger of problems I'd have with the Americans twenty-five years later, I was informed I'd been rejected by MIT.

Dr. Abdullah, however, was not to be denied. Astounded and perplexed, he bypassed the American Friends of the Middle East and wrote directly to MIT appealing the decision. I was admitted. Best of all, the Iraqi government would pay my way, on the understanding that I'd repay the government with one year of service for every year I studied. At the time, it seemed easy enough, and I hardly gave it any thought. Nor did my father, who happily cosigned the forms.

In any event, I was eager to get out of the chaos enveloping Iraq. The military government had quit the Baghdad Pact and was making overtures to the Soviets. No one could predict what was going to happen. Then, in October 1961, came an incident that well could have ended my career. I was walking down then-stylish Rashid Street in Baghdad when I heard machine-gun fire. Pandemonium broke out. People were ducking for cover, running helter-skelter to get away. I started running, fearing I might be picked up in a security sweep. Somebody, it turned out, had tried to assassinate Colonel Abdul Karim Qassim, head of the military regime.

It was Saddam Hussein.

Saddam's assignment, I later found out, had been to provide covering fire for his four conspirators. A lookout was posted in a window, and as Qassim's unescorted, unguarded Russian sedan came down the street, a truck blocked its way. The assassins opened fire with automatic weapons. Qassim's driver was killed, but the colonel pulled out a handgun and began returning fire, even though he was wounded, killing one assailant and sending the others fleeing. Saddam was supposed to deliver the coup de grace, but faced with the colonel's courage, his nerves cracked and he limped away with a superficial leg wound.

The Charles River, dividing Boston and Cambridge, was sparkling with autumn sunshine when I arrived in September 1962. Everything was clean and peaceful, as I knew it would be. On the radio, Peter, Paul and Mary were singing "If I Had a Hammer," and President John Kennedy was sending troops to Ole Miss to escort a young black man to school. What a lucky, lucky country, I thought. Then came the Cuban missile crisis.

Nuclear weapons were no idle curiosity for me, of course. I had come to MIT to study nuclear physics. I had no interest in building bombs—the thought repulsed me. To me, nuclear fission was like the first electrical wire in our house in Diwaniyah: I had to peel back the layers and see what was inside. But the lesson anybody could draw when the Russians retreated was that the United States won because it had more nuclear weapons.

Meanwhile, rumors of coups and conspiracies in Baghdad were constantly swirling through the small community of Iraqis in Boston. One of them, Ahmad al-Chalabi, was particularly articulate. The son of a finance minister to the king, al-Chalabi knew how things worked and who the players were. In early February 1963, news came that military plotters, backed by the Baathists, had pulled off a coup and executed Colonel Qassim, whom Saddam had failed to assassinate two years earlier. One of the coup leaders was Saddam's cousin, General Ahmad Hassan al-Bakr, who became prime minister. The young revolutionist's stock was on the rise.

"We really had the *t*'s crossed on what was happening," the CIA's then–chief of operations in the Middle East, James Critchfield, would recall. "We regarded it as a great victory."

A great victory that was short-lived, as it turned out. As my friend al-Chalabi had shrewdly predicted, the Baathists would be ousted when they clashed with the army. In November he was proved right.

For me, Baghdad, with its military coups and conspiracies, seemed farther and farther from my world. I was throwing myself into my studies, and college life was turning out to be everything I hoped for and more. Late at night I watched Johnny Carson. On weekends I made my way to Harvard Square for a Kurosawa or Bergman flick. Some nights I'd hang out with friends at the coffeehouses where the folk singers were playing. American girls in black leotards, smoking cigarettes, were quite a sight for a boy from Baghdad.

My introduction to American-style dating came with a Greek woman, very good-looking, but at twenty-nine, too old for me. The two main things she offered were sex and a car, neither of which I'd had much experience with in Iraq. My next girlfriend was a Colombian beauty I met at a Harvard graduate student party. We even considered marriage, but that was impossible for me. Nuclear physics was just too demanding.

But life was good. The Iraqi government was giving me two hundred dollars a month, plus three hundred dollars a year for books and clothing on top of tuition. I was also renting out rooms in my house to other students. I occasionally sensed hostility because I was a foreigner, but I was never subjected to a racial epithet or incident. Frankly, despite American liberals' carping about racial segregation, things were better here than in Iraq, socially speaking. I was even befriended by a Jewish-American professor who wanted to translate Arabic texts by computer.

But overnight, it seemed, my spell at MIT came to an end. I had my master's degree, the question now was what to do next. Friends told me about a nuclear nirvana at Florida State University, where there was a new accelerator and unlimited research time. So I applied and was accepted for the Ph.D. It was a good thing, too, because on a brief visit home I was nearly drafted into the army. Connections, I learned, and the right kind of documents were everything in the new Iraq.

Tallahassee was a pretty sleepy place compared with Boston, but a lot better than Baghdad. The riptides roiling the rest of America, civil rights and Vietnam, were hardly felt here, and Southern hospitality was not an illusion. When I went to get a dorm room with some other students, the attractive, well-dressed lady who ran things picked me out of the waiting group.

"Where're yew from, honey?"

Iraq, I replied cautiously.

"Well, God bless yew," she said. "C'mon in." Within minutes, I had a room and a key to the house—no money down, no questions, no application. America. What a great country.

Some of the twenty-five or so foreign graduate students at FSU, however, had a hard time letting go of their old habits. They held on to their cynicism about America and democracy. To be sure, the war in Vietnam, U.S. support for Latin American dictators, the murders of reformers such as Martin Luther King Jr. and Bobby Kennedy, and, especially for Arab students, America's blind support for Israel, were radicalizing influences. Somehow, though, I was able to differentiate individual Americans I met from U.S. policies. For a while I even dated a Jewish girl. If anything, I was becoming more Americanized. I even started playing poker.

An Iraqi friend and I were hanging out at a campus pub where a woman named Kitty was the bartender. Her husband, Gary, was a high-stakes pool player, who taught me how to make a few trick shots. In time, I got pretty good and started to play for money, picking up small change here and there.

No doubt, I was developing a taste for gambling. There was a low-stakes poker game after the doors were closed at night, and Kitty and Gary invited me to sit in. One of the regulars was a guy with a badly deformed hand whose name was Jim.

"Bunch of losers," Jim grumbled one day after an all-night session. "Penny-ante stuff." He asked if I'd like to get into a "real game" with some rich tobacco farmers outside Tallahassee.

Sure, I said. The following Friday night we were tooling out through the flat farmland in my new Oldsmobile Cutlass, which I'd just bought for $3,600. Financially, I was doing pretty well, since FSU was paying me $350 a month as a physics research assistant on top of the monthly salary and tuition I was getting from Baghdad. An hour or so out of Tallahassee, we pulled off the highway and drove down a long, straight dirt road through the tobacco fields, eventually pulling up to a huge estate. Several private airplanes were scattered around a landing strip out back.

Steaks were sizzling on a grill. Beer was piled in ice buckets. A group of pink-faced, oversized men in golfing pants, who were happily chortling with one another and chomping on huge cigars, made me feel right at home. That I was Iraqi didn't matter; they probably couldn't even find it on a map. These were rough-hewn, self-made men. The only thing that mattered was "if you could cut it."

As the cards were dealt, they began reminiscing about the "good old days" before Castro, not so distant in 1968. After an all-night poker game, they'd fly their planes down to Havana, they said, have breakfast, take a swim, hire a girl, and spend the afternoon in the casinos before flying back for another round of poker until Sunday morning.

What a life. And here I was, a Shiite Muslim from southern Iraq, drinking beer and playing seven-card stud on a tobacco estate in Florida.

At first, I won, then the tide turned. The reason was simple: They had so much money, they didn't care if you raised them. They didn't care what I had showing, they had the money and they always called. I lost my shirt, but it was a very good lesson: Don't play with the big boys until you have very good cards.

I had enough work to keep me busy on campus anyway, where I was drawing attention with some breakthroughs in research. But unfortunately, the good life could not last. After a year of postdoctoral work, the university hinted that it was time for me to move on (following the tradition that the school that grants your Ph.D. wants you to teach somewhere else). Out of the blue, I was approached by the dean of a tiny, traditionally black school in southern Georgia, Fort Valley State College. Normally, I might have dismissed it out of hand, but times were not normal: I was suddenly being dunned by the Iraqi government for my scholarship obligation, and the Vietnam War had produced a glut of Ph.D.s who had stayed in school to avoid the draft. So when Fort Valley offered me $17,500 a year, nearly twice the normal salary for an assistant professor, I accepted on the spot. I figured I'd deal with Baghdad later.

The National Science Foundation was ready to give the college a grant to establish a computer center—if they could hire an acceptable caretaker. So I would have two hats, one to teach math and physics, the other to set up the computer center, which primarily involved negotiating for equipment with IBM and Control Data Corporation.

Needless to say, Fort Valley, population four hundred, situated in flat, south Georgia gnat country, had no social or cultural amenities whatsoever. The only other business beside the college was the Bluebird school bus body shop. There were no movie theaters, no restaurants open after sundown. But it was an eye-opener in another way, on race relations in the South. When I dated a few black teachers, I drew disapproving looks from both sides, so I stopped. My black friends at the college were curious, however, about how whites treated me: Did they see me as white or black?

"I don't know," I said. They slowly shook their heads.

Meanwhile, I was shocked by the deprivations of black education. My students weren't just unprepared for college, they weren't ready for high school. Not even in Iraq did college students have such problems with math, or with reading and writing in their own language. If I made a simple error in arithmetic on the blackboard, nobody would catch it. The state and the federal governments

47

didn't help by failing to enforce any standards. Football players seldom went to class but were passed anyway. Not in mine. When I flunked an entire class of students taking a summer course to qualify for high school teaching, the faculty was astounded. Nobody had ever done that before. But the department head and college president backed me up.

Now Iraq roared back into my life. Baghdad authorities, who up until then had been lackadaisical about demanding repayment of their loans, suddenly started playing tough. The legalese in their letters referred to impending government action against "the guarantor" of the loan, my father.

How glibly we'd agreed to that contract years ago, in the euphoria over my admission to MIT. How blithely I had skipped along after I got my Ph.D., having a great time in Florida. Now Iraq had called my bluff, and far different people were in power. On July 17, 1968, there had been another coup, and the Baath Party was back in power. Saddam Hussein, vice president of the Revolutionary Command Council, was now the man to see.

An Iraqi acquaintance of mine in Tallahassee, Tariq Kassar, was rumored to have good connections in Baghdad, especially with Saddam Hussein. I went to see him, and he gave me the bad news first. The new regime wasn't fooling around anymore, he said. If student delinquents didn't pay up or come home, their parents were being picked up and jailed. Some were being tortured.

"These are very, very tough guys, Khidhir," he said evenly. He stubbed out a cigarette, then sipped from a glass of whiskey. We were sitting in his off-campus apartment. The blinds were drawn against the Florida heat. I glanced around at the spacious rooms. It occurred to me that Tariq had an awfully nice place for a student on an Iraqi scholarship, especially one who rarely went to class. His bad grades didn't seem to disqualify him from an extended stay, either.

The good news, Tariq resumed, was that the new regime was being very accommodating to Iraqis who made a good-faith promise to return home when their work was finished. But I had to mean it; I could finish what I was doing, but no more. Then I had to go. Iraq needed engineers and scientists and the new regime wouldn't hesitate to apply the screws to get me back.

And I should go back, he said. Life would be good for me there.

"I've sent several good reports about you to Baghdad," he said, fully making his point. He looked up at me.

"Your work in physics, especially the three-body nuclear reactions, has given you a high standing in the Arab community," Tariq said. "You wouldn't be expected to toil away in the university, teaching stupid farmers' sons." He smirked. I was taken aback that he knew so much of my research.

"I'm sure they would recruit you for a very good job at Atomic Energy or something like that," he said, and offered to help straighten out things for me at the embassy in Washington.

No doubt, he was a player. So during Christmas break, we drove up to Washington in my Olds. I expected he had good connections, but I wasn't prepared for the embassy reception he received. The Iraqi cultural attaché fell all over himself. No less than the ambassador threw Tariq a lavish dinner.

But there was still that little business of my loan to take care of. Tariq ushered me into a meeting with an embassy official, who greeted me with exaggerated respect and kindness. Then he started in on his sales pitch. The Iraqi Atomic Energy Commission, he said, was doing marvelous things in nuclear research and even nuclear medicine. With my knowledge and talents, I could be a big player in those efforts, maybe even head up an entire division. Iraq would be very grateful for my patriotic sacrifice. Was I interested?

I didn't have much of a choice, but at least it sounded like a soft landing. If I had to leave America for a few years to meet my obligation, it might not be too bad. Besides, like most people, I had some feelings for my country. Iraq was coming up in the world, no doubt about it. The government was pouring money into education, science, huge civil works projects, the arts, even archaeology. Women were filling the universities. Saddam could be a bastard, but at least he was modernizing the country and standing up to the mullahs.

In any event, what choice did I have? My father was on the hook. I signed some papers, and the matter was done with. All litigation would be dropped, contingent upon my return next summer. A good job would be waiting for me at the AEC in Baghdad, working on the peaceful uses of nuclear energy.

"Your father will be very proud of you," one official said, chuckling.

Tariq and I spent the rest of the week touring Washington. Under a crust of snow, the capital was beautiful. We visited the Lincoln Memorial and President Kennedy's grave at Arlington. I shivered in the cold. My thoughts were a jumble. I had a hard time believing I was really going back to Iraq.

No doubt Tariq sensed my despair. One day he said he wanted to introduce me to an old friend of his, Basil al-Kubaisi, who was living in Washington.

"Interesting guy," he said on the drive. Al-Kubaisi, he confided, was an Iraqi Baathist, but at present he was working for the Palestine Liberation Organization, the PLO—"at a very high level." He gave me a lingering look.

My mouth probably went a little dry. I knew the PLO had a following among Arabs in the United States, not much different from the cachet Black Panthers had with some American liberals. But I considered most of them armchair revolutionaries, full of coffeehouse braggadocio. Personally, in any event, I had little regard for the PLO. I thought they were good at hijacking airplanes or blowing up school buses, but otherwise full of hot air. A homeland for the Palestinians was a worthy cause, but the PLO's methods were all wrong. I deplored unnecessary violence, whatever the excuse.

When we arrived in Basil's apartment, I was more than anxious. He greeted us at the door, and it was quickly apparent that he had made a special effort, preparing an Iraqi-style dinner of lamb and rice. Within a short time, we were digging in.

"I've heard lots about you," he said, wiping grease from his mouth and raising a wineglass toward me. "You are a smart guy, a physicist. An Iraqi nuclear physicist." He pronounced each word distinctly. "How about that?" He took a gulp of wine, smiled wryly, and then tossed down his napkin. He leaned back in his chair.

"The Israelis are winning," he said. "We can't compete with them in the position we are in. They have nuclear bombs. We have nothing. AK-47s—slingshots. We have no way of catching up to the Israelis as long as they have the bomb and we don't."

I began to listen closely.

The PLO, he went on, was developing a top secret military

research center in Jordan. "We want to assemble a team to make atomic bombs. Are you interested?"

I just stared at him, dumbfounded, I'm sure.

"We're not going to explode one in Israel," he added. "Our plan is to set one off in the desert, announcing to the world our accomplishment. We'll keep the other in reserve. That will make the Israelis listen. They'll be forced to negotiate with us."

I couldn't think of anything appropriate to say. I thought it might even be some kind of trap. So I just fingered my wineglass and remained silent.

"You could be a leader of that team," Basil went on. "Money is no object, since all the Arab oil money is behind it. By the way, there will be no problem for you with the Iraqi government. The PLO will see to that."

He looked up at me. "What do you say?"

Every alarm was going off in my head. The PLO was a collection of terrorist groups, no matter how it presented itself. To the FBI, it was Enemy Number One, or close to it. But its factions were forever quarreling among themselves—and with their hosts, as in Iraq. Saddam, according to the word we had from Baghdad, already regretted letting the PLO into Iraq, because they were making life hell for him. But there were other considerations. If I took the job—and I wasn't sure yet this was an offer I could refuse—I'd eventually come into the crosshairs of Israeli intelligence. Mossad had a well-deserved reputation for hunting down its PLO targets and liquidating them. I'd live in fear my entire life, from all sides. No doubt my own time would come.

I chose my words carefully.

"I don't think this is for me," I told Basil, softly, respectfully. I fumbled for the right formulation. "I respect the aims of the PLO, but . . .

"I am a scientist," I said. "Just a scientist, not a bombmaker. I don't know anything about bombs, really. I don't know how to make a bomb."

I did, theoretically, of course.

"Come on," Basil jibed. "I know what you've studied! You are a first-rank theoretician. You know all the mechanics. You know how to do both." He let out a snort. "Anyway, you can assemble your own team, fill in the blank spots by hiring others." Why not let the PLO fly me to Jordan, he added, where I could ask questions of the top leadership there myself?

I shook my head. How did I get into a spot like this? I had to walk a very thin line, I knew, between rejection and gratitude. But then I decided to gamble, by telling the truth.

"You wouldn't want me," I said carefully. "Like every good Arab, I believe in the Palestinian cause, I believe it is just. But what I see is that you, the PLO, have no real strategy. You talk like you are fighting on all fronts, on all levels, with the whole world behind you. But mostly, you are just killing mothers and schoolchildren."

Basil's eyes flickered, but he remained still.

I shook my head sadly. "I wish the Palestinian people well, I do. But this is not for me, not at all. And I would not be good for you."

Basil stared at me for a long moment and then glanced at Tariq, who shrugged. Then he turned back to me.

"Okay," he said, straightening up in his chair. "No problem. I will tell them."

For the next few minutes we forced some light conversation. There was no more talk of the PLO bomb. Then it was time to go. At the door, Basil shook hands with me. He was cordial, but something in his eyes told me he expected everything about this evening to be kept secret.

It was, not that it mattered. Nine months later, the PLO was evicted from Jordan in the infamous Black September. The Israelis eventually caught up with Basil al-Kubaisi, too. A year later he was shot dead in Paris.

God help me, now I was on my way back to all that.

———

CHAPTER THREE

GOING HOME

FROM THE AIR, Baghdad looked mottled and run-down, like sand castles on a beach. As the wing dipped on the airport approach over the city, I saw the familiar latticework of narrow alleys and tan plaster. At twilight, the stark, fluorescent lights were twinkling along the major boulevards, but large swatches of the city were dark. Baghdad was going to be nothing like the neon-lit, multicolored, fast-moving world I'd left behind in the States.

I was home, but I was a stranger. I'd become half American, or maybe even more in the past eight years. I'd dated girls, bought a car and Beach Boy eight-tracks, rented a garden apartment, played poker, and gone out for beers with my pals. Without the contract that forced me back here, who knows? I might have become just another hyphenated American, shedding the old world like a bad suit. But Saddam had pulled me back.

The airport was badly in need of paint and repairs. And it was hot. Listless porters with tired, vacant faces collected my luggage and pushed their dollies along cracked, dusty floors. Aching from the long flight, I walked out of the shabby terminal and hailed a taxi. A twenty-year-old Citroën coughed to a start and lumbered forward from the shadows. As the driver loaded my bags, I broke out in a sweat from the superheated desert air.

Since I'd been gone so long, I had no place to stay or current numbers for old friends. My family was back in Diwaniyah. As we drove into Baghdad, the driver recommended the Kuwait Hotel in the new downtown. As soon as I got my room and dropped my luggage, I set out for a walk along the Cornice, the riverfront promenade on the Tigris, in search of a favorite kabob from my student days.

No luck. Too many years of fresh sirloins had spoiled me. The minced meat was nothing like I remembered, and the pita bread was stale. More strange, by midnight all the restaurants and bars were closing. In my student days, we might spend the whole night here, drinking beer and eating fish broiled over mesquite. Now the bars were shuttered, a few stragglers were scurrying home as midnight struck. I wondered what had happened.

The Kuwait was owned by a congenial Christian Arab who'd bought the place with a big score in the lottery, he told me. But all he could think of now was going to America. "Things are no good here," he kept muttering, declining to be more specific. Every time I bumped into him in the lobby, he had another question about the good life in the United States.

I took a quick jaunt down to Diwaniyah to see my family. It's a truism that you can't go home again. The bountiful farmland was desolate; the old mounds of fragrant rice were a distant memory. My father had taken a job in a store. Most of the other farmers and peasants, he said, had gone, moved to Baghdad to look for a better life. "And what about you?" I asked. He shrugged. "I am always all right. I will do fine. It's good to have you back."

We drank a few beers in silence. Neither of us wanted to bring up what might have happened if I hadn't come back. Maybe he didn't know how close it was. Maybe I didn't.

I sped back to Baghdad as soon as I comfortably could, to find out what kind of job the government had planned for me. At the hotel, there was a message waiting, from Ali Attia, director general of the Nuclear Research Center at Atomic Energy.

I remembered him, but not too fondly. Ali spent most of his time at the university politicking for the Baath Party. Then he got his Ph.D. in the States by following other students' experiments on a nuclear accelerator. Ali was still probably letting other people do his thinking. And he badly needed help, as I learned when I visited him the next day at his office at Atomic Energy, a cluster of cement buildings ringed by a high steel fence in al-Tuwaitha, twenty miles south of Baghdad.

Ali greeted me with the slick confidence of a party hack, not the somber assurance of a senior scientist. The more he talked, in fact, the more he showed how little he actually knew about nuclear issues. I listened respectfully, however, because now I was in Baghdad, where falling out of favor meant more than a missed opportunity.

I'd already heard about the upsurge in public executions. On paper, aging general al-Bakr was in charge, but the hangings were unmistakably the handiwork of Saddam, vice president of the Revolutionary Council, which controlled budgets and decreed laws. With his additional portfolio as chief of the Baath Party's intelligence apparatus, there was no doubt the mustachioed apparatchik was calling the shots.

Ali made it clear right off that he wanted me as his right-hand man. I'd have the lowly title of researcher in the physics department, and the starting pay would only be about $150 a month, a tenth of what I made in the States. But I'd be close to the levers of power, he bragged, and I could supplement my income lecturing in the universities.

We shook hands, and in that moment it was clear my fate had been settled. As I left the building, I was resigned to throw myself into the work. I'd do the best job I could, satisfy my obligations, and then get the hell back to the United States.

Emergencies flew fast and hard, right from the start. Crop diseases had plunged the countryside toward starvation. With the treasury draining fast from food imports, the regime came up with a drastic solution: It started distributing seeds treated with a mercury compound to kill the fungus. They were supposed to be planted, but the farmers ignored the warnings and instead began washing and using them for bread and animal fodder. Inevitably, traces of the compound remained on the seeds, and before long, mass poisoning swept the countryside, with its characteristic symptoms of mental breakdowns and crippled limbs.

Harsh measures were required. The regime decided to track the tainted seeds and execute anyone who was using them improperly. Since chemical analysis wasn't up to the job, the Nuclear Research Center stepped forward. Dr. Hussein al-Shahristani, a gentle, bearded scientist trained in nuclear analysis at the University of Toronto, trembled with the knowledge that he was passing a death sentence with every finding of purloined seeds, but nevertheless, that's what he did. Ironically, his morbid assignment led to great fame when he began publishing his findings in international journals.

Meanwhile, my own work and duties expanded. I launched a group to analyze reactor experiments. I was given responsibility for all AE publications, including the commission's first annual report and a new quarterly bulletin on the peaceful uses of atomic energy. I started writing an Arab-language book on the same. Because of my work in Georgia, I was also appointed to head a committee to buy a mainframe computer, this one to be used by AE to analyze experimental data collected from the reactor. I got an IBM 360, and soon the oil and defense ministries, as well as the universities, were lining up to use it.

The months flew by. The job, somewhat to my surprise, was turning out to be a challenge. The more responsibility I took on, the more I was given. The Iraq Society of Physics and Mathematics, for example, had been dormant for years. I reactivated it, and joined the board. Another interesting assignment was to implement the New Math in the schools. By then I was also getting some notice for my lectures on theoretical physics at Baghdad University. The minister of higher education asked me to give a series of talks on atomic energy at other colleges across the nation.

Looking back, I know I was being closely watched and evaluated on how I carried out these assignments. The party even launched a background investigation to find out if I were politically reliable, and in particular, whether I had any Iranian blood. The reason was that in Iraq, a Shiite was always suspected of having at least one Iranian in the family tree. During a visit to Diwaniyah one day, I was told by my uncle that no less than the head of the local security service had paid a visit. Naturally, this alarmed my uncle, but the man assured him I was in no trouble and merely being considered for a higher position.

Winter came. The knifelike desert gusts blew down from Syria, gathering cold sand and clearing people from the streets. It was depressing. The economy was in a shambles, with oil revenues falling and farmers leaving the land and crowding the city. I grew restless in my room at the Kuwait Hotel, homesick for my own place and a girlfriend. In Iraq, a single man couldn't even rent a house.

I had to face it: It was time to get married.

I'd been close to marriage once with an American girl, a music student at Florida State. We had an off-campus apartment and vague plans to get hitched, but things soon turned sour. I still had a lot of the Iraqi in me, I guess, issuing commands and expecting a woman to salute. Of course, in late-1960s America, that just wasn't going to work. In any event, that was the past. My problem now was to find another woman, and in Iraq, there was no such thing as a date.

My family was already scouting around for suitable prospects. My Baghdad friends were also looking, but they had come up empty-handed. Then one weekend, I saw her. Her name was Souham, and she was a stunning, lithe beauty. She had just showed up at my father's house with her sister to say hello. I was transfixed.

She came in and sat, and as the evening passed and I watched her talking with my relatives, I grew increasingly infatuated. It turned out she was an orphan who had never seen her father. Her mother had died two years before, and she was living with her married brother, an army officer. But she was young, very young.

"Isn't she beautiful?" my father whispered to me at one point.

"Yes," I answered, "but how old is she?"

"Almost sixteen," he said.

I gasped. "Not even sixteen?"

"No, she is fifteen, but we can fix it with a judge, if it gets to that," he whispered back.

"You know," I said, "in the U.S. I wouldn't even dare to go out with a girl of her age, much less marry her. I'd be arrested. They call it 'corrupting a minor.'"

My father nodded. "Well, thank God you are not in the U.S. now."

Back in Baghdad, I confided in Dr. Abdullah, the acting head of the physics department at Atomic Energy.

"Age doesn't matter," he said, congratulating me for finding an attractive possible mate. "The younger the better."

"Typical Arab view," I snorted.

"No, no," he said. "Marriages like that are more common than you think. Anyway, all the good-looking girls marry early here, so, really, you have no choice."

He had a point.

"Besides," he said, "what's so wrong about marrying a young girl? She sure doesn't lose out by marrying early. She can't date, like in America. Her life is rather dull. So over here, she might as well marry as soon as she can."

But fifteen? Half my age?

"Don't worry," he said, studying my face. "You'll have lots of company."

A few weeks later, a judge looked at my bride's birth certificate in his chambers. Fifteen years old, it said. He squinted at Souham. The document was obviously wrong, he declared. With a flick of his pen, she was sixteen. And we were legal.

Our marriage was solid, but there were other disturbances underfoot. We began to hear rumors of party members killed in highway accidents. The victims were people who'd recently criticized Saddam, it was said. Almost always, their cars had collided with a big red truck from the Ministry of Public Works. Other times the body of someone out of favor was found on the side of a desert highway.

At first, most of the people we knew just shrugged. The party had come to power through murder and intrigue, they said. If they were killing each other, what was the big loss? But as Saddam emerged on the top of the heap, people began to worry. Saddam, everybody knew, was the worst of the thugs.

His family were roughhouse peasants from Ouja, a mud-brick hamlet on the Tigris, a hundred miles north of Baghdad. The closest place of any size was Tikrit, a crumbling textile town whose only claim to fame was as the birthplace of Saladin, conqueror of the Crusaders. It was a backwater of ignorance and guns.

Saddam, born on April 28, 1937, never knew his father, a shepherd who died around the time of his birth. He was raised by his mother and crude uncles, whom he apparently tried to impress by beating up other kids and flashing a gun. When he was only eleven, he shot his teacher, bringing a temporary end to his formal education. The police found him in bed with the still-smoking gun.

Saddam drifted about Tikrit, brawling and drinking like his uncles, until he was seventeen. Most restless youth joined the army at that point, but Saddam drifted into the circles of the Baathists, who espoused a muddy mix of Arab nationalism and left-wing revolution. After his botched assignment to shoot Colonel Abdul Karim Qassim, he fled abroad.

The three years Saddam spent in Egypt and Syria would be his only time beyond the borders of Iraq until he became vice president. By most accounts, he was a brawler, leaving a trail of unpaid restaurant bills and a reputation for barroom fights. In 1963, he sped back to Baghdad for the coup, but played a negligible role, perhaps as a minor gunman. When the coup failed, he was thrown in jail, and one particular stint had lethal repercussions for everyone involved.

It was 1965. The prison warden began a lengthy inquisition, and by many accounts, Saddam spilled the beans. His wife, Sajida, allegedly cooperated, too—and more, according to the gossip of palace intimates years later: She became the warden's mistress and gave birth to a child. The boy, Qussey, grew up with a startling resemblance to the warden, officials whispered, and was soon shunned by Saddam. But when the Baathists shot their way back into power in 1968, Saddam settled the account. He went straight to the jail where he'd confessed and supposedly loaned out his wife, and put a bullet in the warden's head.

Or so went the story, which was repeated only among the most trusting friends in the highest circles of the regime. To me and many others, Qussey did in fact have little resemblance to Saddam, although opinions can certainly differ. What is of no doubt is that the future president obliterated the warden and other witnesses to his jail time as soon as he had the chance. And whatever his true lineage, today Qussey is the odds-on favorite to succeed his father in the presidential palace.

The murders that were rumored when I returned were more attempts by Saddam to wipe out his past. He was cleaning out the party hierarchy. But he was also making a move for popular support, giving speeches to large public gatherings denouncing foreign oil companies. Since the companies were widely loathed, it was a doubly shrewd move, because it tended to undercut the public's growing apprehension over his deadly pursuit of power.

Now, by chance, I felt Saddam's touch. One morning the secretary general of Atomic Energy, Dr. Moyesser al-Mallah, came to my office looking shaken and pale, his stutter worse than usual. He had received an ominous call from Saddam's office, he said. The vice president was asking for all the documentation surrounding our computer purchase from IBM.

Under the new rules, Saddam was supposed to clear any purchase over $250,000. But nobody had bothered to clear it with Saddam, even though it cost twice as much. Apparently, National Cash Register, which had sold a small mainframe to the Electricity Board earlier, was complaining to Saddam that the purchase violated Iraqi laws requiring the publishing of open bids, even going so far as to hint that a bribe had been paid. The company wanted the contract nullified and a new round of bids.

To al-Mallah, NCR's allegations were groundless and silly. But he was also a party hack, and fretted about Saddam. Heads, surely, would roll. Pacing my office, he worriedly asked me to go over my steps in the IBM purchase.

Luckily, I'd done things by the book. We knew about the NCR computer, I said. It was mostly a business machine, not well equipped to handle scientific calculations. A test run showed it to be about twenty times slower than the IBM. I'd gotten a waiver to buy the IBM without soliciting other bids, and the commission had approved it.

All my material was shipped over to Saddam, who took a week to read through all my reports and the AEC contract deliberations. Word came back that he was impressed: The contract was entirely aboveboard and would be honored. But of course, someone had to be punished. Saddam had to show who was boss. The AEC's accountant and legal chief were demoted and transferred somewhere else.

Dr. al-Mallah himself brought the news to my office, nearly sweating with relief, and asked me how I could take the news so calmly. "Don't you know what could've happened?"

I put on a solemn face, and assured al-Mallah I entirely appreciated the gravity of the case. Privately, however, the incident left me impressed with Saddam for different reasons. He had acted with intelligence and restraint, I thought, calmly holding off NCR until he had reviewed the facts himself. Then he had acted fairly, not only exonerating me but rebuffing a powerful American company that had tried to push him around.

But I was new to Baghdad and biased, because Saddam had singled me out for praise. My star was on the rise.

•   •   •

One day I was having lunch in the AE cafeteria with a few colleagues, discussing, as we often did, the future of atomic energy. Dr. al-Mallah strutted in, accompanied by a diminutive, friendly-looking man named Husham Sharif, who had just been appointed to succeed Ali Attia as director of the Nuclear Research Center.

Sharif, it was immediately clear, was a courteous and cultured fellow, the exact opposite of Attia, the abrasive bureaucrat who'd offered Saddam little in exchange for his high-handed ways. He was also a longtime fixture in the Baath Party, with a direct pipeline to Saddam. Unfortunately, he was saddled with a civil engineering degree, a weak hand for dealing with nuclear scientists. Sharif, however, knew what Saddam wanted, and if Saddam was pleased, then everybody could be at ease.

Sharif and al-Mallah asked me to their offices for a cup of tea. When I arrived, they engaged me in some pleasant, aimless banter about my work. Then al-Mallah gave me an odd instruction. He asked me to return to my office, retrieve my briefcase, and go to the gate, where a car and driver would pick me up.

"Speak to no one," he said.

I started to ask what it was about, but he raised a spindly hand. "We just want to talk to you in private, at my house," the secretary general said. "Some things are more easily discussed away from the office."

Al-Mallah's house was located in one of Baghdad's new suburbs, befitting his station, with spacious, high-ceilinged rooms, inlaid tiled floors, and beautifully maintained gardens. His secretary led me to a gracious living room, where I found al-Mallah and Sharif talking in discreet tones.

Al-Mallah's wife then appeared with a drink for me, all smiles. She was a teacher at the College of Arts.

"Why didn't you bring your wife?" she asked me.

"I came straight from the office," I apologized, rising. "Besides, she's probably too young for you to find interesting."

She laughed. "I heard you married a very young girl. Actually, she's probably younger than my students. But bring her next time, I'd love to meet her. Don't worry, I can always put her to work helping me feed you guys."

She left the room, having made me feel very welcome. She was obviously an asset to her abrupt husband, who would do anything to stay in the regime's good graces, including ditching the American woman whom he'd previously married. The Baathists frowned on Western wives.

But al-Mallah, I had been told, had been especially crude about it. He'd had his wife deported without her daughter, and then arranged to have her blacklisted so she couldn't get back in. How the new wife put up with such a cad was hard for me to fathom, but in Saddam's Iraq, she had little room for choice.

None of us did, I was beginning to think. I felt as if I were swimming on the rim of a vortex, a twig slipping into some ominous stream. Over the next few hours, as the hors d'oeuvres and drinks gave way to lamb and rice, and then coffee, the conversation turned to the evening's real agenda, and my apprehension deepened.

At first, it was just shop talk: projects and gossip, the usual stuff when colleagues gather after work. The subject shifted to international developments in nuclear power, upcoming conferences, scientific research. Oddly, however, the mood was rather tense, even glum. Al-Mallah and Sharif kept returning to the theme that Iraq's nuclear program was in the doldrums. Budgets were flat, even declining. Nothing new was going on. The leadership, the code word for Saddam, didn't seem to have much interest in what we were doing.

Then Sharif abruptly turned to me and changed the subject. Had I read the new book called *The Israeli Bomb*? It was written by Fouad Jabir, an American of Palestinian origins.

Of course I had. It was the talk of the Arab intelligentsia. Its theme, which of course I'd heard advanced in a Washington apartment, was that the Arab world faced a bleak future as long as Israel was building nuclear bombs and the Arabs had none. Unless we could create a "balance of terror," we faced permanent, second-class citizenship, with all its political and cultural ramifications. Something had to be done.

I continued eating, uncomfortable with the direction the conversation was taking. The dream of every Baathist, I well understood, was to unify the Arab world and triumph over the Israelis.

"What do you think of Jabir's book?" Sharif suddenly asked me directly.

I was on the spot. I took my time before answering. I knew this was a test, but I didn't care.

"It's a ridiculous study," I said offhandedly, "by somebody who obviously knows nothing about atomic energy and bombs."

The smiles left their faces. They'd obviously swallowed the book whole.

Al-Mallah tried another tack. "We thought it was a very thorough study of the Israeli atomic bomb program," he said.

I shook my head.

"It looks that way," I said, "until you begin to analyze it more closely." I couldn't resist a small jibe. "But you guys must have accepted it without question, because I saw no less than fifty copies in the AE library."

I chuckled, but I'd gone too far. They expected more deference.

"First," I explained seriously, "the idea that Israel has a huge arsenal of nuclear bombs right now is ridiculous on its face," I said. "The Dimona reactor could not produce that much plutonium in such a short time." (Israel had manufactured about a dozen nuclear bombs, according to current reports.)

They nodded slowly.

"Second, in order to compile such an arsenal, they'd have to test at least one or more of them. They're going to make sure the design actually works, because the cost of manufacturing bombs is so huge . . ." I raised my hands in exasperation.

"The cost of making so many bombs is so huge that nobody, certainly not the Israelis, is going to make such an investment—not before they test one and are assured it works. And we have no evidence that they've done this."

They were listening respectfully. Well, I thought, this is what they're paying me for, what they sent me to MIT and brought me back to Iraq for. I might as well tell them the truth.

"It is a good, politically motivated story," I said lightly, "but technically, it's nonsense."

Al-Mallah seemed to break out of a trance. "You mean Israel has no atomic bombs?" he nearly shouted.

"I did not say that," I said softly. "They are in the development stage. So, yes, it's possible they could have a few bombs. But my guess is that they have winnowed their designs to a few workable possibilities, optimizing their budget. They probably have a couple of design versions actually manufactured. But nothing's been tested."

Sharif now came to life. "Don't you expect the Americans or sympathetic Europeans would have helped them select a reliable design? One they don't need to test?"

I nodded. "Maybe," I said. "Maybe. But without testing it's still highly unlikely that they would go into full-scale production. Even if they had, where could they have obtained all this plutonium to make so many bombs? They'd need a ton of the stuff."

"They could have stolen it from American factories," al-Mallah declared.

"No way," I answered. "Not in those quantities."

Al-Mallah's wife had appeared at some point with more coffee and sweets, put them on the table, and withdrawn.

Sharif looked pensive, al-Mallah troubled. Obviously they weren't prepared for my skepticism about the book.

Sharif tried another tack. "If we accept your theory that the Israelis may not have more than a few bombs," he said, "it still means they are way ahead of any of us. It still means that they have the bomb and a production system. And once they assure themselves, one way or the other, that their design is reliable, they can go straight into production, full blast."

Perhaps, I thought. But not likely.

"In any case," Sharif continued, "even if we accept your analysis, what do you suggest we do? We at AE are the only authority in the country in this matter and we have been approached by the political leadership and asked for an opinion."

An opinion. Now we were getting to the crux of the matter.

"What exactly were you asked to advise on?" I hedged.

"Well, is it not obvious?" countered Sharif. "Isn't it? Do or die, that's what we face, isn't it? Or do you think there's another way to handle this?"

Well, there it was, out on the table: an Iraqi bomb. The leadership wanted to see if we could build one—or more. And they wanted to know if I would go along.

My stomach tightened, like it had when I'd gotten the same pitch from Basil al-Kubaisi in Washington. I cleared my throat, as I always did when I was nervous. But my spirits were sinking at the very idea of diverting all that money—billions—from so many other things we needed: doctors, teachers, scientists, lawyers, books, roads, water. The list was endless.

"You guys are authorized to go in that direction?" I asked.

Sharif folded his hands on the table and looked directly at me. "We are Atomic Energy. We need no authorization to make proposals. But if you are worried about wasting your time and energy, I can tell you that I'm confident that if we made a proposal to match the Israeli program, we would have very receptive ears from the highest authority."

It would bail out our floundering program, he went on, renew Saddam's interest in our work.

"If you remember, we could not even send you to a scientific conference earlier in the year because we had no money," he said. "We've reduced our staff and equipment purchases because nobody is interested in atomic energy up there." He meant the presidential palace. "If this continues, we'll be effectively dead, scientifically speaking. The military angle is all they are interested in. If we give them something like this, everything will change overnight."

Sensing my resistance, he threw me an out. "If we had a real live nuclear program, even the peaceful part of the program would benefit."

Now both men seized that angle, clumsily enthusing over the fabulous amounts of money that would flow to AE for nuclear power, nuclear medicine, nuclear research if we got a bomb program going. Anything was possible with Saddam's backing. But the only thing that would get his attention was a bomb.

I parried again.

"Are you going to send your proposal through normal channels?" I asked, remembering the problems I'd had with the computer purchase.

They laughed and looked at each other. "No, it will be going straight to the top," Sharif said. "But again, all we need for now is a plan, something grand but not too detailed. Something that will interest the leadership." He smiled. "And something they can understand."

We all fell silent.

"You can do this, can't you, Hamza," al-Mallah finally said. "Put something on paper." That was an order.

My mind spun. This was deep water. Just this "innocent" conversation had entangled me in state secrets. If I said the wrong thing, Sharif and al-Mallah could have me killed right now, out back. Or by a red truck in an "accident" on the way home. My wife was pregnant with our first child. I wanted to live. I had to put the best face on the situation right now.

I started to nod my acceptance.

"Okay," I said solemnly. "I will do it."

Al-Mallah brightened. Sharif smiled broadly.

"Wonderful!" they both said. "Wonderful!"

I smiled back weakly. I had just taken a first step into a very dark tunnel.

CHAPTER FOUR

———

THE SECRET

OUR HEADQUARTERS would be al-Mallah's house. We started right away.

The mission was breathtaking: Build a nuclear bomb from scratch, starting on a dining room table, far from the technological centers of Europe and the United States. Iraq had no real industrial base, no technological expertise, only our Ph.D.s. Looking back, it was like trying to replicate the *Challenger* from picture books and tinfoil. All we had were books, paper, and pencils. What we needed, just for starters, was a nuclear reactor that could manufacture plutonium in large amounts. And to get one of those, all we'd have to do was find a way to get around international controls on nuclear weapons.

I'd gotten little sleep the night after the meeting at al-Mallah's, getting up several times and pacing the dark house. At dawn, Souham came down and found me in my bathrobe, staring out the living room window at the quiet street. She padded into the kitchen, made me a cup of tea, and, without a word, kissed me on the cheek and disappeared upstairs. Although she was still so very young, I'm sure she sensed I was being drawn into something troubling, but was afraid to ask questions.

I'd run through all the alternatives in my insomnia, and come up empty-handed. There was no way out. Surely by now they had me under discreet surveillance. Even if they didn't, Souham and I couldn't just pack our suitcases and stroll out the airport gates without exit visas.

We'd be stopped. Calls would be made. Saddam's security officers would quietly invite us for an unpleasant conversation. Like-

67

wise, driving overland to Jordan with Souham was impractical. The borders were tight. So I was stuck, at least for now. My only rational alternative, I decided, was to play along until I could think of something else.

As I paced the house, other thoughts crowded my mind, thoughts I would rather have banished. I could barely admit them to myself, much less talk them over with Souham.

Frankly, it was the giddy prospect of conducting immense, hands-on experiments with nuclear fission.

I was, after all, a nuclear physicist. If I got on board there'd be the tantalizing opportunity to observe materials raised to millions of degrees in temperature and millions of atmospheres of pressure. The experiments and simulation programs alone could be fantastic. And it was true: The leap from the lab to an actual bomb would take years, at least a decade, probably more. Who could be sure that the regime would last that long?

Al-Mallah and Sharif were thinking along similar lines. Or at least that's what they implied when I saw them the next day. My ambivalence was probably transparent, so perhaps they were trying to calm me down. In any event, they seemed to go out of their way to downplay the illegality, if not the immorality, of our undertaking.

"Look, Khidhir," Sharif said at one point, "how much can we accomplish? Look at us, with our empty notepads in front of us like students. We haven't even got a reactor that can produce plutonium. We'll be dead by the time a bomb is built—twenty years, at least. Let's just get something on paper to keep them happy." The project, in reality, was ludicrous, they said.

"Them" was Saddam, I had no doubt of that. And I'm sure I showed my doubts.

"We'll get this thing going, get a hell of a lot of money for AE, keep Saddam happy," Sharif and al-Mallah kept repeating.

That was their least convincing argument. I didn't take Saddam for a fool. To the contrary. If I had any doubts about it, they were dispelled with the arrival of a very troublesome fellow by the name of Adnan Meshadani.

Meshadani was a heavyset man in his mid-twenties with a large, porcine nose. On paper a mere research assistant, Meshadani was also one of the glib, swaggering young Baath operatives who were increasingly showing up in government ministries. When he swaggered into al-Mallah's house during our first, top-secret deliberations, I smelled trouble. He could only be a spy, and al-Mallah's craven deference to him underscored the point. His shiny government car spoke for itself. Nor was discretion his particular virtue. Soon Meshadani was inviting some of his Baath Party pals over to al-Mallah's, where they lounged around having drinks while we tried to carry on our discussions in the next room.

There was no how-to book on making a bomb, although the basic principles had been well known for over half a century. Beginning in the 1940s, each country had gone its own way, starting with Germany (the Nazis abandoned the effort as impractical). Their work was picked up by the United States, the Soviet Union, England, France, China, and Israel. India, Pakistan, and South Africa would follow. Every nation had the same goal: to split atoms in a way that mocked a sunburst on Earth.

The Americans, of course, were the first to master the bomb, with a successful test in the New Mexico desert in July 1945. Incredibly, I found their Manhattan Project reports on a dusty shelf in the AE library, under a placard reading, "This is a gift from the United States Atomic Energy Commission." Apparently they were donated to Iraq in 1956 under the so-called Atoms for Peace program. Later, when the Kennedy administration learned the Soviets were offering Iraq a nuclear reactor, it offered an American reactor, but a communist faction in the regime forced the government to refuse it in favor of the inferior Russian model. In any event, I was sure that if U.S. officials knew how valuable its Manhattan Project reports would be to us years later, they would have kicked themselves.

After a few days at al-Mallah's, we decided to follow the path of the Israelis. They'd bought a small research reactor from the French in 1956 and clandestinely turned it to their purposes. We'd do the same, acquiring a medium-size, research-oriented nuclear reactor, along with uranium fuel. But Iraq had its own source of uranium, too, in sulfur deposits in the desert and veins in the northern mountains. The fission of the uranium in the foreign fuel would produce small neutron particles, some of which, in turn, would be reabsorbed by our own uranium in the reactor, producing plutonium.

The task was daunting. We'd also need a clandestine fuel reprocessing unit to separate the plutonium. Normally, at least eleven pounds were needed to make a single atomic bomb. The trick would be getting our own uranium in and out of the reactor unobserved by the international inspectors and their cameras, and hiding the reprocessing operation. The International Atomic Energy Agency (IAEA) had the right to inspect its signatories' nuclear facilities every six months. Israel, India, and Pakistan had never signed. We had.

The enormity of it all nearly had us laughing. But all that was far, far down the line. For now, al-Mallah thought, we at least had enough material to write a report for Saddam.

We wrote a forty-page plan, which was both conservative and optimistic. We made no pledges. We made no guarantees. We promised Saddam only the possibility of a bomb, and then only if he provided the necessary hundreds of millions of dollars in support. Foreign sources would have to be induced to provide the necessary technology. And all along we'd have to get around international safeguards and inspections.

It was a very tall order. Leaping all those hurdles was, I reflected, a remote possibility. But in the meantime, al-Mallah crowed, the money would start flowing like water.

Inevitably, our absences from the office were causing a stir. Dr. al-Shahristani in particular was suspicious. Slim and austere, with a high regard for himself, al-Shahristani was incensed at being left out of the loop on something important, especially after his groundbreaking work on the mercury poisoning. He also had an increasingly open contempt for the regime, a hazardous combination.

"What's going on out there?" al-Shahristani demanded at a meeting of section heads. "You guys have been gone for days now. If there's something serious that requires all the brass to leave, shouldn't we all be informed, or aren't we trustworthy enough for you?"

The new head of the physics department, Dr. Abdullah Abul-Khail, was equally annoyed. "You disappear from the department for days without my knowledge, and then I get an order from al-Mallah saying you are on official business. What kind of business is this that I, your boss, cannot be told about it?"

These were two of my closest colleagues, but I had to be careful. I was living in a hall of mirrors and nobody could be trusted.

"I'm sorry, but if you have any questions about my absences, please direct them to al-Mallah," I apologized, "since I am not authorized to discuss it with you."

Al-Shahristani snorted, waved a hand, and shook his head.

"You guys think you are smart?" he said. "Meeting in al-Mallah's house? We all noticed the official cars parked in front of his house. You think everyone is stupid?"

I didn't answer.

"I think you guys are cooking up something," he said, shaking a finger, "and I'm ready to bet anything that I know what it is."

That unnerved me for a second, but I refused to be baited. It was too dangerous, even if al-Shahristani knew. The obnoxious Meshadani, Saddam's spy, no doubt had every Baathist ear pricked to what I said. So I shrugged my shoulders and left the room.

It turned out to be wise. A few days later, Meshadani and al-Mallah came to my office looking agitated. Al-Shahristani, they said, represented a danger to the project and to himself. He was going around headquarters grumbling about our private meetings, speculating on what we were up to, calling Saddam "a murdering ignoramus who was taking Iraq down the drain." If Saddam ever heard what he was saying . . . They wanted him transferred. Immediately.

I blanched. Sometime soon, I knew, I was going to be made head of the AE physics department. Demoting someone of al-Shahristani's caliber, I said, would be seen as dishonorable and have serious repercussions in the scientific community. I did not want to be associated with it. If they had to do it, then they had better do it before I took over, because I did not want it done on my watch.

Al-Mallah did it in his typically heavy-handed way. When al-Shahristani came to work the next day he was stopped at the main gate, stripped of his official car, handed his transfer order, and curtly told to go away. There was no transportation for him to get back to Baghdad, about twenty miles distant. The world-famous nuclear chemist, standing in the dust, had to hail a cab. In his hand was his new assignment, or more accurately exile, to a small college in the north.

Yet, as ugly as it was, al-Shahristani's firing postponed the terrible reckoning that awaited him at the hands of Saddam. Al-Mallah had been right, as we would eventually learn: Saddam would never swallow a mere scientist's impertinence.

IBM's technicians had been laboring for six months on the installation of our new 360/135 mainframe. We'd sent our people to the company's Middle East training center in Beirut. Now, the gleaming new machine, a full wall of steel and spinning hard disks, was whirring and clicking as smoothly as a Japanese bullet train. I made one last pass through the room, running my hand along the computer's face. Everything, I hoped, was in order.

Saddam was coming for a visit.

It was a typically searing-hot day for Baghdad in August 1973. Grim-looking, heavily armed security agents had arrived early to comb the building, sending our own security force away. Bomb technicians and their dogs scoured the corridors and offices. At the appointed hour, section heads were assembled outside the main administrative building. Soon, a motorcade arrived, and Saddam stepped from his Mercedes.

Until now I'd only seen him on TV. There was the familiar slicked black hair, dark mustache, and thick eyebrows. As usual, he was wearing a well-cut linen suit. But everything else was different. On TV, he was always surrounded by fawning officials and adoring crowds, always smiling, trading pleasantries, even joking with the people around him. Not so this morning. His face was dour, concealing some unfathomable rage. He ignored al-Mallah's welcoming remarks and, after a brief touch of our hands along the reception line, strode briskly into the main building.

Al-Mallah caught up and tagged along, fawning and fluttering as Saddam moved through the corridors. But the vice president showed little interest in al-Mallah's spiel about the new computer and its capabilities, instead interrupting him with banal questions about the building. We cringed at the embarrassing spectacle, all the more because of al-Mallah's stutter, which worsened with every minute.

Eventually Saddam came to the computer center, and it was my turn to show him the centerpiece of the program. I was, of course, nervous. He walked slowly along the mainframe with me, touching it once or twice, but then quickly lost interest. I was surprised, considering the fuss we'd had over the contract. I'd half-expected he might even make a joke about getting his money's worth. Instead, he appeared bored by my presentation and anxious to move on to inspect our offices.

He stopped in the corridor outside my warren of rooms. On the wall by the door I had tacked up a scroll of photo portraits of history's greatest scientists, from Copernicus to Einstein, donated by IBM, nearly a hundred in all. It was hardly more than high school fare, but it gave some color to the bare corridor.

Saddam stopped and studied the pictures. Then he raised a hand and pointed.

"What are those?" he asked, barking out in his rural Arabic. "Who are they?"

I smiled weakly. "Sir, those are the greatest scientists in history."

He turned to me, looking agitated. Then, suddenly, he combusted into a cold fury.

"What an insult this is! All these great men, these great scientists!" He jabbed a finger at the pictures.

What? I was dumbfounded. I didn't know what he was talking about. My mouth was open.

"You don't have enough respect for these great men to frame their pictures?" he demanded. "You can't honor them better than this?"

"I . . ." But the pictures were hardly more than magazine photos, I began to explain. Just a temporary decoration. They were not really worthy of frames.

I glanced at al-Mallah, who gave me a curt shake of his head. I stopped in mid-sentence. Saddam was silently glaring at me. I lowered my eyes and murmured assent as Saddam resumed his harangue.

"How could you show such disrespect? This is entirely unacceptable," he declared. I stood stoic as he babbled on, saying nothing.

At last, he walked away.

Hours later, when my shakes finally went away, I figured it out. He'd sensed some independence in me, and made the only point he wanted to make: He was in charge. Anyone who challenged him did so at the risk of his life. It had nothing to do with the pictures.

For months, at a distance, I'd assessed him as rather clever. But now I saw he was a killer. And an ignorant one at that.

What's the IAEA? Saddam demanded. His memo landed on our desks like a mortar.

The International Atomic Energy Agency, headquartered in Vienna, had been organized by the United States and other members of the nuclear club to monitor the proliferation of atomic reactors, which, pushed by the major plant manufacturers, had been spreading rapidly to Iran, Israel, India, Pakistan, South Africa, and other countries who might use them to make a bomb. There were reactors in South Vietnam and the Philippines. Even Taiwan, nominally leashed by the United States, was secretly toying with the idea of making a bomb from the by-products of nuclear reactors. Iraq had a small Russian reactor that was not really adequate for producing fuel for a bomb.

Members of the IAEA pledged to open their atomic programs to international inspection. Iraq's pro-West royalist government, which had also signed the 1961 Nuclear Nonproliferation Treaty, had joined the IAEA at its inception.

Eventually, we figured out the answer Saddam wanted and gave it to him: The IAEA was essentially a U.S.-dominated international spy agency, whose purpose was to prevent countries like Iraq from getting the bomb. His response: Get inside it and turn it to our purposes.

A tall order. Under the indifferent watch of our ambassador in Vienna, Iraq's involvement in the IAEA was nonexistent. Our first priority would be to mount a strenuous campaign to get Iraq onto the IAEA's board of governors, which held elections for half of its twenty-two seats every year. At the same time, we wanted to get an Iraqi appointed as a nuclear inspector. That way we'd have our own spy on the inside, as Saddam wanted. But we had to get to Vienna and work the rooms.

In September 1973, we flew to Vienna, the cradle of Haydn and Mozart, Franz Joseph and Prince Metternich. Supposedly, the ambassador had paved the way for our plan. But when we arrived, no political work had been done, and we didn't even have hotel rooms. To our furious complaint, the ambassador responded with a diffident shrug. Obviously, he hadn't grasped the fact that we were sent by Saddam. The next day he was removed as head of our delegation.

Our new chief flew in from Baghdad. Thin and intense, Dr. Husham al-Shawi was the regime's Oxford-educated minister of education, a portfolio obtained by virtue of his leadership of an Arab nationalist group aligned with Saddam.

The change was electric: Al-Shawi was brisk and authoritative, quickly grasping our difficulties and issuing instructions in his clipped British style. It was also clear that he was closely following Saddam's script. Over the following days he studied Saddam's cables like a schoolboy, making sure he missed nothing and understood every word.

At first glance, we faced impossible odds. Our rival, Iran, with plans to buy twenty nuclear power stations, had been campaigning for the board's Middle East seat for a year and was backed by the United States. It appeared to have the votes locked up, even among Arab delegations, including the Saudis, who apologized profusely but informed us that diplomatic niceties made it impossible to change their votes. The Soviet bloc was also in the Iranian column. Al-Shawi immediately apprised Saddam.

To our utter shock, within a few days a parade of delegations began showing up at the embassy to announce, in solemn tones, that they were changing their votes. Of course, we were curious. We learned that Saddam had simply called his foreign minister on the carpet and let him know his job was riding on the IAEA vote. Midnight cables had gone out to Iraqi ambassadors in each target country and summonses were issued to foreign ambassadors in Baghdad. The message was as subtle as an oncoming train: With oil prices high and supplies tight in the wake of the Arab oil embargo, Iraq was ready to cut prices to its special friends. We also had huge standing orders for their nuclear and other technologies. Friends would be rewarded, enemies punished. Overnight, the vote started swinging our way.

It was the talk of Vienna. But then the Americans got angry. Four U.S. presidents, going back to a CIA coup that returned Shah Reza Pahlavi to the Peacock Throne, had backed Iran. Teheran was the linchpin of U.S. security interests in the Middle East, second only to Israel. The United States was not about to allow the upstart Iraqis to push the Iranians aside. Soon enough, as I was sitting in the Iraqi delegation's seat at the IAEA assembly, I felt the full heat of Washington's frustration. An American diplomat approached me, his face twisted in anger.

"We know what you're doing," he said, wagging a finger. I looked around. This was very undiplomatic behavior. Nearby delegates saw the commotion and glanced our way.

"You should save yourselves the trouble and just quit," the American continued, oblivious to the stir he'd caused, "because we are on to you, and we will never—never—let you win." With that he turned on his heel and stalked away.

All in all, the incident was fairly amusing, but when I told al-Shawi about it, he frowned. He fidgeted in thought for a brief moment, and then announced crisply, "It means that we cannot pursue that seat now." Directly challenging Washington would be a mistake, he said. We had to consider alternatives.

As if on cue, a super-delegation of several South American countries showed up. They suggested we drop our fight with Iran, which was tearing the assembly apart, and instead accept a "floating seat" traditionally reserved for an African or Asian country. The seat was now held by Egypt, but its term was up. If we agreed to take it, the assembly would approve.

It was obvious that Washington had put the South Americans up to the scheme, but we decided to play ball. A floating seat was a seat, after all.

The next day, however, we learned we'd been double-crossed. An Iraqi source in the IAEA told us that Egypt in fact intended to hold on to its seat.

Now our necks were really on the block. Saddam had made it perfectly clear that we were not to come back to Baghdad empty-handed. In our desperation, we decided to call Egypt's bluff.

As soon as I spotted the Egyptian ambassador at the evening banquet, I approached him very discreetly. Arm-twisting was supposed to be off-limits during the dinner.

"As you know, Mr. Ambassador, we've been offered the floating seat," I said quietly, "but if you still want it, we'll step aside. It's not our intent to pick a fight with our Egyptian brothers."

The ambassador's eyes narrowed, but he was on the spot. There was no way he could admit Egypt's double-dealing. So he drew himself up, managed a smile, and assured me there wouldn't be a problem. "We have no intent to pursue that seat," he said. "To the contrary, I have strict instructions from my government to campaign for you."

"Thank you, Mr. Ambassador," I responded. "That's very kind of you. I'm sure Iraq will remember this selfless act." With that I smiled and withdrew.

On election day we split the delegates among us. I took two aisles, al-Mallah took two, and another member of our team took two. We told the delegates that Egypt had withdrawn its nomination and wanted its votes thrown to Iraq. In the end, we moved just enough votes to win (and not long after, to get an Iraqi appointed as a nuclear inspector). After the tally, I happened to pass the Egyptian ambassador, who looked at me with murder in his eyes. The U.S. ambassador was nowhere to be seen.

We flew home relieved, like a football team that had won on the last play. Nothing those delegations could have done would have equaled Saddam's fury. And sure enough, classified information began to flow from our spy inside the IAEA. Saddam had been right.

He was always one step ahead of everybody, I was learning. Saddam had studied our first bomb program memo very closely.

There would be no perks, he responded. There would be no Atomic City, as we had suggested building. Concentrating everybody in one place would provide too tempting a target for the Israelis; one air raid would wipe them out. To the contrary, he'd scatter the units all over the country, under innocuous-sounding covers. Likewise, there would be no pay raises. It was stupid to create an island of prosperity in the middle of underpaid government employees, he said, which would only call attention to the project. On the other hand, he assured us, if things went well, everyone would reap fabulous rewards. As just one mark of his interest in our work, he was taking over the reins of Atomic Energy himself. Al-Mallah was out.

He should have seen it coming. The planning sessions at his house had turned into a circus, with Baath operatives hanging around, their cars littering the road outside. Then there was a stink with Adnan Meshadani, who'd muscled al-Mallah into hiring his girlfriend at AE. When she refused to marry him, he had her fired, but she didn't go gently into the night. She complained directly to Saddam. Al-Mallah had tried to please everyone, and lost control. Our secret was coming unglued. The final straw was Vienna, which al-Mallah had treated like a foreign junket.

Saddam moved swiftly, without fanfare. One day al-Mallah simply didn't show up. Days passed, and still he was gone. His office gathered dust, the chair stayed empty. Al-Mallah had disappeared. Weeks later he was seen puttering around in an undefined role on the AE board.

There had been no announcement, but everybody knew: Saddam was now in charge. The office of the secretary general was canceled. Sharif was also out. Of the three men who had started toward the bomb, I was the only one left.

My new boss was Khalid Ibrahim Saeed, a short, gregarious young man who'd been retooled under Saddam's personal direction. When I first arrived at the AE, Saeed was a chubby young research assistant in the physics department. Soon after, he disappeared to England. When he returned three years later, he had a Ph.D. in solid-state physics. How he managed that in such a short time nobody knew. The credential, however, gave him a leg up on Sharif among the nuclear scientists at Atomic Energy. Saddam was then able to put him into the top job at the Nuclear Research Center, shoving Sharif aside.

Only thirty-three, Saeed was now Saddam's own man at Atomic Energy. His first act was to send for me and inquire about the security breaches at al-Mallah's house. He said that he'd heard about the fiasco from Iraqi intelligence agents in England. From now on, he said, party members would have no hand in running the AEC, and security matters would be handled professionally, through proper channels. All party operatives who used to have the run of the AEC, he declared, had been reassigned.

Saeed also made it clear that he was unhappy about al-Shahristani's abrupt transfer, and was going to get him back. Their connection went back a long way, I knew. Both started college in the Soviet Union, but when they realized Moscow was using them mostly for propaganda, they managed a transfer to England. Al-Shahristani got his degree in chemistry, Saeed in physics. Al-Shahristani then went to Canada to get his Ph.D., Saeed to the United States for a master's. Now, with the bomb project approved by Saddam, Saeed said, he needed al-Shahristani more than ever, no matter how difficult he was.

But there was someone else, even more important, whom he wanted back, he divulged: Jaffar D. Jaffar, the brilliant experimental nuclear physicist who had exiled himself to Europe. Jaffar, he said, was "the key to our project. And we've got to get him back."

The dinner was at an expensive supper club in Jadriyah, Baghdad's Beverly Hills. The club had been cleared out at Saddam's order, though he would not be personally attending. In his stead, anchoring the center table, was Ghanim Abdul-Jalil, his hideous chief of staff. Few would grieve later when Abdul-Jalil, accused by Saddam of conspiring against him with Syrian president Hafiz al-Assad, was executed. On this night, however, Saddam's man was the laughing, amiable host, presiding over a dinner designed to flatter Jaffar D. Jaffar into returning. All the department chiefs were there.

About the time I came back from America, Jaffar had left for Europe, annoyed by al-Mallah's imperious ways and lack of support for nuclear experimentation. But his footprints were everywhere at AE, I found. He'd had a hand in ordering every piece of equipment. He loved designing experiments. He was also the department's social lion. Slim and darkly handsome, he'd led a posse of pals on the rounds of Baghdad's nightspots.

Jaffar's royalist pedigree was well known but forgiven. His father had been a finance minister in the king's cabinet, but the family money came from his grandmother, who was the daughter of a major Shia-sect headman in India. Legend had it that Jaffar's yearly take came in bags of money and jewelry. Whatever the facts, his family once owned huge swaths of real estate in Baghdad, including the land on which Saddam's own palace was built.

Jaffar's education was private school, followed by college in Britain and a Ph.D. in high-energy nuclear physics from the University of Birmingham. He was only twenty-four when he finished his degree and came back to Iraq. He interviewed to teach at Baghdad University, but the head of the physics department was put off by his stutter. So he went to the AEC, where he was quickly allowed the run of the place. A Russian reactor was about to be commissioned, so Jaffar took a team to the Soviet Union, studied the technology, and fell in love with fission. Soon he was head of both AE's reactor and physics departments and designing experiments. Just at that point, however, the malaise set in at AE under al-Mallah and he left for a job with the European Center for Nuclear Research (CERN) in Switzerland.

With Saddam's green light, Jaffar was flown back for a whirlwind week, capped by a lavish dinner, offers to return all his family's confiscated land or reasonable compensation, and a sparkling new job at AE. By April 1974, he was back on staff. The time would come, of course, when he bitterly regretted it.

The Iraq Air jetliner rumbled down the runway at Baghdad, lifted off, and banked north over the desert. It was June 1974. I sat back in my seat, closed my eyes, and dreamt of what was ahead. We were headed to France to buy a nuclear reactor, the first big step toward making a bomb.

The purses had suddenly opened. A few months earlier I'd asked for about four million dollars' worth of equipment. To my utter amazement, my full request was swiftly approved. Then I was told I'd head the delegation to Paris.

There were three others making the trip: Jaffar, Abdul-Qadir Abdul-Rahman Ahmed, a Kurd with a background in nuclear chemistry, and al-Shahristani, who'd been miraculously rehabilitated.

When he first came back, al-Shahristani was subdued and ill at ease, no doubt embarrassed by the ordeal he'd been through. But in no time he was back to his old self, making caustic jibes about the Baathists.

"Hey, another party meeting," he cracked one day as Saeed returned to his office. "How many people were condemned today?" Saeed merely rolled his eyes and walked on. Al-Shahristani had no idea how fortunate he was.

Our tattered old jet, a British castoff that was costing the government a bundle in spare parts, descended over the green French countryside. We were carrying a pittance in pocket money, but the embassy got us first-class rooms at the Intercontinental. I'd persuaded Saeed that there was no way we could travel like rug merchants and make a credible offer on a nuclear reactor, so he made a few calls.

The week ahead would be an elaborate put-on, suitable for Gilbert and Sullivan. Why would Iraq, sitting on a sea of oil, be investing hard-earned millions in nuclear power? On the face of it, our cover story didn't pass a smell test, but as we would learn again and again, nobody cared. Everybody wanted our money.

The French were first in line. Saddam had already cinched the reactor deal in principle with Prime Minister Jacques Chirac, undoubtedly as a quid-pro-quo for oil concessions in Iraq, Iraqi imports of French cars, the award of a lucrative contract to develop a lake resort outside Baghdad, and promises to make a huge purchase of French military planes. Whatever it was, something had cast a potent enough spell on legendary Gallic cynicism to permit the sale of a sophisticated reactor "for peaceful applications." Of course, for a militant Arab leader with fathomless oil reserves, the reactor could have only one true purpose: to produce fuel for a nuclear bomb.

The French were turning out to be easier to manage than my two colleagues, al-Shahristani and Jaffar, who kept sniggering about our "firecracker project." Word had come down that they were not to be read into the true aims of our project until their reliability was beyond doubt. I was forbidden, therefore, to discuss the bomb project at all.

Of course, the proposition was utterly fantastic that the two nuclear scientists couldn't figure out what was going on. On the other hand, I had to accept the possibility that they were being used against me in a double game to test my own reliability. Whatever the truth, I played my role, kept a straight face, and waved off their jokes. The disclosure wasn't going to come from me. No matter how absurd, my mantra was that we were buying a reactor to conduct nuclear experiments, until I was told to change the script.

The routine was typically French. Each morning we started out at Saclay, headquarters of the French atomic energy agency, on the outskirts of Paris. We'd take a leisurely tour of the facilities, then at noon, we'd be taken to a reserved cafeteria. We'd have a couple of drinks before lunch, which would then be washed down with wine.

After lunch, more drinks would be served. It would be three or four in the afternoon before we'd have another go at negotiations. We had decided right off to purchase the Osiris reactor (named for the Egyptian god of the underworld). The rest of the sessions were about specs and ancillary equipment.

After a few days, however, I had to ask the French to ease up on the liquor. It was hard enough to keep my eyes open, much less engage in complicated technical talks. Every night, there'd be another drinking binge at dinner.

True to form, Jaffar wanted to hit all the clubs, particularly the ones off the Champs Elysées that catered to Arab oil money. One night he took us down a side street and knocked on an unmarked, ornate door. A bouncer cracked it open. Disco music poured out, and behind him we glimpsed a hall full of Parisian beauties and only one or two men, dressed in the white suits typical of Gulf Arabs.

The bouncer took one look at us and closed the door.

"What happened?" I asked Jaffar. He was already bounding down the street, undaunted.

"Too many of us," he said. "That place, they like single men they can pick off."

He wanted the company of a beautiful woman. Ahmed and I looked at each other and shrugged. Down another side street, he landed us at another door. This time we got in. A couple of smiling women in sequined dresses quickly appeared at our table. Jaffar sized them up and asked one if she'd like a glass of champagne. Ahmed and I rolled our eyes. She sat down, and many hundreds of Jaffar's francs later, she left. So did we.

Walking back, I was tingling with the magic of Paris at dawn. Here I was, a boy from Diwaniyah buying a nuclear reactor.

The next day our hosts arranged dinner for us on the upper deck of a tour boat on the Seine. We floated down the river under the lilac sky, taking in the sights. The French were in a jovial mood, and why not? They had a three-hundred-million-dollar deal in the offing.

Dinner began with pink champagne. When the waiter arrived, I asked what the national dish was. *"Cuisses de grenouille,"* he said. Frog legs. "Fine," I said, smiling, "I'll have that." Moments later I was digging into the purest garlic I'd ever tasted.

Amid all the bacchanalia, however, we managed to closely study the reactors, particularly the Osiris, the EL-3, and the EL-3 Prime— all plutonium-capable plants. We'd also decided what kind of equipment we'd want to add. Other negotiations revolved around training, spare parts, and, of course, prices.

Every day, the French were hiking the bill. Their initial estimate for the whole package was $150 million; after two weeks, it was $300 million. When we howled, they dismissed our complaints and suggested we go elsewhere.

But they knew we would take it. French companies dealing with Iraq routinely multiplied the actual cost of a contract by four. In our case, they'd multiplied it by ten at the end, knowing we had no choice: They knew Saddam wanted the French reactor and would take it at any price.

All their information about us, in fact, was very good. They were intrigued that Jaffar had left CERN after such a short while to go back to Iraq. They knew that his father had been the king's finance minister. They asked me why I'd left a professorship in the United States for a low-paying job in Iraq. Closer to the bone, they asked why, if Jaffar and I were the only real nuclear physicists in Iraq, we needed the Osiris reactor for research. Wasn't our Soviet reactor sufficient? At some point I must have squirmed, because our hosts broke out laughing.

"Don't worry," one said with a wink, "we just need this stuff for our report."

The cruise down the Seine came to an end with handshakes all around. As we walked along the quay, the Eiffel Tower was twinkling against a purpling sky. The light summer breeze promised endless possibilities. But I was wondering: How long could our secret be winked at, before somebody paid a price?

CHAPTER FIVE

———

THE LIFE OF THE PARTY

THE EGYPTIAN BELLY DANCERS jiggled across the stage, shaking their bellies like quivering bowls of crème brûlée. The oudh players strummed themselves into a dither. The violinists sawed away.

It was a typical night at the Hunting Club, the private cabaret for Baghdad's elite. With a difference: Normally the band had the audience on its feet, clapping and whistling the dancers to greater and wilder gyrations. But not tonight. On Thursday nights we sat glued to our seats, sipping our drinks and checking our watches. We were waiting for Saddam.

Sometime between nine and ten o'clock, he appeared in the doorway. His oiled black hair, brush mustache, and rheumy-looking eyes had not yet earned the instant, global recognition they would when he sent his armies into Kuwait, set oil wells afire, and terrorized the world with the threat of chemical weapons. In the mid-1970s, few Americans outside the Middle East knew his name. To Washington, however, he was someone to track as his hands got a tighter grip on power.

I watched Saddam move deliberately through the crowd. With his gold Rolex, French cuffs, and entourage trailing behind him, he evoked nothing less than an expertly tailored, well-barbered gangster. He brimmed with casual self-confidence, the same smiling image so ubiquitous on TV. We, his senior ministers, scientists, army generals, and party faithful, so desultorily sipping our scotches only a moment before, rose from our tables, obsequiously offering applause. Gliding through the club, Saddam returned a half-smile, a nod, or a brief wave, soaking us up with his onyx eyes, betraying

85

nothing. In the unlikely event he missed anything, security cameras, watching through pinholes in the walls, got it all.

We knew Saddam's spies had compiled dossiers on each of us favored enough to enter this sanctuary, set on a vast estate of green grass, tennis courts, and other enticements next to the racetrack in the high-end Mansour district. The Hunting Club was Saddam's private preserve. He personally approved the guest list; he personally managed the decor. He had made the club part of his empire, and gradually turned it into a social center for the country's elite. But no one doubted the identity of the club's most privileged guest. He picked the entertainment and went over the reports supplied by his private police on the patrons. The sauna and swimming pool were off-limits in the mornings, just in case he dropped in for a swim. The glass eyes of mounted boar heads, deer, and antelope stared out at us from plaques along the walls. Display cases held collections of shotguns and knives. The Hunting Club was thoroughly Saddam's.

Most of us would spend hours, or even days, trying to decipher his gestures on these nights. Did he smile our way? Did he seem pleased to see us, or annoyed? We lived in a gilded cage.

My pay and perks were steadily rising. I had the Hunting Club membership, a government car, a nice new home, and tailored foreign suits. Saddam was very good at this, doling out carrots while wielding a very big stick. But along with the rewards we also heard new whispers—of torture, murder, disappearances into a vast network of secret prisons. The perks helped us look the other way.

I watched Saddam and his entourage take their seats at the front row of tables, which had been empty until now. A flurry of waiters groaning with trays of drinks and aperitifs appeared. A bottle of Saddam's favorite, Johnnie Walker Blue Label, was reserved for him at the bar. Everything, of course, had been screened in the kitchen by Saddam's own taster, who led a worrisome life. If he intercepted a poison, he could die a terrible death. If the vice president developed a cramp, he might be arrested, and the entire kitchen staff threatened with death. The same went for his physician. A story went round that Saddam came down with diarrhea at the palace one day and ordered a squad of security agents into the kitchen. For hours the cooks and food handlers quaked under the gun barrels while the doctor examined the boss. Only when a common cold was diagnosed was the kitchen staff released.

The likelihood that Saddam would eat innocently tainted food was highly remote, because it was screened by Atomic Energy. Most of it was flown in daily from Paris, where a special embassy detail purchased the best beef, lamb, lobster, and shrimp. Then it was sent to our technicians, who employed multimillion-dollar machines to check for poisons, radiation, or even trace elements of metals, such as mercury, lead, or arsenic. If there was the slightest question, the food would be sloughed off in the public markets or restaurants. The same went for Saddam's toilet articles, clothes, and the black dye for his hair, which were likewise screened for toxins. The Iraqi embassies in London and Paris employed men of Saddam's exact size to shop for his wardrobe.

Saddam had a terrible fear, perhaps paranoia, about germs. A physician was always stationed outside his office to look over visitors. Even his closest aides were interrogated on whether they had a cough or runny nose before they were permitted to enter, with their eyes, ears, and mouth examined for signs of disease. No one was permitted to touch Saddam, unless it was an occasion carefully choreographed for television. Those who forgot or simply didn't know were beaten beyond the camera's eye. Although he was a nominal Muslim, Saddam permitted only Christians to work on his housekeeping staff, convinced they were cleaner than his own people.

Tonight, Saddam and his companions nibbled at the food on their plates at the front of the club, which seemed drained of pleasure. Fear had put a stop to that. I surveyed the room, taking in glimpses of the other high party members and officials who, like me, enjoyed the exalted status of an insider. There was Tariq Aziz, the portly sycophant who would become Saddam's foreign minister and a fixture on CNN. There was Adnan Khairallah, the boisterous and deadly army general and cousin of Saddam. There was Humam al-Ghafour, who would become the sophisticated chairman of Atomic Energy. And there was my former boss, Moyesser al-Mallah, who seemed to be chuckling at a private joke, perhaps how he'd inveigled Saddam into spending millions on a nuclear bomb. What a fool. The subversive thought crept into my head: Was a social evening with Stalin like this? Did Hitler's aides clink glasses, knowing they could be shot without warning?

The dance floor was empty. I noticed that the women at Saddam's tables, draped in diamonds and dresses from Paris showrooms, started to fidget and look bored. Then suddenly a folded piece of paper arrived at our table, addressed to al-Mallah. He opened it up. It was an "invitation" from Saddam—to get up and dance.

Al-Mallah knew what was expected. He pasted a smile on his face, rose from his seat, took his wife by the arm, and led her to the floor, where they put on the semblance of a happy two-step. The waiters circled the room dropping little pieces of paper on the tables, and other couples joined them. Soon, the dance floor was filled.

One could never be caught looking at Saddam. Or his table guests. Excessive talking or drinking was also dangerous. One night a friend of mine had a little too much to drink. He was regaling the table with a funny story and his voice got a little too loud. Soon two security men materialized. One bent down to whisper in his ear. He flushed, meekly rose, and walked out of the room, the security men trailing. The next day his name appeared on the club bulletin board. He had been banned for unseemly behavior.

He was lucky. Another man was sitting in a swanky Baghdad restaurant one night when Saddam and his entourage arrived unexpectedly. The man innocently reached into a briefcase for a pack of cigarettes. Security men jumped from nowhere, knocked him to the floor, and held him at gunpoint while his briefcase was searched.

Saddam made it impossible to relax. The couples tried, but their dancing was wooden. Laughter was forced, conversation dwindled. The drinks soon tasted sour. But the awful truth was, there was nowhere else we would have been. Thursday night at the Hunting Club was the top of the heap, the sexiest perk of the regime. The Arab world's best entertainers, the city's best food and liquor were ours for almost nothing. If life in Saddam's Iraq was becoming a glimpse of hell, so far it was worth having.

For three years now we'd been on a long leash at the Nuclear Research Center, especially the few of us sharing the secret of the bomb. Anyone connected with it seldom had a request rebuffed. I'd recently negotiated an affiliation between Atomic Energy and the International Center of Theoretical Physics, in Trieste, Italy, for example, and taken Souham and our three-year-old son, Firas, on a monthlong trip there.

It flashed through our minds to leave Iraq, but we had neither money nor prospects. And where would we go? What would we do? The bottom was falling out of nuclear research in the West, so there was no need for a nuclear physicist from Iraq. While I attended seminars, Souham shopped, and we came home with extra suitcases packed with clothes, appliances, and electronic goods.

Souham didn't know about the secret program—I'd purposely kept it from her to protect her—but she sensed something dramatic was going on at the office. Meanwhile, she enjoyed the club membership, the bigger house—we'd moved—the growing friendships with the wives of high officials, and the respect accorded the wife of a senior official. But she was smart enough to put two and two together. As I struggled to fix a pipe under the kitchen sink one night, she jibed, "That's not as difficult as making an atomic bomb, is it?" I'm sure I banged my head.

Ironically, considering all the dating I'd done in the States, my arranged marriage with Souham was working out. Although she'd been chosen for me in the Muslim way, mutual passion and respect had taken root. I'd fallen deeply in love, and she was the twenty-year-old mother of our boy. We not only nightclubbed together, we cooked together and played with Firas on the floor. She'd also become my professional collaborator, taking dictation and helping me assemble my books. She was tight-lipped by nature as well, which made her the perfect wife during these times as people began to disappear.

Security, meanwhile, had gotten cloying. Gate inspections had become more rigorous and intrusive. One day a guard started going over me twice, until I complained to the chief of security. Another time a dirty-fingered guard picked through a sandwich I'd brought. Another time, one of our researchers was so incensed by a body search that he dropped his pants and yelled, "You better make sure I'm not hiding anything else."

A more troubling problem, however, was the badgering of scientists whose wives were foreigners. Jaffar, who was married to an

Englishwoman, and al-Shahristani, whose wife was from Canada, were apparently exempt. But two other researchers in the department were constantly harangued about divorcing their wives. Another man, head of our laser section, simply refused to return after a scientific conference abroad.

Foreign contacts were increasingly scrutinized. The purchasing department was the only channel authorized to buy foreign equipment, preventing scientists from advising on crucial decisions. Overall, the number of security personnel at AE had more than quadrupled. Most of them were guards, with nothing to do beside clutter the hallways, but poorly educated Baathists were again being assigned to us in droves. It was becoming clear that the new project was going to be featherbedded by incompetent party hacks. The excuse we got was that they were reliable, security-wise, but our first concern was whether they knew anything about atomic energy. Most knew little beyond basic physics, if that.

We began to complain, resulting in confrontations with administrators and a further lowering of morale. More than a dozen scientists demanded transfers. Other scientists left the country rather than accept orders to work under such conditions. One physicist wrote to President al-Bakr that he wouldn't come back unless an order was issued transferring him to the University of Baghdad. Lucky for him, he was.

The ruckus was finally picked up by Saddam, who called a two-day conference to address the rising discontent. Jaffar and I drove together to the meeting hall, on the grounds of the presidential palace. When we passed through the gate, he pointed to an empty lot.

"This is where my house is going to be," he said.

"But this is inside the palace grounds," I said, surprised.

"Yes, but it's still my family's land," Jaffar said, "like a lot of the palace compound."

Unquestionably, it was one of the most valuable pieces of real estate in Baghdad, roughly equivalent to the East Lawn of the White House. But the downside to living even near the palace was that the guards were trigger-happy. Stories abounded of people being shot because they didn't heed a signal to stop. One night a man who'd had a few beers drove past a sentry without hearing the order to halt.

His car was raked with machine-gun fire, killing his ten-year-old daughter. Since Jaffar's main pleasure was staying out all night, I thought it would be a hazardous place for him to live. As it turned out, however, the time would come when he would prefer being shot.

When we arrived at the hall, some two dozen senior scientists, department heads, and administrators were waiting for Saddam. A high-backed chair sat on a raised podium at the front, along with a water pitcher and a couple of glasses. Soon, a security man walked in, poured water into a glass, took a sip, and swirled it slowly in his mouth—quite a show for our benefit. Then Saddam entered the hall, and we all rose. He gestured for us to sit down. Flashing a comfortable smile, he looked like a man without a care in the world. Tea was served to us all, and he started into his lecture.

"This meeting is to get to know you, and also help you to resolve some of the problems you may have," he said, looking us over and still smiling. "It's apparent that in our bureaucratic system, sometimes real-life problems are ignored."

He began walking the stage.

"Do you know what a bureaucrat is?" he asked. He made it sound like a living room conversation. We looked at each other.

"A bureaucrat is a person who looks at the world through a flow of paper across his desk," the vice president said. "He has no knowledge of the real world except what he reads." His smile began to evaporate.

"We try not to be bureaucratic, but our administrators slip into it naturally as an inherited tradition of our system of government."

He paced a few more steps, letting his message sink in.

"You have to excuse me, my doctor says that I should walk two hours a day."

We affected concern.

"I will give you an example," he resumed. "Suppose we have a problem with a certain country. To get some inside information on that country, I will read our ambassador's reports. But do I get anything realistic from these reports? Anything to help me deal with the problem? No. Most of the time I don't. They are the reports of a bureaucrat, totally disengaged from what is really going on.

"But," he said with a shrug, "this is the system that we inherited, and we have to keep working on it until we finally change it."

Then he turned to us.

"But you also have faults," he said. "I hear that you're running some kind of dictatorship over there, a dictatorship of department heads."

He braced us again.

"Our administrators can't place new people in your departments because you keep objecting." He wagged a finger, and his voice turned guttural with his rural Arabic accent. "You must accept the people we send you, because in real life, we have security needs. In real life, we sometimes make appointments not based solely on academic criteria."

I felt my chest tightening.

"A scientist," Saddam went on, "a scientist must be security-conscious, otherwise he is useless. And we don't want him."

He looked over his audience. All of us stared straight ahead.

"Security should be uppermost in your minds," he said, "and it can take many forms. One way is to pretend that you don't know much. Hide what you know and don't flaunt it. But sometimes it is difficult for you to evaluate your foreign friends and acquaintances. So we do this for you."

He wagged a finger again. "From now on, any foreigner you correspond with has to be on our files. You will report him and tell us whatever you know about him."

A window was closing. And then another.

"I hear that you scientists want to go abroad for a year at a stretch on these so-called sabbaticals, even though you've done plenty of studying during your Ph.D."

He rubbed his hands together. "What I say about that is, for now, your doctorates are good enough for us. We don't need you to study even more."

My heart sank.

"Also," he continued, "we don't need money from the IAEA anymore. We'll pay for our own trips to conferences and buy our own equipment with our own money."

The drawbridges were being raised all around.

Saddam's speech went on for another half hour, and it was all downhill. The party half-wits were here to stay. Research was closed.

Then he suddenly looked concerned.

"I know some of you have real problems," he said. "Anybody with a real problem should write to me."

Not me. But some would, which meant we'd all have to eventually, or be conspicuous by our silence. When, as it turned out, the first few sought an audience, they walked away with cash or some other reward, which quickly made the rounds. What it meant was Saddam was adopting the timeless Arab way of dealing with public funds: The treasury belonged to the ruler, to distribute as he pleased. It was a system that had always kept us weak, subservient, and backward.

But there we were. Saddam went on for a while longer, and then we glumly filed out of the meeting. The party had been given new life, resistance would not be tolerated. Feeling the noose around their necks, some scientists fled. One was Ghazi Ayoub, the head of AE health physics, responsible for monitoring radiation. He left for a conference in England and never returned. But Ayoub had a foreign wife and automatic citizenship abroad. The rest of us were trapped. To strengthen his hand, Saddam ruled that anyone who divorced a foreign wife would have his costs paid by the government and get a hefty bonus. A few took him up on the offer.

There was another aspect to Saddam's conference that didn't go unnoticed. Whenever he needed someone to run an errand, he turned to a boyishly handsome man in his early thirties by the name of Humam al-Ghafour. We soon learned that al-Ghafour had managed, through party contacts, to finagle a scholarship to England, where he had gotten a master's degree in physics. An army reserve officer, rumor had it that he'd been writing to Saddam through party channels about the possibility of using AE to make atomic bombs. When he came back, even though he had only a master's, al-Ghafour was billing himself as a foreign-trained nuclear physicist, and in the party hierarchy he was becoming the resident expert on nuclear affairs.

Saddam, we abruptly discovered, had made al-Ghafour his new point man for AE. A colleague of mine who'd gone to college with al-Ghafour was nonplussed. "He wasn't the worst student there," he quipped. "But he was the second worst."

Now the smooth-talking young man was Saddam's atomic energy gofer. The party's "resident expert" moved quickly to put his stamp on things.

One of al-Ghafour's enthusiasms was the idea of using something called laser isotope separation to enrich uranium. The Israelis had made a major breakthrough in the technique, according to the scientific journals, and the Americans were working on it, too. Al-Ghafour was feverish about acquiring the process. He summoned me to his office in the presidential palace, which was only two doors down from Saddam's. My application to go to the United States to purchase a nuclear accelerator, he said, would be approved on the condition that I take a colleague along for a conference on lasers in Santa Fe, New Mexico, where the subject of the Israeli breakthrough might come up.

Of course, I said. I respected Hadi al-Obeidi very much.

The young apparatchik nodded, then leaned back and gazed out the window. He was silent for so long, I thought the meeting was over. I started to leave.

"One moment," he said. I sat down. He turned back to me.

"There's something else I want to talk to you about." He lit a cigarette and exhaled. "I'm afraid that I have information that Hadi is going to join his British wife in England and will not come back with you," he said. He took another drag.

"I want your personal guarantee that you will not let that happen, that you will bring him back with you," he said, pointing at me.

I looked at him. A dozen possibilities flew through my mind, none of them good.

"With all due respect, I don't think I can do that," I finally said, evenly. "Do you expect me to put him in shackles and lock him in a room so he can't run away?"

I leaned forward to explain.

"In the United States, I'll be under American laws," I said. "If I prevent his movement at all, he could have me arrested for kidnapping. So if you're serious, I'd rather have you cancel the trip. Because, I can tell you right now, if Hadi wants to flee, I can't get in his way unless you want me to end up in jail."

I stood up and started to leave.

Al-Ghafour raised his hands. "Wait," he said. "Wait, wait, wait."

I turned around. "Listen," he said, "come to think of it, if Hadi wants to leave, then let him leave. You just go ahead with your trip and regard this conversation just as, you know, an alert to a possibility that we know about it."

He got up from his desk, came around, and offered his hand. "Okay?"

I was still smoldering, but I took it.

"Good luck," he said. "Have a good trip."

I wanted to wash my hand as soon as I left his office. But al-Obeidi wasn't going to be a problem. The problem would turn out to be a Palestinian by the name of Serwan al-Satidah, a short, swarthy man in his late thirties with the patter of a con man and the soul of a pickpocket. In Iraq, he went by the name of Merwan.

A protégé of PLO chairman Yasser Arafat, Merwan had a very special deal in Iraq running a very hush-hush operation called the Al-Hazen center for Research. He had a parade of Americans and Brits visiting the center and unique connections with an American university. He was probably Saddam's major tutor on the subject of Arab self-reliance in science and guns.

"The military sector," he said at a small lecture I attended, "is the most critical, and yet sometimes the easiest, sector to get into. Take a tank. A fully functional, fully automated, ready-to-go tank costs us a bundle. But suppose we buy a stripped-down tank, an older tank. We get the rest of the pieces and equipment and install them ourselves."

He scanned the room. He had the audience with him.

"You know, doing this simple process will save a considerable amount in the cost," he said. "The Israelis do it all the time."

Merwan was working on installing laser range finders on guns and sending students to the University of Arizona's Optics Science Center, the world's leading laser research facility. That alone was an astounding scientific coup for any Iraqi institution, even with our cordial, if not warm, in 1975, relations with the United States. Washington no doubt was taking quiet note of Saddam's steady rise, but to most of the West, we simply looked like an industrious Arab nation putting its oil billions to good use. Merwan's coup spoke for itself; it was astonishing. He would, of course, be going along with al-Obeidi and me to the States.

Just before the trip, he stopped by my office. We engaged in chitchat and gossip. The Palestinian was being oddly deferential, even obsequious. He was obviously angling toward some sort of favor.

"You know, Dr. Hamza," he finally began, "in the States before, they knew me by a different name."

I listened.

"It was . . ." For the life of me, I cannot remember it now. But it was probably his real one, Serwan al-Satidah, and he wanted to make sure I wasn't surprised if I heard it called out when we boarded a plane, passed through U.S. Customs, or met people in the States. He asked that I pass along the word to Hadi al-Obeidi.

"Sure," I said. "No problem." I was beginning to feel like a chaperone on a school trip. But the fact was, the transliteration of Arabic names on Western documents was always a headache. My own name had been spelled so many different ways on visas and other documents that I always traveled in fear of being yanked out of line at some airport and interrogated, especially since PLO terrorists were hijacking planes left and right.

But what the hell. "No problem," I told Serwan. What intrigued me more, frankly, was when he showed up at the Baghdad airport with a bevy of assistants and a thick wad of money. To al-Obeidi and me, Serwan looked like a man who was trying to put one over on Saddam, a very dangerous game. The fact was, his Al-Hazen research center was shrouded in mystery and off-limits to all of us at Atomic Energy—odd, since we were trusted with Saddam's deepest secret. What we knew was that Al-Hazen was generating millions and millions in contracts for foreign equipment, but none of us saw anything produced. We suspected that the money was disappearing into Serwan's pockets—this in a system where Saddam was the chief thief and tightly guarded his prerogatives. Something inside me told me to keep my distance, and it was one of the smartest things I did.

America was a breath of fresh air. I'd almost forgotten what it was like, although Souham and I lived as close to an American lifestyle as we could. I'd taught her how to make hamburgers and pot roast, mashed potatoes and gravy. We were raising our boy on Dr. Spock and feeding him vitamins from Johnson & Johnson. I'd rewired the house so that our U.S.-made humidifier, air purifiers, and our Sears electric blanket would all work. But they didn't add up to the real thing, as I was reminded on the drive from Albuquerque to Santa Fe. The spontaneous variety of America was astounding, especially after being away almost five years. The United States, simply put, was free.

And I yearned to be back. My loan obligation to Iraq was nearly up, but I knew Saddam would never let me go now, not without a struggle. My wife and child were virtual hostages while I was gone. I'd heard scare stories about Saddam's assassins tracking down exiles abroad. What would be the point of running if you were going to be tracked down in Virginia? In any event, the job market for foreign nuclear physicists in America was nil. In Iraq, meanwhile, I led an extraordinarily challenging and comfortable life. My job and prestige were unmatched. I could only hope, as al-Mallah and Sharif had so giddily assured me, that we'd never get to a bomb.

The conference and hotel were both in downtown Santa Fe, which was convenient since we didn't have major credit cards to rent a car. But when a side trip to Los Alamos, the birthplace of the atomic bomb, came up on the docket, we were momentarily stumped. Luckily, a guy from Hughes Aircraft volunteered to take us. He turned out to be a laser expert, so I decided to broach the subject of the Israeli patent as we rolled down from the mountains and into the desert.

Nobody, he stated flatly, had managed to reproduce the Israeli results. In his opinion, the reports were a hoax, probably meant to throw Arab research in the wrong direction. If it couldn't be done yet in American labs, he said—and everyone had tried it—then it couldn't be done at all.

I glanced at al-Obeidi. It was obvious we shared the same delectable thought: If the guy from Hughes was right, then the young party upstart al-Ghafour had swallowed the Israeli bait whole. Even before we left Baghdad, we'd learned he was planning a full-scale program into laser enrichment. We nearly broke out laughing.

As soon as we got back to Santa Fe, we began making discreet probes during breaks in the conference, eliciting opinions from other laser scientists about the reported Israeli breakthrough. The consensus was unanimous: There was nothing to it. The Israelis didn't have the cash or the technology to make it work. The report was "disinformation," a product of Israeli intelligence.

Serwan, meanwhile, was walking the corridors like a rock star, surrounded by people from Arizona. They included the Optics Science Center's most notable scientists. No doubt he'd worked some magic. Our guess was that he'd tapped Saddam's coffers for some impressive grant money, on top of paying the university tuition premiums for every Iraqi student. I momentarily considered trying to set up something along the same lines in America for our Nuclear Research Center, but quickly discarded the thought: With Saddam and his security people breathing down our necks, it would never get off the ground.

But our trip to Los Alamos had been a shock. Its huge Laser Fusion Project was demoralizing to Third World scientists like us. If the Americans could produce energy by using lasers to fuse atoms together, as they appeared close to doing, then it would be impossible for the rest of us, because they'd hold the patent and classify the details. With the exception of the Soviets, no one else could do it. The billions of dollars, industrial base, and technological feats required were prohibitive. The Los Alamos managers were so cocky that they'd opened the laser facility to all of us.

What moved me most, though, was the museum. Inside were replicas of Fat Man and Little Boy, the atomic bombs dropped on Japan. I ran my hand across them, feeling their power. If we managed to build our own, they would look very much like these.

We needed a nuclear accelerator, which was essential for research in low-energy nuclear physics. It can be used to study the structure of atomic nuclei, examine the makeup of materials, even change their properties. It's indispensable for many modern technologies, such as making computer chips. Or help making a bomb.

Because they were so common, our announced intention to buy an accelerator didn't raise any red flags. There were no export restrictions. Jordan was getting one from Germany, Egypt had one, and so did many Third World countries.

Earlier, I'd been approached by a man named Walid Mourad, a Syrian-born salesman for the National Electrostatic Corporation. I told him of our interest in an accelerator, and he invited us to visit his company headquarters in Madison, Wisconsin. We flew up there as soon as the conference ended.

Madison, perched amid lakes cratered by retreating glaciers, is one of the most charming small cities in the United States, home to the University of Wisconsin and the brightly lit dome of the state capitol. With strong programs in advanced math and sciences, the university drew students from around the world, including China, which just three years before we arrived had broken a quarter-century of estrangement from the United States.

Dr. R. G. Herb, a white-haired, ascetic-looking university professor, and winner of the Bonner Prize in nuclear physics, was the president and chief executive officer of NEC. Dr. Herb had invented a new method for generating the millions of volts needed to charge the dome of a nuclear accelerator. Instead of employing a belt of the kind used by MIT's Van de Graaff accelerator, which threw off sparks and destroyed critical parts, Herb's accelerator used a chain of small cylinders, or pellets. Hence, the Pelletron accelerator. His invention was not only more stable, but generally more advanced than other accelerators on the market. And we needed it. It was our gateway to ionizing atoms, and thus uranium enrichment, a fallback in the event our reactor program failed to yield plutonium. It was our ace in the hole.

NEC was anxious to make the sale. Like its rivals, it was eager to recoup the millions it had spent on developing its product, for which there were very few customers. In that way, accelerator inventors were like salesmen for Lotus and Maserati. Or nuclear reactors. They needed to make the sale.

Dr. Herb was very pleasant, and curious as to why we needed an accelerator. I gave him a full range of possibilities, from research in nuclear physics to the investigation of solid matter. I talked about our work in nuclear medicine. I preempted the question of why oil-rich Iraq would invest in nuclear power by pointing to similar investments by Iran, Brazil, and even Kuwait, which was also trying to negotiate a reactor deal. He laughed at my story of the Kuwaiti who appeared at our main gate one day, fully robed in headdress and cloak, asking for information on how to buy a reactor. It turned out there had been a Kuwaiti advertisement soliciting bids for a nuclear reactor and he wanted to get the contract by making the lowest bid. We sent him away with a couple of names of manufacturers. Finally, I didn't forget to roll out our mantra: "The oil won't last forever."

Dr. Herb offered to sell me an accelerator for $1.5 million, which would include training in the United States for our people. We shook hands with mutual wishes for a rewarding collaboration. He said we'd always be welcome at his facility.

It was time to go home.

Dr. al-Obeidi, meanwhile, took me aside, leveled his eyes into mine, and asked for a favor: He wanted to go visit his wife. I took a deep breath.

"Cover for me," he pleaded. "You can truthfully tell them I attended all the meetings." He searched my eyes for mercy. "I'll meet you in London," he begged, "and we can fly back together from there."

It pained me even to hesitate. But my neck was on the line. If al-Obeidi didn't show up in London, I'd be crazy to go back to Baghdad without him.

Al-Ghafour summoned me immediately as soon as I got back. I was still jet-lagged from the New York–London–Baghdad trek, my head feeling like it was stuffed with flannel. Already, America seemed like a dream. I drove carefully across the city in my old Toyota, feeling like a tourist in my own hometown.

Thank God al-Obeidi had shown up at Heathrow, grinning from ear to ear. Al-Ghafour, ever the party apparatchik, had been calling my home for the past two days, leaving stern messages to call as soon as I arrived.

Saeed was in al-Ghafour's office when I got there. The party boss got right to the point.

"What about the Israeli lasers?" he asked.

I reeled out what we had learned in Santa Fe as diplomatically as possible. I knew that he'd jumped into lasers for uranium enrichment with hundreds of thousands of dollars. So I let him down as gently as possible, couching what the experts had told me. But then he scoffed one too many times.

"Look, the patent is irreproducible," I said evenly. "It can't be done. The Israelis made it up. That's the consensus of every expert we talked to. It was a trick."

Smoldering, al-Ghafour picked up the telephone. The Science Research Council had a section responsible for tracking international patents. He got somebody on the line.

"Is it possible to file a false patent claim?" he barked. Apparently, whomever he was talking to wanted to know what the problem was. He couldn't answer such a broad question.

Frustrated, al-Ghafour handed me the receiver.

I explained the question more thoroughly. The researcher started to give me an elaborate answer that boiled down to: It was possible. As I was listening, al-Ghafour grabbed back the phone.

"Tell it to me." After a few moments, he hung up with a defiant glare. He wouldn't give up.

"Do you think the Israelis would tell you, or the Americans, for that matter, exactly how they go about enriching uranium?" he asked me. "Just like that?" He snapped his fingers, pointed to the telephone, and added, "That man says that patents are full of falsehood! Drug companies do it all the time. Nobody tells you exactly how they did it, they just tell you the end results."

He wagged a finger at me. Saeed stayed rooted in his corner chair.

"The Americans are in with the Israelis," al-Ghafour sneered. "Didn't you yourself say that the Americans brushed off your questions about the laser enrichment of uranium and said it was classified?"

"Yes," I agreed. "I said that."

"Well, why should they tell you anything? There's no free lunch!"

He got up and moved from behind his desk. He was stroking his mustache.

"We're just going to have to find out how to do this on our own," he continued. "And we will. We have the means. The party is behind it."

Oh, I bet they are, I thought. What do they know about laser physics? Or, for that matter, atoms? As Serwan had said, most never graduated from high school.

"By the way," al-Ghafour was going on. "I don't want to hear any talk about this down in the department, because it will demoralize the laser group's morale. God knows we've had enough trouble getting people to work on this project."

He looked angrily at me.

"Now you want to demolish it on some hearsay in a conference."

After a few minutes more of this, I was dismissed. I walked slowly back to my car.

Well, I thought, science certainly took a beating in there. Not even science, really—intellectual honesty. I hadn't, of course, pressed my rebuttal once al-Ghafour got on his stump. The facts were beside the point in Saddam Hussein's Iraq.

I coughed a bitter laugh as I turned the key to start my car.

Well, I thought, the Israelis certainly will be happy. No doubt their spies would find out we were throwing millions of dollars away.

CHAPTER SIX

CRUNCH TIME

Saddam Hussein flew into Paris like an Oriental pasha on September 10, 1975, leading a retinue that included grim-looking bodyguards and a troupe of Iraqi fishermen bearing Baghdad's specialty, Tigris River fish roasted over flaming barrels of pungent sticks.

Saddam let nothing go unchallenged in his world, ever—not bureaucrats, not scientists, not dissidents, not even cooking in the capital of culinary sophistication. He invited *tout le Paris* to a cooking demonstration on the banks of the Seine, ignoring the titters of high French officials led by Prime Minister Jacques Chirac, who gamely swallowed fish served up Baghdad-style on aluminum foil for the benefit of the cameras. Watching the newsreels back home, we cringed in mortification as Saddam proudly beamed over his fishermen, whose leathery faces, unkempt hair, and crumpled peasant clothes suggested they might have slept with their catch.

But Saddam was enjoying his own private joke. He knew Chirac would eat old tires from the Tigris if it got him our nuclear deal, worth hundreds of millions of dollars, along with a prospect of cheap oil. For us back at Atomic Energy, however, Saddam's ballyhooed state visit to France epitomized what was quickly becoming a troubling fact: Our secret was coming unglued, with consequences that could only be bad.

The first warning had come out of the blue, with an unsettling visit from Abdus Salam, head of the International Center of Theoretical Physics in Trieste. A blunt-spoken, almond-faced Pakistani who would win a Nobel prize in 1979, Salam entertained us with effusive compliments about our nuclear program, then cut right to the chase.

"Why don't you guys finish the job and make an atomic bomb?" he said with a matter-of-fact smile. "Israel has a few, at the very least. You have not only the right but the duty to defend your country."

Jaffar, Saeed, and I were stunned. We all knew Salam was advising the Pakistani prime minister, Ali Bhutto, on nuclear matters, which most certainly included making a bomb. The Indians had conducted a nuclear test in 1974.

"Don't tell me you haven't thought of it," he said. "It's the first thing you think about when you have a nuclear-armed enemy—the first thing in the morning and the last thing at night."

We listened like stone statues.

"I can understand if you're reluctant to discuss such an undertaking with me," Salam continued breezily. "After all, you barely know me. But let me tell you a story. . . ." With that, he relaxed as if he were in the Harvard Club instead of the offices of the Iraqi nuclear program. He folded his hands, looked out the window, and waited for just the right beat to continue.

"After their first hydrogen bomb test, the Chinese government invited me over for a visit," he recollected. "When I got back to Rome, the U.S. ambassador called me up and invited me to lunch." He waved a hand.

"Even before we ordered lunch, the ambassador asked me, point-blank, if I had seen the Chinese nuclear facilities. Did I know how they made their bomb?"

Salam chuckled to himself at the memory.

"I answered him simply. 'Even if the Chinese were foolish enough to tell me,' I said, 'I wouldn't be foolish enough to tell you.' " He chuckled again.

I glanced at Saeed. I could tell the story hadn't gone down well with him. Nor had it with me. The implication seemed to be that Salam wanted in on our project somehow. Or was sniffing for information, and not too subtly at that.

Saeed decided to cut it short. "We have no intention of making atomic bombs, Dr. Salam. Our pursuit of the French reactor is strictly peaceful."

The physicist looked back at us, incredulous, then snorted. With that, Saeed stood up. "You must be very tired from your trip," he told the visiting scientist. "I don't want to keep you any longer." We all shook hands stiffly.

When the door closed, Saeed and I looked at each other with dismay. Of course, the idea that we could keep the program secret for long was, in retrospect, silly. The fact was, we weren't just opening a new factory, we were on the road to making a billion-dollar nuclear bomb. We were oil-rich Arabs buying a sophisticated nuclear reactor and ancillary equipment, and sending some four hundred technicians abroad for training. To be sure, an argument could be made—and we certainly made it—that our intentions were totally innocent. But the nuclear club was small. And now Saddam, with his uncanny knack for pushing the limits, had apparently decided that justifying the *concept* of a Muslim bomb would be better than staying silent and inviting the worst conclusions. On the eve of his Paris trip, he'd told the leading Arabic-language newsmagazine that Iraq should be *helped* to obtain atomic weapons to balance the Israeli arsenal. And then he'd flown off to France to sign a nuclear cooperation treaty amid much fanfare. For an extra few millions, the French were persuaded to throw in a Ph.D. degree from the University of Paris for the party physicist, Humam al-Ghafour. The Israelis howled.

The reactor, however, wouldn't be ready for another five years. That meant we'd have to start preliminary work with our old Russian reactor, which had sprung a leak. When we explored the cost of repairs, the Russians were frantic that they'd have to accept payment in the rubles they'd paid into an escrow account at the International Atomic Energy Agency, as required of every member. When Saddam heard about that, he merely smiled and told the Russians he'd give them a half million U.S. dollars, but the rest would be paid in their own worthless cash—take it or leave it.

Real money, meanwhile, was disappearing down the rat hole of uranium enrichment by laser, chasing the Israeli rabbit.

"Al-Ghafour's road to the bomb is going nowhere," I remarked to Jaffar one day after going over the budget.

"Everyone wants to make their own bomb around here," the aristocratic beanpole sardonically replied.

But al-Ghafour was getting stressed. The laser group was stymied, which was no surprise to us. They had decided that the key to the mystery had to be out in the world somewhere, so they convened a conference on lasers in Baghdad, where they hoped to wheedle some secrets from one of the foreign experts who might show up.

Little did they know that Iraq's pursuit of lasers had already become an open joke. Even more comical, the Iraqi technicians working for al-Ghafour were under orders not to ask anyone at the conference directly about it, but to confine their questions to enrichment in general. Of course, nobody was fooled. The hapless Iraqis came off like Inspector Clouseau. Finally, near the conference end, as an Italian scientist was giving a lecture on a closely related topic, a British expert on the panel had had enough of the charade.

"Why don't you just talk about uranium enrichment and let's get it over with?" he said impatiently. "Don't you see that they're not interested in anything else?" The audience erupted in wild laughter. I was sure the echoes were heard as far away as Santa Fe—and Tel Aviv.

The world as we knew it, meanwhile, was about to disappear. On February 1, 1979, a bearded, hollow-eyed Iranian cleric boarded a chartered Air France flight in Paris with a hundred and fifty of his rabid followers and a large contingent of international journalists. The plane flew southeast. When it landed in Teheran five hours later, our lives would be forever changed.

The triumph of Ayatollah Ruholla Khomeini not only stunned Washington, which lost its key regional ally and a reliable source of cheap oil, it shook Saddam Hussein to his boots. The Iranian Revolution, with its virulent germs of Shiite fundamentalism, threatened the sovereignty of Iraq.

Saddam was coiled like a snake as he watched the turmoil in Teheran, only a two-day drive across the desert from Baghdad. Suspicion of the Iranians was endemic, historic, embedded in his DNA. Iraq and Iran were eternal enemies, going back to a battle with the ancient Persians at al-Qadisiyah in A.D. 637. The rivalry had never really ended, but in the past decade the struggle had taken new life, with each side arming their Kurds to keep each other off balance.

Saddam was convinced the ayatollah and his Revolutionary Guards coveted the hundreds of thousands of restive Shiites who lived in southern Iraq. They were Khomeini's fifth column, as far as he was concerned, along with any Iraqi of mixed Iranian heritage.

Ironically, Saddam himself had greased the wheels for Khomeini's triumph a year earlier when he expelled him from Iraq's own Shiite holy city, An Najaf, where he'd lived in exile from Iran since 1965. As long as the bearded cleric hurled his fundamentalist ravings at the U.S.-backed shah next door, Saddam could tolerate Khomeini. When he began to excite Iraq's own Shiites, however, Saddam booted him out. But Paris, the media center of continental Europe, gave Khomeini an even better bullhorn with which to broadcast his message to Iran. When the shah wobbled and finally fell, Khomeini flew in and picked up the pieces. A wave of terror began, with ad hoc religious courts condemning and executing thousands of Iranians suspected of past employment by the shah's secret police, ties to the U.S., or merely insufficient Islamic fervor. Not surprisingly, the Muslim proselytizing began to spill over the border.

"This place hardly seems like part of Iraq," Saddam grumbled one day as street mobs of Iraqi Shiites chanted Khomeini's name in the holy cities of southern Iraq. "They don't even speak Arabic."

No one who knew Saddam doubted he would move quickly to snuff out the agitators. His excuse came with the 1980 assassination attempt—some think it was staged—on his foreign affairs adviser, Tariq Aziz, by Shia fanatics. When the funeral procession for Aziz's slain companions was attacked, Saddam declared a crackdown. More than thirty-five thousand Shiites and Iraqis with Iranian blood were rounded up at night, stripped of their money, possessions, and papers, and dumped at the Iranian frontier. Eventually more than a hundred thousand people were deported, including Christians. When Western churches, including the Vatican, protested, Saddam relented, but continued to purge the Shiites.

Murders were part of the terror. The well-known Shiite leader Baqir al-Sadr and his sister, Bint al-Huda, were picked up and tortured. She was repeatedly raped in front of her brother before they were both killed. Just the rumor of pro-Khomeini sympathies was a death sentence, as I discovered when a second cousin of mine disappeared in Diwaniyah. Security agents summoned his older brother a couple of weeks later. When he arrived at their office he was directed to a room in the back, where he found a pile of bodies, which he had to sort through to find his brother. He carried him home by himself.

The fallout reached Atomic Energy. Even a party man like al-Ghafour wasn't immune. His younger sister, married to a Shiite of Iranian origins, was a target. When al-Ghafour got word of the deportations, he was able to warn her in time for them to escape. In Paris, meanwhile, one of our AE researchers, training on a French reactor, heard that his family had been deported. He panicked and immediately fled to Iran.

Worse news came. The father and the brother of the deputy head of our French project, both Shiites by birth but hardly religious, were swept up in the sting. The Iraqi Chamber of Commerce had invited Shiite merchants to a meeting with the minister of commerce in downtown Baghdad. About seven hundred businessmen showed up, including Ibrahim Shakarchi and his youngest son. After everyone arrived, security agents locked the doors, announced a bomb threat, and hustled everyone into buses. They were driven to the Iranian border, ordered to walk across the frontier, and told to never come back.

A red alert went off in my head. We could not afford to lose Dr. Shakarchi, who I suspected was preparing to flee from his post in Paris. I went directly to al-Ghafour. In great dismay, he immediately called Saddam's secretary, who came back with an order in less than an hour: Bring Dr. Shakarchi home and let him work on getting his family members back from Iran; Saddam would pay all his expenses plus a hefty bonus. Eventually Shakarchi did retrieve his father and brother, slipping them out of Iran through Kuwait and Syria, aided by wads of hundred-dollar bills and Iraqi passports provided by Saddam. But his father's heart condition worsened from the ordeal, and when he died, the younger Shakarchi bitterly blamed Saddam. Atomic Energy officials, fearing he might defect, stripped him of his security clearance. His brothers were purged from the intelligence service.

While Saddam was preoccupied with Iran, we at AE were nervously eyeing Israel. The Jewish state and Iraq had been in a virtual state of war since 1948, when Palestine was dissected to make room for Jewish settlers. In 1948, and again in 1967 and 1973, the Arabs and

U.S.-backed Israelis had fought three apocalyptic wars, the last one under the shadow of a possible Israeli nuclear strike.

By then, knowledge that Israel had amassed a small arsenal of atomic weapons was an open secret. As early as the late 1950s, U.S. intelligence had gotten wind of the Israeli program from U-2 over-flights. In 1963, the CIA produced a White Paper, "Consequences of Israeli Acquisition of Nuclear Capability," for President Kennedy. But from the first discovery of Israel's clandestine purchases of yellow cake uranium from South Africa, the U.S. attitude toward Jerusalem's nukes had been a mixture of ambivalence, denial, and private resignation. In principle, the United States decried the spread of nuclear weapons, but in Israel's case it averted its eyes and hoped they'd never be used. When Tel Aviv turned down a sixty-million-dollar loan for a much-needed nuclear desalinization and power plant, rather than open up its facilities at Dimona to IAEA inspectors, Washington merely shrugged. By then, besieged in Vietnam and wary of swelling Arab radicalism, the Americans were even more willing to give the Israelis a free pass. On the other hand, the Israelis were not about to give Iraq the same.

The Israelis knew exactly what the French deal with Iraq meant, if only because they had pioneered the route. In 1956, Israel bought a French reactor and clandestinely began making plutonium. So, even before Saddam flew to Paris, the Israelis began making a stink. When four years of protests fell on deaf ears, they decided to handle the problem themselves. At dawn on the morning of April 6, 1979, a muffled explosion was heard outside a plant at La Seyne-sur-Mer, near Toulon. The cores for our two reactors had been sabotaged.

The news arrived swiftly in Iraq. I went immediately to Jaffar's office and found him gathered with a group of his scientists. They all looked shaken.

"Have you heard?" I asked. Jaffar nodded, and signaled for the others to leave the room.

"The head of the Iraqi group in Paris is following up on this," Jaffar said, closing the door. "I've requested more information on the extent of the damage."

He sat down. "It had to be Mossad," he said.

"But how did they get such easy access to the most important part of the reactor?" I asked. "The French must be in on it."

"Maybe," he said. "But I think it's more likely it was a French sympathizer, somebody on the inside who helped them. I don't think the French would help the Israelis, as a policy."

I wasn't so sure. "But how about the lack of security where the reactor cores were located?" I said. "Don't you think that would take some official help?"

Despite his studied nonchalance, Jaffar hid his anxiety badly. The core was the most difficult part of the reactor to manufacture. It had to be forged to demanding specifications, tough enough to withstand the intense radiation generated by the reactor. The slightest fault in its manufacture could lead to a nuclear incident. A few days later, when the French showed us the X rays of the cores, it was clear the damage was significant. The explosion had caused hairline fractures. The cores were still good enough to be put on line and fired up, but they'd eventually crack. Manufacturing a new one, the French told us, would take about two years.

Far from being apologetic for not safeguarding the equipment, however, the French were haughty, even dismissive: We could take it or leave it, they said. If we took it, we'd have to sign a waiver releasing them from responsibility in the event of an accident.

Which put us in a quandary. It was Jaffar's call, and I could see that he was wringing his hands. To my surprise, however (until now he had been an indifferent bureaucrat), he decided to accept the damaged core, sign the waiver, and hope for the best. Apparently, he'd decided that the prospect of a nuclear malfunction was nothing compared with the heat he'd get from Saddam if the project was delayed.

When the news got out that the French were resuming shipment of the cores, the reaction from Israel was ominously muted, we thought. Their sabotage had failed. The next time, we feared, they wouldn't go after the equipment. They'd go after one of us.

For the past few summers I'd been spending a month in Trieste, losing myself in questions of pure research. My usual morning routine was to pick up a copy of the *Guardian* at the train station and read it on the twenty-minute bus ride to the International Center of Theoretical Physics. The British paper had superior coverage of the Middle East, and I was interested in any follow-up to the recent news that Saddam had shoved aside President Ahmad Hassan al-

Bakr and made official what had been de facto for years: He was running the country.

In the back of the paper I found it, and my blood chilled. Saddam had begun a purge. Over the following days, I would learn that hundreds of officials had been summoned to a mass meeting and whipped into a chorus of mutual denunciations. Saddam then picked on various officials to prove their mettle by drawing pistols and carrying out the executions of their colleagues. Over two hundred men had been killed outside the hall, many of them the party's most prominent Shiites.

Saddam's suspicion of Iraqi Shiites predated the Iranian Revolution. Back when I was still a student in Florida, a friend of my father's, a man named Nadhim Gzar, was later drawn into a plot on Saddam that hardened the vice president's distrust.

When they first met, my father and Gzar would meet almost daily at a local coffee shop to play cards or dominoes. Gzar was a mild-mannered man, but after the Baathists took power in 1968 he seemed to change, my father said. He joined the party's intelligence section and rose rapidly, becoming security chief of the new regime. It was an unusual attainment for a Shiite, and sure enough, in a short time, Gzar began to notice that the plum jobs were going to Saddam's Tikriti clan. Pretty soon, he got wind that he was targeted for elimination. Deciding to preempt the strike, Gzar surrounded himself with fellow Shiites and concocted a plan to kill both President al-Bakr and his deputy Saddam when al-Bakr returned from a trip to Europe. As luck would have it, however, the president's plane was delayed and Gzar lost his nerve. He fled in a car with some of his conspirators, but Saddam's military helicopters caught up as they neared the Iranian border. Saddam tortured them himself before they were shot.

The lesson for Saddam, of course, was never to trust a Shiite. Over the years he kept purging them from the security services and the army, and when the Iranian Revolution caught fire, he went at them with a fury. The terror now consumed both sides of the border. Saddam was becoming the ayatollah's doppelgänger, a Khomeini without the turban.

Just before I was scheduled to return to Iraq, I bumped into the Trieste center's director, Abdus Salam, in a corridor. He must have seen the worry on my face. He showed great concern.

"Are you going back?" he asked.

"Sure," I said with false bravado. "Why not?"

He searched my eyes, then smiled with a slight sneer.

I'm sure he was concerned, but I couldn't take any chances. I'd never forgotten his earlier prying about our program. I had to be careful, because after the Israelis hit us in France, who knew who was working for whom?

"Well," he said kindly, touching my arm, "let me know. And if I don't see you before you leave, I hope you'll write and stay in touch."

I think he meant it. But there was no way I would write. All of our letters now were being opened by the Mukhabarat, Saddam's intelligence organization.

Things seemed oddly normal when I got home, but after only a few weeks in the office I could tell that the young party members, once so full of themselves, were really shaken up. Overnight their bosses and mentors had been fingered as traitors and shot. How deep the purges would go, nobody could know.

Then I got a glimpse of the terror. It came my turn to be the night duty officer. As I was working one evening, one of the senior party operatives stopped by my office and invited me down to his room for a cup of tea. When we got settled, he asked if I'd like to see a movie.

"Sure," I said, "if it's not too boring."

"Don't worry," he said, "it's not." He got up and slipped a tape into his VCR.

A grainy, black-and-white video flickered on. Saddam was at a head table in a large meeting hall haranguing rows of gloomy officials. From the camera's jerking around, I immediately realized what I was watching: a private newsreel of the party denunciation meetings. The night of the long knives.

I stared at the screen.

An official at the podium was reading names. At each name, a man would stand up. Guards would come and get him and lead him to an exit. At the door, he'd be asked to recite the party oath: "One Arab nation with a holy message! Unity, freedom, and socialism." Then he'd be led out.

This performance continued for several minutes, with one after another name being read and men being led from the room. Armed guards stood along the walls, ensuring that no one could leave. Occasionally the camera jerked over to Saddam, who seemed to be laughing at some private joke. He was the only one smiling, however. Farther down the head table I noticed Taha Yasin Ramadan, another member of the ruling council, crying openly in his seat.

Suddenly the camera cut to a new scene, outdoors, in a courtyard, perhaps behind the meeting hall. Men were kneeling with blindfolds over their eyes, wrists tied behind their backs. Then a close-in shot. A hand, a gun barrel, a shot. The men jerked and crumpled over, blood oozing from their heads into the dust.

Horribly, some of the gunshots were inaccurate. A few victims were still alive. Either the shooters were not professionals, or they'd lost heart at their task. Then I saw an arm come into the frame, with a pistol. It put a finishing shot on each of the heads.

The screen went white.

I sat there mute for a moment, a cold cup of tea in my hands. My friend stood up and turned off the television. He looked at me intently.

"How about taking a walk?" he said. The walls had ears.

It was a typical early winter night in Baghdad, chilly and dry, with just the wisps of seasonal clouds drifting across the moon. We strolled in silence, down through a grove of cypress trees to the edge of the AE grounds. The dark, glassy Tigris flowed by below.

We stopped to look at the river, and he turned to me.

"You know," he finally said, "despite what you think, I really don't need this job."

I started to speak, but he shook his head. He gazed out at the river, seemingly unsure of how much to say.

"I'm sick of this job," he started again. "Before this, there was some hope of democracy, some integrity to the party." He stopped again.

"But now we've turned into a group of murderers and thugs." He sighed again, then looked me in the eye.

"You know, tomorrow, if Saddam gets mad at you and decides he wants you dead, you know how he will do it? He'll put a gun in my hand and order me to shoot you."

I just listened.

"And I will do it, you know, because this is a new form of cannibalism that Saddam has invented. The system eats itself."

I wanted to take him by his fancy lapels and shake him. "You fool," I wanted to say, "you stupid fool! It's a cliché that revolutions eat their children! Do you think Saddam is something new? Don't you know anything? Where have you been?" Instead, I just sucked my teeth in silence and stared at the river.

He glanced sidewise at me. Now he was sneering.

"By the way, do you know who one of the main executioners of our friends on that tape was?"

I cocked my head.

"Humam al-Ghafour, that's who," he said. "Your friend. He shot another one of your friends, Ghanim Abdul-Jalil. That was his arm with the pistol that you saw on the tape."

My mouth went dry. Abdul-Jalil had presided over the lavish dinner to lure Jaffar back from Switzerland. The guns were getting close.

"And that other friend of yours, Roges al-Hadithi?"

I had a sinking feeling. Roges was a kindly, meek man who had been sent over from the presidential palace to be our chief of staff.

"What about him?" I said as calmly as possible.

"Oh, I noticed that you always take your morning coffee with him. You also lunch with him frequently," he said casually. Now he was toying with me. He *loved* this job.

"And of course you remember Adnan al-Hamdani, don't you?"

"Of course," I said quietly. He'd signed our nuclear treaty with France. We'd met several times at the Hunting Club.

"Well, al-Hamdani was executed by another friend of yours, al-Hadithi," he continued. "And that one was really a hatchet job! Al-Hamdani was writhing all over the ground and al-Hadithi just stood there shaking like a leaf."

I looked at my companion with barely controlled shock. He was stifling a huge laugh.

"Then Barzan," my interlocutor went on, chuckling, referring to Saddam's notorious half brother, "Barzan had to put a couple of bullets in his head to finish him off." A few more chuckles. "Al-Hadithi's been transferred out, because he didn't show the required steadfastness."

I turned away and began to walk back to my office. My friend scrambled to catch up. I wondered why he'd told me all this? What was the point? Was he trying to scare me? Or warn me? Or was he just a psychopath?

How unimaginably horrible it must have been for my friends, and not just for the victims. Would the day come when I would have to pick up the pistol myself? My God, I thought, what have I gotten myself into? And how did I ever think I could outmaneuver these butchers?

On December 17, 1979, Iranian zealots stormed the U.S. embassy in Teheran, taking 66 Americans hostage and putting the ayatollah and the Revolutionary Guards back on center stage. The crisis would go on for 444 days.

Saddam saw where the Shiite fire was heading, but he wasn't going to wait for his own house to burn down.

About the same time as the embassy takeover, Atomic Energy was sealed off one day without warning. Armed guards locked the doors and filled the halls, along with their bomb-sniffing German shepherds. A motorcade of black Mercedes, surrounded by plainclothes agents with submachine guns, was idling at the curb. All this meant only one thing: Saddam was coming to visit.

And not for a courtesy call. That was clear from the way he stomped into the building, trailing a jackbooted retinue, and walked directly to the office of his deputy for atomic matters, Abdul-Razzaq al-Hashimi. Guards were posted in the hall, and the doors slammed shut. When the party hack Saeed tried to go in to greet Saddam, he was rudely pushed aside and told to wait.

Inside, Saddam demanded al-Hashimi round up his top nuclear officials. Al-Shahristani and Jaffar were summoned by telephone. Al-Ghafour arrived. With Saeed in tow, they all entered the room and closed the door behind them. As it happened I was in New York on U.N. scientific business, but I was later able to piece together what went on.

Saddam was in no mood for preliminaries. He stood without speaking until everybody was assembled. Then he looked over the room, assessing his audience. By the time he spoke, the officials, all grown men, were nearly trembling.

He had only one question.

"When are you going to deliver the plutonium?" he said. He glanced from man to man, but no one answered.

"I said," he repeated slowly, "when are you going to deliver the plutonium?"

Again he looked around the room. By now everyone's eyes had drifted over to al-Shahristani, the brilliant little scientist fond of wisecracks about the party. Saddam followed them there and stopped.

Al-Shahristani wasn't making any jokes now. He was in charge of plutonium extraction. But suddenly, he seemed befuddled. For all the jokes he and Jaffar had made about my "firecrackers" on the Paris trip, he genuinely seemed confused.

"Plutonium for . . . for what?" he asked. Saddam stared at him. The room was as quiet as a tomb.

The president spoke again, in a voice that seemed to come from a very dark cave.

"When will you deliver the plutonium for the bomb?"

Al-Shahristani now was rattled. "Bomb? We can't make a bomb," he sputtered. "Well, theoretically we can make a bomb, if we made enough plutonium, but . . ."

He stopped. His eyes searched his colleagues, desperately beseeching them for help. They were stone-faced. He turned back to Saddam, whose gaze was pinned on him.

He tried again. "We cannot use the French and Italian projects for plutonium production," al-Shahristani said in a thin voice. "They are covered by the nuclear nonproliferation treaty, and we will be held in violation of our treaty obligations."

It was his death sentence, as everyone knew, perhaps even himself.

Saddam drew himself erect and wagged a finger. "Treaties," he told al-Shahristani sternly, "are a matter for us to deal with. You, as a scientist, should not be troubled by these things. You should be doing your job and not have these kinds of excuses."

Saddam stared at his quarry, who was speechless and pale. Then he cocked his head, a signal for somebody to take al-Shahristani away. He turned his back while the trembling scientist was led out of the room.

Saddam then crossed his arms and assessed his remaining officials. They waited with eyes downcast, like serfs.

"Well," Saddam said. He shook his head slowly. And with that, he had no more to say. He turned slowly on his heel and left.

Saeed, al-Ghafour, and al-Hashimi waited as the sound of the retreating boots disappeared down the corridor. When Saddam and his motorcade finally pulled away, they all rushed to the bathroom and threw up.

Al-Shahristani was shipped off to a dungeon. When Jaffar heard the news, he rushed to his colleague's house to protest, and got into a scuffle with a security agent. A few days later, he was arrested, too, and disappeared into the gulag.

When I came back from New York several weeks later, I got the news of their arrests. And worse.

Now I was in charge.

CHAPTER SEVEN

ACCIDENTS WILL HAPPEN

FROM MY OFFICE WINDOW in the Nuclear Research Center, I could see just a slice of what Saddam's oil money had built in less than a decade: a sprawling complex of nuclear facilities, scattered over ten square miles, poised to deliver us the bomb. It was called al-Tuwaitha, in Arabic "the truncheon."

It was 1981. I looked out on our campus, a half-hour's drive from Baghdad. Across the way was our two-story library, already crammed with the latest scientific literature from foreign sources—the United States and Soviet Union, France, England, Italy, India, and Pakistan. When I first came to Atomic Energy, our neglected shelves held just a few musty books, outdated journals, and the reports of the forty-year-old U.S. Manhattan Project. The files were chaotic, but soon we'd have the greatest nuclear technical library in the Middle East, outside of Israel.

Saddam had lived up to every promise. Below my floor was fifty thousand square feet of office space and laboratories, sparkling with new equipment, where hundreds of technicians were running nuclear experiments. Outside to my left was our chemical reprocessing plant, where we would enrich fuel for a plutonium bomb. Down the street was our domed Russian reactor, newly renovated with Belgian electronic controls, which made it capable of generating radioactive material for nuclear triggers. Past that was our French-supplied neutron generator, and next to that our electronics labs, and then a four-story building that handled spent nuclear fuel, full of hot cells and new remote-controlled equipment overseen by platoons of white-jacketed technicians. All this was a long, long way from the dining room table where we'd scratched out our first memo for a bomb in 1972.

Rising up behind my office, however, was al-Tuwaitha's jewel in the crown, the aluminum dome of the French reactor, glittering in the blue desert sky. Osirak was the most advanced reactor of its kind, crammed with such up-to-date equipment and technology that visitors were amazed that the French had ever agreed to sell it to us. Little did they know that the acquisition of Osirak, an incredible feat on its own, was merely a decoy: Saddam wanted us to copy the French design and build another, secret reactor, where we would produce the bomb-grade plutonium beyond the prying eyes of foreign spies and inspectors—the same thing to him. It was called Project 182.

Now even the Russians were begging us for access to the facilities, which had hardware they couldn't afford and American technology they'd been refused. To us, with few exceptions, the Russians were a joke—badly trained, often drunk, sluggish at work, more interested in buying clothes and electronic goods unavailable in Moscow and sending them home than doing their assignments. (One Russian I knew bought up suits by the hundreds and found a machine to flatten them into boxes.) Everything at al-Tuwaitha was bought and built for only one purpose: to construct a nuclear bomb. We didn't even make a pretense of generating power. Our electrical output was nil. And our only actual service to date was screening Saddam's food and clothes for poisons and radioactivity. Al-Tuwaitha was his billion-dollar X-ray machine.

It was a heady time for me. Only yesterday, it seemed, I'd been teaching math to nearly illiterate students at a tiny college in rural Georgia. Now I was chief of the theoretical division of a future nuclear-armed power, in charge of designing the actual bomb. For the next stage of development alone, I was drawing up a budget for one hundred million dollars. The serious money would follow.

Some of it was fattening our own wallets. I was making twice the pay of a university professor. When I went on trips to Europe, al-Ghafour's secretary usually came by with an envelope containing an extra thousand dollars or two, saying it was a gift from Saddam to buy toys for my kids or gifts for my wife. One day a new Mercedes was in my driveway. And I was handed a deed for new land.

Souham was enjoying it. She could go to the Hunting Club every week. She was draped in tasteful, European-cut clothes and jewelry. Our social calendar was full. The boys went to good schools.

Our firstborn son, Firas, was turning out to be extraordinarily bright, at the top of his class right into fourth grade, which filled his papa with tremendous pride. Our second boy, Sami, who came along in 1978, was a roly-poly, black-eyed child whose birth had been troublesome.

I was in Italy when Souham felt her first labor pangs. She started to panic; the last thing she wanted was to have a baby by herself in an Iraqi hospital. When she called, I rushed straight home.

The problem with Iraqi health care, starkly put, was that doctors didn't make bombs. They didn't add to Saddam's wallet or power in any way. Saddam didn't care about them. They were drastically underfunded. Unlike scientists at Atomic Energy, they were poorly educated and poorly paid, making hardly more than clerks. When they graduated from an Iraqi medical school, they were usually drafted into the army. If they survived a five- or six-year hitch, they went to work in a poorly run government hospital. Those who were lucky enough to be sent abroad for advanced training rarely came home. If they did, the price of office space in Baghdad, and a closed medical society, made launching private practice a forbidding proposition.

Souham's labor pains turned out to be a false alarm, which made my frantic return from Italy the butt of jokes around the office. But the real thing came soon enough, and we rushed Souham off to Al-Wia (Daughters of Mohammed), a semi-private hospital in an upscale part of town.

Even there, the corridors were dim and the walls looked like they needed a good scrubbing. Beds went unmade, soiled linen was piled in the corners. Nursing stations were as chaotic and disorganized as a check-in counter at Iraqi Airways. The storage and tracking of medicines and doses was haphazard. Pharmaceuticals were often out of date.

But the main reason I had to be with Souham in the hospital was social. The sad fact is that in the Arab world, men have authority and women don't. Without my presence doctors and nurses wouldn't hesitate to stick her with a used syringe. The complaints of females were generally ignored. After all, they were only women.

So I stayed by her side as much as I could, and when I had to leave, Souham's sister took over and called me whenever there was trouble. And trouble there was. Arab medicine's disrespect for women extended even to the sacred act of childbirth. Without a man at bedside to insist on proper treatment, our women were pretty much on their own.

As it turned out, Souham's labor was difficult, lasting days. In the end, she gave birth to a handsome, twelve-pound boy with thick, straight black hair. But not before many more hassles. The one compensation for such torment—beside having delivered a healthy son, of course—was that Atomic Energy paid for it all.

AE also was one of the few government agencies that could snatch a young man from death's jaws at the Iranian front. Saddam never questioned our requests to exempt or retrieve certain men from military service and have them reassigned to AE. But there was an agonizing downside to this godlike privilege. When word got around that I could get someone off, Souham was besieged at home or even on the street by crying mothers who begged her to lobby me to save their sons from almost certain death on the battlefield.

We were not without compassion, far from it. Our hearts ached with every coffin we saw, and they were adding up as the Iranian war dragged on. But solving one problem created another. Families whose sons were stuck at the front bitterly spread the word that AE officials were taking bribes. In fact, one of our junior executives was under investigation for accepting ten thousand dinars (about thirty thousand dollars) for getting someone off. So I had to be careful, limiting myself to exempting only my former students or other young men I could really make a case for needing. This, of course, enraged all my friends and relatives, especially my brothers-in-law, who denounced me for abandoning them to their fates. Poor Souham had to bear the brunt of all this, fending off constant importunings or insults from her sisters.

The raging war, ironically, was turning Baghdad into a party town. Saddam had a theory that a soldier on leave needed not only entertainment but reminders of the secular values he was defending, especially in contrast to the stark religious life of the Iranian enemy.

An endless string of entertainers filled the clubs, along with luxury foods and foreign liquors at cut-rate prices. Souham and I started going out twice a week, instead of our usual Thursday night at the Hunting Club. The good times rolled on until, eventually, the price of the war came home with a thud.

But that was still a few years off. In the meantime, I was still being singled out for special care. Others at AE were getting perks, but none so lavish. One day, for example, al-Ghafour sent for me. The party operative invited me to sit down in his office and closed the door.

"Are you in trouble?" he asked, settling into his chair.

"No. . . . Why?" I said. My heart thumped. In this regime, you never knew.

"We heard you stopped the work on your house," he said.

"Oh," I said, exhaling. "It's nothing. The bank loan ran out. I just need more money to finish it."

Al-Ghafour studied me for a moment, then got up and went to his desk. He opened a drawer and came back with a thick envelope.

"It's a gift from the president to finish your house," he said, handing it over. I looked inside and thumbed the bills. It was the equivalent of about seventeen thousand dollars. When I looked up, al-Ghafour was studying me again. It was another test.

"Well, thank the president for me," I said. "It's certainly enough to finish the house. I'm very grateful. Thank you. Thank you very much."

And it *was* plenty to finish the house. Especially after I'd traded my Mercedes for a Volkswagen Passat.

All that loot was softening me up, I don't deny it. But it was the project itself, the enormity of the task, and the pure, scientific challenge of cracking the atomic code that excited me more.

I mean, how many people get to make a nuclear bomb, just to see if it will work? Not to drop it on anybody, just to see it go off—the double flash, the instant darkness, the roar of the wind and dust over our trenches, the mushroom cloud rising over the desert. Everything they had seen at Los Alamos at the dawn of the nuclear age in 1945.

It was a thrill. I was knocking on the door of membership in a very, very small club, with names like Fermi, Hans Bethe, and

Oppenheimer. With stars like that racing around my head, I was able to put my throbbing conscience to sleep.

And I *did* have a conscience. My mind's eye sometimes flickered with visions of a postnuclear Teheran or Tel Aviv: charred, smoldering holes, with hundreds of thousands of people vaporized and the living envying the dead. If only because it was such a horrifying nightmare, however, I quickly banished it from my thoughts.

The fact was, I was so consumed by the scientific challenge before me that I'd become a prisoner of the bomb. One step had led to the next, and to the next. Every excuse I stood on had collapsed like a trapdoor beneath my feet. I rationalized: We were finessing Saddam, taking his money and putting off the actual making of a bomb. Then Jaffar and al-Shahristani had been arrested. So I constructed a new rationalization for my collaboration, which went more or less like this: If the balance of nuclear terror had prevented a war between the United States and the Soviets, as many cold war intellectuals thought, might not the same be said someday of Arabs and the Israelis once we had the bomb? Whatever my thoughts, the fact was that Israeli prime minister Menachem Begin, swaggering with nuclear bombs in his own holsters, had rebuffed every Arab idea for peace. That left us one recourse, we thought: surrender or a nuke.

Should I have refused to make the bomb? At what point? When could I have bluntly said no and lived to tell this story? After my colleagues were tortured? Before? Whatever the answer, by 1981 the bomb had become my "Bridge on the River Kwai," I confess, a project so engaging that I forgot I was a rat in a guilded cage. I often dreamt of saying no. But when I thought of Jaffar and al-Shahristani, I was jolted back to reality.

Security at al-Tuwaitha was astounding, starting with the heavily armed main gate on the edge of Riyadh, a filthy slum town on the banks of the Tigris. With my new prerequisites, a driver picked me up at seven every weekday morning and delivered me through the gate with hardly a wave. But most employees, and all visitors, were required to park their private cars outside the gate, pass through airport-style metal detectors and a search of their briefcases, then hop AE buses for the trip to their offices.

The front gate, set in a brick wall, was actually the most pleasant-looking part of the perimeter. The wall rose sharply as it stretched away from the gate, gaining a spiked fence, barbed wire, and periodic guard towers as it circled the ten-square-mile complex.

Sometimes an employee opted to avoid the congestion of Riyadh and go in through a back gate. But going in that way had its risks, especially at night, when the area was dark and desolate. The gate was flanked by a twenty-foot-high barbed-wire fence and watch towers bristling with machine guns. One night a couple of officers arriving at the gate had the misfortune of having their car stall just as the guards ordered them to back up. As they fumbled to get it started, the guards mowed them down. In most countries the soldiers would at least be rebuked, but Saddam gave them commendations. There were also precautions to keep people from walking around unescorted. One dark night two soldiers tried to walk out the back entrance when their ride failed to show. Unfortunately, free-running police dogs found them and tore them to shreds. After that, we half-joked about the gate as the "Back Door to Death."

The sprawling complex was also a testimony to the porous safeguards of the Nuclear Nonproliferation Agreement. And it was, of course, a major target for our main enemies, Israel and Iran.

Saddam ordered his agents to be suspicious of everybody. The foreign laborers we'd hired for construction work were the first targets. An Egyptian construction worker, for example, was unmasked as a saboteur in 1980. A particularly rugged guy, he was suited for heavy outdoor work but kept insisting on doing tasks in the offices. Iraqi security agents quickly became curious. A few days later he was followed to the house he shared with other workers and searched while the place was turned inside out. Items that could be used for bomb components were found.

The man was arrested and interrogated, and allegedly said that Egyptian intelligence had ordered him to get a job at the reactor and wait for future instructions. Nobody in Iraqi security would believe such a story. They were sure the Israelis were pulling the strings. I heard later that he expired under interrogation.

This revealed glaring holes in Atomic Energy's security, although with all the checkpoints I had to pass through every day, I would have thought it impossible to sneak anyone in. Four security organizations worked within AE, each one reporting on the others. Their reports, in turn, were cross-checked by Mukhabarat and the SSO. After the Shiite conspiracy was smoked out, the chief of security was transferred and the officers in charge of the gate were imprisoned. The new chief of security, a man from Saddam's hometown, was more thorough. As a test, he started smuggling bomb components in with workers. Each time one got through, the officer in charge at the time was beaten and demoted. Next, entire bombs, deactivated for the test, were smuggled in, with the same results. After that, security got tighter.

The stifling defenses and pressures to show progress sent morale plummeting and fear soaring at AE. As long as Jaffar and al-Shahristani were around, Saddam could blame them for our shortcomings and lack of progress on the bomb. But now other necks were exposed, including mine.

The fates of both Jaffar and al-Shahristani were giving me nightmares. Both had initially been taken to Mukhabarat's headquarters, a forbidding place of screams and despair behind high walls in the wealthy Mansour district of Baghdad. Later I heard al-Shahristani had been transferred to Abu Ghraib, Iraq's crude version of Leavenworth, a maximum-security facility about ten miles northwest of Baghdad, with electronically controlled doors, surveillance cameras, and several levels of isolation.

After an initial round of beatings, the once elegant Jaffar broke down and agreed to cooperate, we'd heard, and his treatment improved slightly. But al-Shahristani's case was handled differently, most likely because of his Iranian roots. He'd been tortured so badly at Mukhabarat headquarters that his children didn't recognize his bloated face when they were finally permitted to visit. The visits, it turned out, were just a prelude to a show trial by a special security court, where he was handed a life sentence.

I'd always suspected that Jaffar's procrastination and aristocratic habits would eventually catch up to him. He could not spend seven hundred million dollars without results and be surprised when Saddam noticed. Jaffar's wife, meanwhile, an attractive British woman with a lacerating wit and a taste for good times, was getting tired of living under Saddam's heavy-handed regime. Perhaps sensing her mood, Jaffar had sent her out of the country, but not before she slapped a rude security agent at the airport. She would never come back.

Al-Shahristani's fate was preordained. The ascetic, self-righteous academic with the propensity for loud, sour jokes about party operatives had already been exiled once, to a soft landing at a remote college. Given a second chance, he had still failed to grasp that the name of the game was "make a bomb." How he could do that was beyond my comprehension. I certainly had no such misapprehensions.

But I was shaken. I knew them both well. They were my colleagues. I was pacing the house at night imagining the tortures the two scientists were enduring. Whatever the failings of Jaffar and al-Shahristani, they did not deserve to be beaten, hung by their thumbs, or shocked with electrical wires, all standard tools of the prison sadists. Abu Ghraib was not the kind of place where you were locked up and left alone.

From England, Jaffar's wife began organizing attention to his plight, which, along with al-Shahristani's arrest, was featured in *New Scientist* magazine. Posters of al-Shahristani were showing up in the Paris subway, probably the work of pro-Iranian groups.

Jaffar's jailing was having other effects. It scared off a young physicist I had sponsored to go to MIT. When he refused to return, the Iraqi embassy in Washington began to threaten him. Much to my secret joy, I heard he went right to the FBI, which warned several Iraqi embassy employees, including the cultural attaché, to leave him alone or they'd be deported. In France, an electrical engineer we'd sent for training at Saclay had married his German girlfriend, gotten a job with Siemens, and refused to return.

Jitters about being marked by the Israelis had begun to wash over Atomic Energy even before the sabotage in France. Tempers began to fray even among the party leaders as our lack of progress in reactor experiments became obvious. One day al-Ghafour exploded in an open staff meeting.

"I hear that Begin can't sleep nights because he's so worried about our reactor," he shouted sarcastically, referring to the Israeli prime minister. "The poor guy. I have a solution for him. All he needs to do is to come here as my guest. I'll give him a personal tour and after that, he'll sleep like a baby."

As it turned out, Begin was indeed planning a visit.

• • •

The jets swept over the rooftops with a ground-shaking roar. I was standing outside a garage on the dusty highway leading to Atomic Energy when they came over, heading for al-Tuwaitha, about a mile and a half up the road. There was an explosion, then another, then another. The jets were buzzing like hornets over the aluminum dome of the French reactor, bombing and strafing. Then our anti-aircraft guns opened up in staccato bursts. For the next few minutes the jets swooped and soared. Then as quickly as they came, they darted back west across the desert.

And then there was silence.

I stood on the roadside, watching a plume of black smoke curl over the far end of town. Then came the wail of an ambulance. Next, several cars came racing down the broken highway from the direction of al-Tuwaitha. I waved at a car I recognized and the driver pulled over. His face was full of resignation.

"It's the reactor," he said. "They destroyed it. I think it's the Israelis this time."

Of course. Only the Israelis had those kinds of aircraft, F-15s and F-16s, the hottest fighter-bombers in the U.S. inventory. Nine months earlier the Iranians had hit the nuclear center with F-4 Phantoms, a much older warplane, and managed only a few holes in a couple barrels of radioactive waste. But the Israeli pilots were professionals, flying state-of-the-art American jets.

It was June 7, 1981. When I got home my wife was frantic. I told her what happened. She said the television had gone haywire at about the same time. Now I knew it was the Israelis. The Iranian planes didn't have the jamming radar to cause that.

I made myself a drink and called the reactor's deputy director.

"The big reactor is gone," he said. The Israeli jets had blown open the dome and obliterated the cooling pool.

"Isis is okay," he said, meaning the smaller of our two French reactors. I didn't care. Isis was almost useless for plutonium production.

"The Italian labs are safe," he added, referring to the chemical reprocessing facility. "So is the Russian reactor."

I hung up and sat down on the couch. Only dumb luck had kept me away from my office when the reactor was bombed. A pickup truck had slammed into my Volkswagen Passat a few days before and I was getting it painted when the jets screamed over.

The day after the bombing, I went to AE and found the air force's explosives-disposal detachment crawling over the facilities. The place was a disaster. The reactor dome was completely gone. The reactor cavity, kind of a swimming pool where the fuel rods were cooled, was cratered beyond any hope of repair.

The uranium, however, was safe. Eight or nine men had been killed or seriously wounded, most of them, it turned out, from our own antiaircraft fire. Trying to bring down the dozen or so jets whizzing around them, the gunners had lowered their sights and ended up shooting each other. One or two more deaths were attributed to the Israeli bombs, others from jet gunfire.

The investigators were totally demoralized. The fact that Iraqi gunners had failed to inflict even a single casualty on such a large number of warplanes in such close proximity in daylight was the ultimate in haplessness. The air force had to be thinking of their own warplanes' sorry performance in Iran, where, rumor had it, losses were heavy and their ordnance was failing to explode.

More troubling, however, was news that the antiaircraft unit had been taking a dinner break at six every evening, shutting down its radar! Surely it wasn't a coincidence that the strike came at 6:25. An Israeli spy had done his job. When Saddam heard about it, he ordered the officer in charge shot.

I walked around the reactor. Several unexploded bombs littered the facility. One was lodged in a hundred-foot-long tunnel running between the reactor and a large laboratory where experiments were carried out. That the tunnel had been selected for special attention was more evidence that the Israelis had inside help. The day before the strike, in fact, I'd been walking by the facility with a colleague and noticed a closed van parked next to the tunnel. When I asked what it was, he said it contained radiation detection equipment the French had just delivered. In the aftermath of the bombing, investigators reportedly found a guidance transmitter inside.

There was other odd behavior on the part of the French, it turned out. Late the day before, French technicians working at the site had gone off to a meeting—not at their offices adjacent to the reactor, as usual, but at a village especially constructed for them about half a mile away. They'd scheduled their meeting for five P.M., and attendance was mandatory. One of the technicians, however, had refused to go, pleading work that had to be finished. The technician's friends had been so insistent he leave that a scuffle broke out. He'd stayed behind and died in the bombing.

Another odd incident came to the investigators' attention: Iraqi guards and cooks in the village said that loud quarrels had broken out among the French late into the night following the Israeli attack. The next day, one of them was found floating in the village swimming pool. Either he drank or said too much.

Needless to say, Saddam reacted poorly to each piece of bad news, finally giving a grim, fulminating television speech that not only accused the French of complicity with the Israelis but, much to our own distress, denounced the leadership of Atomic Energy for lax security, including a failure to construct Osirak in a way that anticipated a military attack. It was Saddam's way, of course, of distancing himself from the smoking, very expensive ruins.

He well knew, however, that we'd fought hard to put the reactor underground, where it would have been safer from attack. But the French would not agree. They were prepared to go along with our bomb deception only to the extent that they could plausibly deny it. And the only reason to put a nuclear reactor underground, considering the huge costs required, was to manufacture plutonium in secret and protect it from a military attack. The French weren't going to take the fall for that.

The first effect of the destruction of Osirak was the elimination of the plutonium route to the bomb. Al-Ghafour suggested an alternative, enriching uranium using centrifuge technology, for which at first I had little enthusiasm: It would require the clandestine acquisition of even more highly sophisticated, foreign technology, with a tremendous risk of exposure. But with Jaffar in jail, Osirak in ruins, al-Ghafour calling the shots, and his laser project going nowhere, it looked like that was the way we would go. Anyway, who was I to say no?

The centrifuge process involved extracting bomb-grade fuel by spinning a uranium compound–gas inside a fast-rotating cylinder. The lighter uranium at the center of the cylinder is enriched by the fuel. Repeating the process many times over brings it up to bomb-grade levels. This was the method the Pakistanis had adopted, according to our reports, and it had two distinct advantages: No reactors were required, and no dirty plutonium was produced.

Unwittingly, as it turned out, the Israeli attack might have made our job easier: We could let the world think we'd been crippled, but we still had the uranium from Osirak.

Yet despite those bright spots, the atmosphere had changed for the worse again. Now we were at war on two fronts, with Israel and Iran. The war with Iran was brutal and open, two armies slugging it out in a contemporary version of trench warfare. The war with the Israelis had been covert, a back-alley struggle of hide-and-seek. Until now.

The Osirak bombing signaled a new and terrifying phase in the conflict. The Israelis, we knew, were ruthless when it came to the defense of their country. The bombing meant we wouldn't be safe at home or abroad. Some of our colleagues had already died mysteriously abroad.

It did not take long for word of our heightened fears to reach Saddam. He turned up at AE one morning decked out in his wartime getup of black beret and olive drab army sweater, a pistol slung on his hip, and launched into his version of a pep talk.

Cowards, he called us.

"If you're scared now, how do you think you guys would do in a real shooting war?" he asked contemptuously. A wave of discomfort, even shame, swept the room. We had all seen the amputees, the coffins arriving on taxis from the front, the weeping families.

Every Iraqi, Saddam said, had to be a fighter. Every Iraqi had a role to play in the war. Everybody was a soldier. We needed to toughen up. There was no victory without suffering.

Angrily pacing the floor, he wagged a finger in our direction.

"You think the Iranian mullahs are weak? You think those bearded fanatics will give up?

"No, they are not weak. They will never give up. Those Iranian boys dying at the front are *twelve and thirteen years old*, and they're happy to be going to heaven! They can't wait to die for Allah!"

Now he was openly sneering.

"Do you know who your enemy is?" he asked. "The ayatollahs. If we let them get to Baghdad they'll shroud our women in veils and beat us to the sidewalks for not growing beards.

"No more good times for you guys then," he chuckled derisively.

And where were the Iranians getting their new weapons now? The Israelis!

"So," he asked, "do you think you are tough enough to stand up to them?"

Around the room, heads nodded woodenly. Nervous smiles and a patter of applause broke out, mostly from the party stalwarts.

"Good," he said. And then he dropped another little bomb. In recognition of the good work many of us had done, he said, he was leaving a gift: twenty-six new cars. We could decide among ourselves who should get one. There were hundreds of employees.

With that, smiling widely, Saddam left the room.

I felt a familiar wave of nausea in my stomach. His reassurances, as usual, meant very little. Saddam had created our nuclear nightmare. And there was more than a little suspicion among us that Saddam himself was behind some of the misfortunes that befell our colleagues overseas.

Yehia al-Meshad was a shy, quiet nuclear engineer from Egypt who came to us from Alexandria University, where he'd earned a reputation for reliability and academic conservatism. In his mid-forties, stocky, with dark features and a droll sense of humor, al-Meshad was a relief to have around.

And he filled a hole. By 1980, we were losing engineers left and right. Young Iraqis sent abroad for graduate training, especially in the United States, had stopped coming back. They'd all discovered human rights. Suddenly every Iraqi student seemed to know about Amnesty International. When the thugs came around to apply pressure to return, they'd fire off a letter to the Iraqi embassy in Washington warning that if there was any more harassment, they'd stir up trouble. For a while, at least, it seemed to work.

But it hurt us. Soviet-trained Iraqi engineers were still around, but they were useless, more fluent in Marxism than physics. So al-Meshad, trained first in the United States and later in the Soviet Union, was a great asset, especially since I was overburdened with other things. I was glad to delegate someone to deal with the French.

Initially, the French had offered us bomb-grade uranium because they knew we would pay any price for it—nothing was too expensive for Saddam. At that point we had plans not only to produce illicit plutonium with the French reactor, but to build our own secret reactor with the enriched uranium as a fuel. In any event, the amount we'd agreed on was fifty-eight kilograms, easily enough to make two bombs. But then, under pressure from Israel and the United States, the French tried to back out of the contract, offering us the so-called Caramel fuel, a much lower grade. We refused, and sent al-Meshad off to nail down a deal.After a few days at a nuclear facility south of Paris, he checked into the Méridian Hotel. He had a few more days' work with the French nuclear agency at Saclay ahead. A lesser-paid colleague traveling with him moved on to a cheaper hotel.

On the day he was scheduled to fly back to Iraq, a hotel maid found al-Meshad's body lying in a puddle of blood on the floor of his room. He had numerous stab wounds, including a deep gash in his face. Two days later a French prostitute by the name of Marie-Claude Magalle, who'd had some sort of encounter with al-Meshad, was knocked down by a hit-and-run driver and killed.

The murder made big headlines in the Paris press, with all arrows pointing to the Israelis. One version of the story was that Mlle. Magalle had made a pitch to al-Meshad but he wasn't interested. Then, after he entered his room, she waited in the hall to see if he'd change his mind. When she heard voices in the room, she gave up and left. Or so she said. When the French police sought to question her again a few days later, they learned that she'd been run over by a car.

Saddam dispatched two Iraqi intelligence officers to look into the case. With long experience in such matters, they didn't believe in accidents. If all she did was hear voices, they reasoned, then why was she killed? To the Iraqis, the prostitute's death meant only one thing: She'd been inside al-Meshad's room and in some fashion paved the way for the killers.

Next to enter the crosshairs was Salman Rashid, an enthusiastic young electrical engineer. Rashid, educated in the U.K., had been working with Jaffar on designing and building a magnet for uranium enrichment. But neither was strong in math, and they'd been having trouble with the design calculations. Jaffar used his connections with the European Center for Nuclear Research (CERN) in Geneva to get Rashid a fellowship.

Now, with Jaffar in jail, Rashid was struggling. A Swedish company, Brown Boveri, was contracted under the cover of a peaceful research project to help with the design, and late in the summer of 1980, Rashid went off to see them in Geneva, along with a contingent of assistants and a security officer. It was going to be a two-month-long session. He urged me to come with him, but I begged off, citing my workload. The main reason was that I wanted to stay home with my family.

No doubt word spread that an Iraqi scientist was in Geneva asking all sorts of questions about a magnet that would be useful for enriching uranium. On the eve of his return, Rashid suddenly came down with what looked like a bad case of the flu. But it was a flu like he'd never had before. He had difficulty swallowing; he started to bloat. The doctors at the American Hospital in Geneva seemed perplexed. Saddam sent in an Iraqi doctor, but he was stumped as well. After about ten days, Rashid died. Poisoning was cited, but the exact cause was unknown.

The officer in charge of his security claimed that Rashid was under his watch all the time. But internal Iraqi embassy reports told a different story. Rashid had been seen many times in the local bars and restaurants, either alone or in the company of his colleagues at CERN. There had been many opportunities to slip something into his food or drinks—or jab him with a ricin-tipped pin, the way a Bulgarian dissident was assassinated in London in 1969. Whatever the cause, we had no doubt whatsoever that Rashid had been murdered. Of course, it meant someone was tracking our travels.

Six months later, another of our engineers was murdered. Abdul-Rahman Abdul Rassool died after swallowing an unknown poison at an official French banquet. Again, it was easy to suspect the Israelis in the killings. But with our experience in Iraq, other possibilities came to mind.

The killing of al-Meshad was particularly troubling. He was, after all, a minor figure in our program, a foreigner working on a yearly contract. He was just a nuclear engineer, who could be replaced without a day's loss in the project. If indeed the Israelis were behind his murder, they had taken big risks to kill a small fish in the heart of the French capital.

It also developed that perhaps al-Meshad was being debriefed by Egyptian security during his vacation trips home. The Egyptians would very likely pass along his information to the CIA, which in turn would pass it to Mossad. If that were truly the case, then Saddam would have reason to kill al-Meshad himself, in a setting that would absolve him and point to "the Jews."

Somebody, obviously, wanted to make a point: No one was safe. No one. Certainly not me.

CHAPTER EIGHT

SPIES AND LIES

Jaffar finally came back.

For the first few days after he returned to Atomic Energy, he stayed in his office, a secluded ghost of his old, vivacious self.

When I cracked open his door, he froze like a deer in the headlights. Only when he saw it was me did he relax and lower himself back into his chair, smiling weakly. Gently, I came in and sat across from his desk. I'd missed him terribly.

We did not talk of his time away, and certainly not his torture. The subject was unspeakable. Neither of us knew how to bring it up. What would I ask? "Was it terrible?" "How terrible was it?" Of course it was. So I waited for him to broach the subject. And when he didn't, it floated between us like a fly that we both chose to ignore.

A slight tremor shook his head and his bony hands, I noticed. His aristocratic self-assurance was gone.

There was a knock at the door. His eyes swerved as if he was expecting a firing squad. It was just his secretary. She poked her head in and asked if we'd like some tea.

"She's a pain in the neck," he said when she left. "She talks on the telephone all the time. She talks too loud. I'm going to have to get rid of her."

Jaffar had been restored to us without prior notice. One day in September 1981 we heard that he'd been released from house arrest at Habbania, the French lake resort eighty miles north of Baghdad. But no one had ventured a visit to his elegant home. Then one day he just appeared in the office at the side of al-Ghafour.

"I told you last week that I'd have a pleasant surprise," the boss said, beaming—he being the man whose hand I'd seen on the boot-legged tape putting a bullet into the head of the official who'd presided over Jaffar's recruitment dinner in 1975.

Jaffar was smiling but he looked extremely fragile. We wondered what he'd given Saddam to win his freedom.

Everyone crowded around Jaffar, shaking his hand and slapping him on the back. We all chatted for a while, and then I decided on a whim that he could use a boost. That afternoon I arranged for a small dinner in his honor at an Italian restaurant, attended by just the senior physics department staff, something casual and light. As it turned out, it was a cheerful reunion, with jokes and laughs over several rounds of drinks and plates of pasta. Even Jaffar seemed to loosen up. Of course, everyone was happy to see the handsome beanpole back, even in his diminished state.

He was still the gourmet, remarking discreetly how the quality of food had declined while the prices had gone up since he'd been away. It was the war, I told him. Fresh ingredients were harder to come by and foreign kitchen staffs were leaving, mainly because of new restrictions on how much currency they could convert and send home. The cooks apparently figured that if they had to dodge Iranian air raids and missiles, it might as well be worthwhile.

Jaffar's stutter had nearly evaporated, we all noticed. Was it the torture? I wondered. Or the psychiatric care he'd been getting for his prison trauma? Nobody dared ask.

We also noticed now how quickly he tired. Jaffar's stamina was legendary. In the past he'd routinely put in twelve or fourteen hours a day without a lunch break. He'd have a sandwich on the run while he was discussing some aspect of our work. And then he'd party all night. Now it wasn't even ten o'clock and his eyes were drooping.

The next morning, he called me.

"Can you come over?"

"Sure," I said. "Where are you?"

"In the trailer behind the library," he said.

The trailer. I'd wondered where he'd settled. His old office was right next to al-Ghafour's, but I got the impression that relations between them had cooled. The ruthless party operative had replaced al-Hashimi as deputy chairman, no matter that he'd flushed millions down the drain in pursuit of Israel's laser enrichment scam. But then, Jaffar had sunk millions into his own failed crusade to make plutonium. So far, the bomb program was a billion-dollar lemon. Atomic Energy wasn't even producing atomic energy.

Jaffar looked at me with a weak smile.

"So," he said, "I hear you don't like the idea of enriching uranium by centrifuge."

I was surprised and laughed. "You read my report?"

"Yes. And I agree with you," he said. "It's harder to enrich uranium that way."

He picked up a thin folder and tossed it toward me on his desk. "Here, read this."

I opened the folder. There were several handwritten sheets. On the top of the first page was "Using the Method of Diffusion to Obtain Bomb-Grade Uranium." It was addressed to Barzan al-Tikriti, the chief of central intelligence, the Mukhabarat. He was also Saddam's brother-in-law.

So this is how Jaffar got out of jail, I concluded. It was his renewed commitment to manufacture bomb-grade uranium.

I looked up at him. "Are you going to do this?"

He was watching me closely.

"No," he said. "You are."

I nodded slowly. Finally, I asked, "And what about you?"

"Back to enriching uranium using magnets," he said.

"I see." It made a certain sense. The Americans had used magnets a half century ago to enrich the uranium for Little Boy. The process wasn't a secret, and Jaffar's expertise, after all, was in magnets. Osirak was in ruins; there was no question of buying a new reactor.

But why have me work on something else? I quickly deduced that Jaffar wanted to show Saddam he was pulling out all the stops. Having me work on diffusion, the current standard, would be his backup. The only problem was that key elements of the technology were in the West—and classified.

There was a knock on the door. Jaffar motioned me to turn the report facedown.

"Yes?"

A uniformed officer of the Presidential Guards stepped into the office. Jaffar visibly stiffened and sat up.

The officer saluted, then walked to Jaffar's desk. He placed a set of keys on it.

Jaffar hesitated, then reached forward and picked them up.

"A Mercedes," he said, smiling wanly.

"With the compliments of the president, sir," the officer said.

Jaffar looked embarrassed. "There is no need for this," he nearly whispered.

The officer made no move to leave.

Jaffar pulled himself together and looked up at the officer. "I thank the president and appreciate this gift," he said firmly.

The soldier smiled curtly, turned on his heel, and left.

Jaffar and I went to the window. Parked outside was a shiny new Mercedes 450. I'd already walked past another new Mercedes parked in the lot, a sleek 280S, which I assumed was also Jaffar's. He looked chagrined.

First the stick, now the carrot; torture, then a Mercedes. So it went in Saddam's republic of fear. Apparently they were going to give Jaffar a string of new cars until he settled down and forgot what they'd done to him. I looked at his aristocratic profile. Born to wealth and privilege, with hundreds of millions of dollars' worth of real estate in Baghdad alone, he would need a lot more than a couple of shiny new Mercedes to make him forgive or forget twenty months of beatings and humiliation But it was the only thing they knew.

I had more immediate concerns. I wanted to know what Jaffar's status was and what our relationship would be.

"What's the next step?" I asked. "What are we going to be doing?"

"Establishing a new umbrella for our work," he said. "You're going to help me set up a new organization, which we'll call the Office of Research and Development." Its sole responsibility would be to deliver enriched uranium for the bomb.

I nodded. "Do we work through al-Ghafour?" I asked. "Or are we going to have the same problems we had before with him and al-Hashimi?" By that I meant party interference and delays.

He scoffed, as if I were way behind the times.

"Al-Ghafour and AE will have no say in what we do," he said. "We are completely independent now. Our authority comes straight from the president. From now on it's just you and me."

I had a fleeting vision of my head going back on the block. No promotion, no added responsibility came without peril in Saddam's Iraq.

"We might use al-Ghafour as a functionary to take our requests to the presidency," Jaffar continued. "But in reality we have the direct authority of the president, and he will be merely the messenger. At present, however, I have no system to handle money, or purchases, and no staff. So for now, AE will provide staff and space for us. What we need right away is a plan for a whole new structure to carry out the uranium enrichment."

He must have seen the question forming on my lips.

"As for building the bomb itself, it's not my worry," he said with a wave of his hand.

I didn't like that. The implication, of course, was that the bomb design and construction was my worry—alone. His responsibility was only to come up with the fuel, and only the fuel. While I was being drafted to help him out, the bomb was still on my neck.

"I won't have the time to worry about the everyday details of running the new enterprise," Jaffar was going on blithely. That, he said, would be my responsibility. I'd be transferred to his command. But I should know that we'd both be working directly for Saddam.

And, oh, by the way, he added, Barzan al-Tikriti would be working with us to clear away any bureaucratic underbrush or security problems.

Great. The head sadist. "That will certainly make people hop," I agreed wryly.

At that point I was in such a haze I can't remember the other organizational details we discussed. Immediately afterward, however, I dropped in on al-Ghafour.

"What's Jaffar's status now?" I asked.

"Fully rehabilitated," he answered.

"He wants me to work with him," I said.

"Do whatever he asks," he said, shifting his expanding bulk in the chair. "Our orders are to cooperate with him. For now.

"Keep in mind," he added, "that you're going to have to leave him at some point to design and build the bomb itself. Don't commit yourself too deeply to him. Just help him for now. After all, if you don't have fuel, you can't build many bombs."

Ever the bureaucrat, al-Ghafour had clicked his heels at Saddam's new imperative and gotten out of the way. In any event, all I needed to know was that Jaffar was in charge now. The question was whether Jaffar himself fully knew what he had signed on for. I had a feeling that, in the end, he'd be held responsible for more than just producing uranium.

We spent the next few days planning for the new office. The immediate problem was a lack of current information. Despite dramatic additions to our library over the decade, we still lacked details on the intricacies of uranium enrichment, particularly current technical reports. Nor was this the kind of open material we could order from Blackwell's, our British purchasing agent for books, journals, and publications—especially with increased attention to our nuclear program following the attack on Osirak and the Israelis' continued complaints. We assumed that foreign intelligence agencies, particularly the Israelis, were keeping even closer tabs on us now.

We were also missing critical items for calibrating our nuclear experiments. Iraqi intelligence agents, so good at pulling out fingernails in the dungeons, had proved inept at acquiring sophisticated materials abroad. After much discussion, Jaffar and I decided I should go to London myself. It was not a happy prospect.

Souham begged me not to go, pleading and weeping on her knees, clutching my hand. Three of our people had already been assassinated, and she rightly feared the same would happen to me. She was a young mother of two boys, unprepared to be a widow. In the riptides of conspiracy and murder engulfing the presidential palace, she feared what would happen if I weren't around to protect her. Even senior officials were being replaced left and right, some disappearing into the dungeons or their bodies showing up on the roadside. She feared she'd be caught in the undertow if I weren't around.

"I have no choice," I explained patiently. We were all Saddam's captives now, whether we were holding high office or sitting in a cell, awaiting the firing squad. Plus, the war was going badly, the fanatical Iranians were pounding at our door. Who else could save us from the glassy-eyed Shiite martyrs but Saddam? For a while, we just had to hold on and hope that somehow things would get better.

142

Souham sniffled and wrung her hands. But there was really no alternative, I said softly: I had to go.

The murder of our officials in France and Switzerland had changed some of our security procedures. Now there was a man at AE in charge of handling our passports, visas, and airline reservations. Of course, he was connected to the Mukhabarat.

New procedures were put into place to reduce the chance that foreign spies, and particularly Mossad, could obtain advance notice of our travels. The AE security man arranged with Iraqi Airways to book our advance round-trip tickets under one set of names, then switch them to other names on the day of departure. Air France, which we flew on the London–New York leg, had close relations with Iraqi Airways and would go along with the changes. Later, when the international reservation system made late changes more difficult, the security man would switch my name two or three days before the flight but use phonetic and other variations on the Arabic to throw off the scent. Most foreign ticket agents and Customs officials could care less about the difference between Khidhir Abdul Abbas Hamza or just Khidhir Abdul Abbas. In any event, since Abbas and Hamza were both so common in Iraq, even attentive observers would have a hard time ascertaining which one was really me. As another layer of camouflage, I was issued a new passport for every trip. The same techniques, I would learn, were used to disguise the movements of Iraqi hit men and international terrorists like Abu Nidal in and out of Baghdad.

Another challenge we faced was reestablishing relations with the international science community, which, ironically, was giving Iraq the cold shoulder because of Jaffar's jailing. (And that of al-Shahristani, too, who still languished in prison.) CERN, for example, critically important to helping us contract for a magnet design, was now refusing to cooperate at all. In addition, Dr. Salam, the Pakistani who headed Italy's International Center of Theoretical Physics, was still angry at Saddam because his inquiries about Jaffar's prison status had been rebuffed by Saddam. Iraqis studying science abroad, meanwhile, were further poisoning the well by using the New Scientist's articles about the jailing of Jaffar and al-Shahristani to bolster their pleas for asylum.

"We have to start mending relations," al-Ghafour told me on the eve of my trip to London. He said I should go to Trieste first and patch things up with Salam.

"Explain to him that Jaffar's fine now and everything has been fixed up with him. Tell him that the Iraqi government didn't have anything against him personally when we didn't issue him a visa to come here and investigate Jaffar's case. Just say, 'It was a bad time, you know, with the war and all that.' Then you can go on to London from there."

I doubted Salam would be placated so easily. His nose had been bent out of shape by Iraq's rebuff and he wouldn't forget so easily.

Al-Ghafour had something else.

"Due to the length of the trip, we're also sending along a Mukhabarat security officer, to guard you," Al-Ghafour added, clearing his throat. "Try not to make him stand out—cover for him."

Cover for him? A Mukhabarat security officer? It would be easier to cover a potted plant.

Before I got a chance to bring that up with Jaffar, he wanted to talk about something else.

"You know, my wife is in England right now," he said. I knew all too well. Just the mention of her made me think back to better days and the cocktail parties at their house, her lively wit and wickedly funny mocking of the regime. She'd been lucky to escape with her head after slapping a security guard at the airport. Now, from London, she was raising a ruckus about Jaffar's treatment.

"She doesn't think she'll ever be able to come back," Jaffar said in an understatement. "So I'd really appreciate it if you would take the rest of her personal stuff to England for me."

There were two large travel bags in the corner. Was it a trap? Not from Jaffar, I decided. I carried them out and put them in my car. When I drove off, I realized I'd forgotten to ask him about the guy from Mukhabarat.

Iraqi Air had recently acquired a new Boeing 707. I sat in the first-class section on the flight to Rome. Fortunately, my "bodyguard" was shunted to coach. In only a few minutes' conversation at the airport, I'd quickly sized up "Hussein" as a typical Mukhabarat stiff who'd get in my way more than protect me from harm. I'd gathered that it was his first trip outside the country.

Aside from wider seats and free drinks, first class on Iraqi Airways had none of the amenities of an international airline. Dinner was a case in point. Incredibly, it was stew meat with beans and rice, an everyday dish in Iraq, but hardly appropriate as first-class fare. I looked on it with dismay.

The man in the next seat, it turned out, was an Iraqi Airways executive. We traded glances. The reason we weren't getting first-class treatment, he explained, was because the government reserved first class for officials like myself and the airline didn't make any money on us. Often, he said, government agencies didn't even bother to pay for the tickets they had booked, like mine. The airline would be stiffed for the fare.

That was wrong, I mumbled.

"It is," he said with a chuckle. "But who do we complain to?" He sipped his scotch. It was a rhetorical question.

"So that's why you get that," he said, tipping his glass toward my tray. "We have to make up for it somewhere." First-class amenities weren't appropriate anyway, he added, with the war going on.

"Look at us," he said, "flying like thieves in the dead of night for fear of Iranian fighter planes. You'd think we could get a fighter escort out of our own airspace."

The conversation soon tapered off. I pulled a blanket over my shoulders and slept as best as I could.

At the airport in Rome, I waited in vain for my bags. The suitcases for Jaffar's wife were there, but none of mine. When I confronted the Iraqi Airways clerk he wasn't even apologetic. He made no offer to recompense me in cash, as other airlines routinely do, or even to provide some basic temporary necessities. When I sputtered that I was a ranking official and they'd surely hear about it later, they merely shrugged and told me to do whatever I had to do. It reminded me of what the Russians had said about the Soviet system. Customer satisfaction took a backseat to staying in favor with the party bosses, in this case Saddam. The head of Iraqi Airways had even divorced his wife so Saddam could take her as his mistress, or so we'd heard. (She later became his second wife.) Why would he care about us? He had it made.

I rounded up some new clothes at considerable out-of-pocket cost, then went to the Iraqi embassy with my bodyguard and checked in with the Mukhabarat station chief, as instructed. When he found out I'd made arrangements to meet Salam in Trieste, he wanted to go along. I despaired. This wasn't a junket, but of course I didn't say that. I cautioned him that it might be better to wait until I felt out the situation with Salam. He insisted, however, and of course I gave in. I didn't really want to antagonize a man whose boss was Barzan al-Tikriti.

As it turned out, Salam was attending a conference in Rome. His secretary made a call, and a few hours later I was waiting uncomfortably in a hotel lobby with the two goons from Mukhabarat when Salam came in.

He sensed my discomfort. "Who are they?" he whispered discreetly when we got to his room. The intelligence guys were already distracted by the opulent furnishings.

"This one is the cultural attaché from the Iraqi embassy," I lied, referring to the Mukhabarat station chief. "And the other one is one of our workers at Atomic Energy."

Salam looked at me, then sized up the bodyguard, who looked like a bouncer.

"Ask him to leave," he said. I nodded and went over to the young man, and in a low voice asked him to wait outside. He left.

"So how is our dear Jaffar?" Salam asked, taking a seat.

I rolled out the best spiel I could, letting him know that Jaffar was just fine after a "disciplinary" stint away from Atomic Energy. He was back and working enthusiastically, I said.

"Good." Salam smiled. He asked me to send him his best. Then he nodded in the direction of the station chief, who was off in a corner toying with an expensive figurine.

"Why is the other gentleman here?" Salam asked.

I explained that the "cultural attaché" had come along to extend an official welcome to him in the event he'd like to visit Baghdad again in the near future. This is the man who would expedite his visa, I said.

Salam weighed my words silently. Then he turned to me with a brittle smile.

"You'll have to excuse me," he said. "I have another meeting I must attend to." At that he stood and offered me a stiff handshake.

That was the last time I would ever see Salam. Clearly I'd violated our friendship by bringing along the government goons. As I walked through the hotel lobby with the Mukhabarat men in tow, I vowed I would never make that mistake again.

Back in my room, however, I couldn't shake my young bodyguard. He hovered around, asking me about Jaffar's case until, finally, I said, "It's none of your business." Then I threatened to report him for a security violation unless he stopped pestering me.

That was the magic bullet. Suddenly he paled and begged me not to report him. I thought he was going to have a nervous breakdown on the spot.

"Don't worry," I finally said, feeling some sympathy. He was just a rube, after all. Unfortunately, now he mistook my pity for friendship and started bugging me to help get him a call girl. He didn't speak English well enough to do it on his own.

Good God, I thought. If the whole trip's going to be like this . . .

We went out on the Via Veneto, Rome's main drag, to look for a girl he'd seen earlier. When we finally found her, she agreed to go with him for a hundred dollars an hour. For two hundred, she said, he could have the whole night. Against my advice, he eagerly forked over the cash, then handed me his passport and wallet for safekeeping.

I was lying on my bed reading a half hour later when he was back, looking sick. He said she smelled so bad "down there" it made him vomit. I almost laughed, but then he told me how he'd kicked her out of his room. The way he described it made me think he might've slapped her around.

Not good. The hooker could well come back with her pimp and make a scene, possibly beat him up. It was not the kind of incident I could afford, considering the mission I was on. The Israelis had ties to the Italian police.

"Call the desk immediately and demand a switch in rooms," I told him. "Make up any excuse." The whore and her pimp could be coming back any minute, I told him, so he'd better move fast. He scurried from my room.

That was enough of Mukhabarat for me. As I pondered how to shake him, I got a break from the British embassy: It had denied him a visa to enter the U.K.

The British constantly amazed me with their information. Whenever we sent a list of AE employees over to the British Institute in Baghdad for English-language courses, for example, the Mukhabarat always tried to slip a few of their agents onto the list. When it came back, the British had invariably scratched off their names. They obviously knew who my companion was. I shot off a telegram to Baghdad saying I couldn't continue the trip with him. Thankfully, al-Ghafour's answer came back the next day, with orders to proceed by myself. My poor bodyguard was on his own now.

Several hours later I ran into my own hitch at Heathrow. An imperious little immigration officer was convinced I'd come to Britain for free medical care. We went back and forth over it for several minutes, until, exasperated, I finally said, "Look here, Officer, I'm here on a business visa, as you can plainly see, not to see a doctor. Furthermore, if I had a medical problem, I'd certainly be more inclined to see a doctor in the United States where I got my Ph.D., instead of here."

At that the bureaucrat pulled himself up to his full five feet, glared at me, and stamped my passport. Outside, an Iraqi security agent from the embassy asked me what the fuss was about. When I told him, he said the British were constantly harassing us because Baghdad routinely denied them visas. A spy war, I guessed.

The next day the agent came by my room and moved me to a different hotel. Ever since the murders of our people in France and Switzerland, we'd been trained to move frequently. In Rome we had changed hotels three times in nine days. It was a tiring and counterproductive idea, I thought, which would only draw more attention to us, since every new registration was routinely reported to the police. They might even think we were terrorists. After a few days I went to the Iraqi embassy and persuaded the Mukhabarat chief to rent an apartment for me. He found one in Kensington with a door guard and hotel services. It was definitely better than moving from one bustling hotel to the next.

Other new security measures had been put in place. To avoid poisoning we were instructed not to eat in the same place twice, to locate cafeterias where we could choose our own food, and to decline impromptu invitations from strangers to restaurants or private homes. Never leave food in your room, we were told, or drink any hotel water. Buy your own. Keep personal items, such as toothbrushes and razors, with us at all times. I followed the rules to the letter.

The Iraqi chief of intelligence in London was actually a Syrian national, which was not as odd as it may sound. Many Syrians lived in Iraq or worked in Iraqi embassies abroad. Both Syria and Iraq officially ascribed to Baathist ideology, even though they were deadly rivals for leadership of the Arab world. Some of the branch leaders of the Iraqi Baath Party, whom I often saw at the Hunting Club, were Syrians. All the same, I was uncomfortable with a Syrian knowing anything about my mission, for the simple reason that his allegiance could be suspect. So when I learned he was asking questions about my mission, I went to see our ambassador, Husham al-Shawi.

Al-Shawi had swung through the highest rungs of the regime since I'd last seen him in Vienna in 1973, when he took charge of our mission to penetrate the International Atomic Energy Agency. He'd been minister of higher education, and then chief of the president's staff, before Saddam tapped him to be our ambassador in London. He'd come a long way from teaching political science at the University of Baghdad.

Highly cultured and literate, al-Shawi was more comfortable as a diplomat than a government henchman. He was not a Baathist, nor did he really fit in with Saddam's thuggish clique, especially the president's power-mad relatives. All in all, he was a model diplomat. When I was shown into his office, he politely asked me to take a seat and apologized in his Oxford accent that he had to finish writing a cable to Baghdad for the next diplomatic pouch. When he finished, we had tea and a pleasant conversation, catching up on events since our last meeting a decade ago. Finally, I broached the subject of the Syrian station chief.

Al-Shawi nodded sympathetically as I spun out the story of the hapless Mukhabarat agents in Rome. When I told him about his Syrian asking questions, his eyebrows arched. When I finished, he spoke to me in a low, discreet voice.

"Don't let those Mukhabarat guys near you," he said. "If you go around with them, you might as well put a sign on your back." British intelligence knew who the Iraqi agents in the embassy were, he said, including their names. Any association with them at all would prompt British security to conclude that I was either a spy or some other official who merited their special attention.

"Either way, you lose," he said. He sighed. The embassy was honeycombed with party hacks and security men, he complained. They always gave him headaches.

I told him I was grateful for his advice. In return, I confided in him about my mission. The ambassador listened intently. He said I could use the embassy as a safe house for my materials, but advised me to seal the bags or envelopes in a way that discouraged anyone from opening them. He'd have the embassy staff put the stuff directly on the Iraqi Airways flights, sidestepping the usual security procedures.

He didn't like butting heads with the intelligence people, he said wearily. They were trouble. The accuracy of their reports was also suspect. Later, I would find out how true this was: The regime would spend millions of dollars on bogus documents and ersatz plutonium hustlers.

The ambassador wished me luck.

Later, the Syrian station chief was nonplussed when I told him I was turning down his services. He insisted that I couldn't possibly travel around London alone.

"It's my neck if something happens to you," he declared.

"Don't worry," I cracked. "I won't blame you if I'm killed." He failed to see the humor in it.

"Look," I said, "I've had enough of Iraqi security. You people have almost gotten me killed." I told him about Rome. I reminded him that our man Rashid supposedly had the protection of Mukhabarat when he was poisoned in Geneva.

"So that's it," I said. "I'm going alone from now on. If you don't like it, complain to the ambassador or my boss at Atomic Energy. Or the president himself. Tell him what a good job you're doing. Meanwhile, I've got work to do."

I stood up and walked out.

The biggest barrier to technological advancement in Iraq (and in the Third World altogether) was the lack of good information. The Internet would radically change that, but in the 1980s, routine breakthroughs in science and technology were available only in specialized reports that were expensive to buy and time-consuming to obtain. Even keeping up with indexes on what was out there was difficult.

Compounding our problem was the fact that dictatorships tend to restrict information flow. The articles about Jaffar and al-Shahristani in the *New Scientist* had provoked Saddam to block the import of even popular journals. Only specialized ones were now allowed in, and those only to a select few. This kept us so isolated that we did not know what people were writing about *us*. When one of our scientific societies complained to Saddam, his answer was quite revealing: He wouldn't open the door to foreign publications, he said, but he'd help them publish their own journals to circulate information—under his strict supervision. I lobbied al-Ghafour about it several times before he relented and allowed some publications to resume—on a tightly restricted basis.

In London, I decided to spend my first week in the British Science Library, part of the British Museum, and to make the rounds of various technical societies and bookstores. I bought hundreds of books and magazines and photocopied tons of material from scientific journals and reports. I'd decided to postpone buying any nuclear-oriented equipment. For starters, I didn't have enough time or good help. But I was also concerned that any sensitive purchases would set off alarms at British intelligence, which seemed to be keeping close tabs on us. Instead, I left instructions with the embassy to pick up several large photocopy orders I'd left at the Science Library. It was against my better judgment, but I had no choice. The next time I'd bring a few assistants. Meanwhile, I spread the photocopy orders over as many days as I could and interspersed them with innocuous-sounding requests.

At the end of two weeks it was time to leave. When I got to the airport, I learned that a van full of books, journals, and photocopied materials had been loaded onto the plane without any inspection.

Jaffar spent the next several months diddling with his experiments, as was his style, meticulously going over and over his results without much hard progress. I'd agreed to help him on the diffusion method, which involves passing gaseous uranium compounds through the very fine pores of a barrier again and again to separate the lighter uranium suitable for a bomb. It sounds easy in principle, but the pioneers of nuclear technology were aware of the implications of enriching uranium and had kept some of the critical elements of the technology secret. Except for very simple barriers such as aluminum oxide, the process of making barriers was classified. And even for the aluminum, we could not get all the manufacturing details.

But I did not want to be dragged into the everyday details of enriching fuel, I told Jaffar. I'd help him get started with calculations, but I needed to move on to research for the bomb itself.

He was unhappy. Jaffar wanted somebody responsible for diffusion, me in particular. I told him that enrichment was his responsibility, not mine, and that if he wanted me to do that he'd have to reassign me officially. Since al-Ghafour agreed with me, he backed off.

Now I was off the hook with Saddam on the fuel. Uranium was Jaffar's job. However he wanted to do it, I'd help him get started. Diffusion, magnets—I didn't care. The important thing was that my neck was no longer on the block. Getting bogged down with Jaffar was a bad idea, I had decided. We'd already waited three years for him to deliver.

One thing Jaffar certainly knew how to do was spend money. He'd mapped plans for multibillion-dollar factories to enrich uranium. He'd begun importing equipment at the rate of a hundred million dollars a clip. Over the next five years, we would buy everything from electronics to lasers, fiber optics to machining equipment, some hundred million dollars' worth of U.S. technology alone on the open market.

Meanwhile, we were raiding outside our walls for personnel. First we drew up lists of every science and engineering professor in Iraq. Then I visited the universities and asked around about promising students. After suitable interviews with Jaffar and me, we'd pass their names to Saddam, who would instantly order their assignments.

The same went for scientists at government ministries, such as oil or industry—we just took those we wanted, even critical personnel. After we stole a technical chief from the only functioning steel factory in Iraq, it went out of business. Even the National Energy Board wasn't beyond our reach. We stole so many of their electrical engineers that they complained they couldn't repair grids damaged by the war. Our reputation for getting people out of military service, meanwhile, was driving other recruits to our door. Within a year, every branch of the government was crying foul. It fell on deaf ears, of course. Saddam wanted the bomb.

Some of the equipment we needed was available only in the United States. So in early 1984 I packed my bags again.

We needed an electron microscope, for example, to take pictures of the barrier pores for the uranium diffusion enrichment process. We needed advanced computers for nuclear calculations and controls, and specialized air filters to protect our electronics labs. Most of these things were perfectly legal, but our official purchases tended to languish in the bowels of U.S. export control agencies. Al-Ghafour ordered me to go to the States and buy what I could myself—with cash.

He warned me, however, not to do anything illegal. "We have more expendable people for that," he said. An Iraqi intelligence agent in our Washington embassy, for example, had arranged for an engineer of Indian origin to buy a restricted computer and its programs. The Indian delivered the computer to a Florida parking lot and turned it over to one of our scientists, who broke it down into parts and shipped it back to Iraq in his luggage. Over the ensuing years, Iraqi agents would use such contacts to acquire all sorts of illicit materials, including nuclear triggers.

Most of what we needed required my personal nuclear expertise and easy familiarity with the way things were done in America. My cover for the trip would be to attend a space conference at the University of Michigan, in Ann Arbor. (Saddam had an active interest in U.S. spy satellite capabilities.) I was taking along my new assistant, a graduate of the University of Michigan, to help me gather reports and take care of photocopying.

The visa officer at the U.S. embassy in Baghdad was unusually pleasant, stamping our passports with a year's worth of multiple entry visas, an early sign of the Reagan administration's tilt toward Iraq in our war against Iran.

From Paris, we flew on Air France's 747 Special to New York, my assistant in coach, I in first class. The complimentary champagne and caviar were especially tasty after another dreadful trip from

Baghdad on Iraqi Air. In the upstairs lounge, I met an Egyptian who was the chief of a major U.S. soft drink maker's Middle East division. He was a pleasant and lighthearted guy, and after a while I felt comfortable enough to kid him about how bad the Iraqi version of the soda tasted compared with the real thing in the States.

They had no control over that, he said. "Have you ever tasted the Egyptian variety?"

No, I said.

He winced. "It's pure poison."

We both laughed.

Funny. But I asked him why that was. He rattled the ice in his glass.

"It's the governments," he said. "Back there"—Egypt and Iraq—"the bottling plants are owned by the government. The directors are chosen for their connections, not performance. They've never had inspections and almost no quality control. But who's going to shut down a government plant for health or quality reasons?"

It was the same story with Iraqi Air, of course, and so many other of our industries.

"So how does your company work in Iraq?" I asked.

"We just sell them the basic ingredients," he said. "Your people mix and bottle it. Your equipment's old and you have poor quality control. I've tried to improve things, but . . ." He chuckled again, but his eyes were mirthless. "Anyway," he said, "I live far away, in Beirut. And thank Allah for that." He smiled and drained his glass.

We landed at Kennedy late at night. The Customs man was not as friendly as the clerk at the U.S. embassy. He started grilling me about the money I'd listed in my entry form—why a scientist attending a conference in Michigan was carrying forty thousand dollars in cash. Because Baghdad banks didn't issue credit cards, I said. Plus I planned to buy a lot of things I couldn't get at home in poor, war-ravaged Iraq. He pestered me for several more minutes, with two Iraqi intelligence agents lurking on the far side of the gate. When I pointed out that I'd obeyed the law by declaring any cash in excess of ten thousand dollars, he finally let me go.

Although it was almost midnight, I told the agents I wanted to be taken directly to our ambassador to the United Nations. A half hour later we pulled up in front of the Iraqi U.N. mission at 14 East

Seventy-ninth Street. The ambassador arrived looking highly put out. What was so important to draw him away from an important function at midnight? he asked, taking a seat behind his desk. I wondered what kind of diplomatic event the ambassador could go to in jeans.

A graduate of the University of Paris, Riyadh al-Qaisy was a rising star in the Iraqi diplomatic corps, highly regarded as a levelheaded and practical man. I'd had friendly dealings with him at meetings of the Space Committee in Baghdad. I profusely apologized for calling on him so late, but I explained that it was an emergency. We were flying out early in the morning and needed the benefit of his advice on making sensitive purchases in the United States.

Now his eyes really flashed with anger.

"This is a diplomatic mission," he declared. "But you guys in Baghdad seem to regard it as your personal purchasing and shipping headquarters. You've given the FBI a full-time job just keeping track of all the Iraqis coming and going."

I wanted to protest that it wasn't us, it was MIMI, the military industries empire run by Saddam's son-in-law, Hussein Kamel. But the ambassador was on a tear.

"They've been bringing stuff here by the truckload! But they made the mistake of taking their purchases to a packing company to get them ready for cargo transport on Iraqi Airways. Of course they figured out too late that the packing company was an FBI front. The FBI checked the stuff and found some of it was being exported illegally. So they arrested two of the MIMI guys, and now our accountant is under a deportation order."

The ambassador shot a look of contempt at the two intelligence officers at the back of the room. They were bristling.

"You know," he continued, "Iraqi Air has the largest cargo hangar at Kennedy Airport. A lot of stuff that goes through that hangar comes from the embassy. It's very stupid . . ." He shook his head as if he were talking about errant teenagers. "It's very stupid to use an intelligence-infested community, such as an embassy, to do illegal operations. You *never* do that. You never mix the two. It's the easiest way in the world to get caught."

Especially, he said, when "all or most of the office temps working at the embassy were probably FBI informants." He shook his head.

"Wait outside," he told the agents. When the door closed behind them, he came out from behind his desk.

"The best thing for you to do," he told me in a low voice, "is to stay away from here. Do your business outside the embassy. Even if you're doing nothing illegal, as you say, the FBI will still be watching you on the assumption that you are doing something illegal. Especially after MIMI's fuck-ups." He was still simmering over the ineptitude in his own embassy.

"Look," he said. "Don't ship through Iraqi Air. It's under more scrutiny than other airlines. Ship through the Jordanian airline, Alia. They'll take your stuff, without question. It's a lot safer."

I wanted to protest again that I wasn't going to do anything illegal, but thought better of it. It was late, almost one A.M. Instead, I thanked him and left.

Too much work makes Hamza a dull boy, I decided, and postponed our flight for a couple of days. Whenever possible on my foreign trips, I took in movies and stocked up on books and videos that wouldn't be likely to show up in Baghdad. The Barnes & Noble stores were my favorites, because I could get everything from the latest Travis McGee by John D. MacDonald to fiction best-sellers and biographies of famous scientists. I filled shopping bags with the stuff. But just walking down Broadway and breathing free air was invigorating, an experience too many Americans take for granted. I didn't care if the FBI was shadowing me or not. What would they find out—that I liked books and Szechwan chicken? I walked for hours, all the way to Chinatown and back. In Times Square I stood in line at TKTS and snagged a last-minute seat for *Oh! Calcutta!*— a rousing show for a Shiite boy from the Iraqi backwoods. I loved New York, just like the bumper stickers said.

So did my young assistant, whose eyes were stuck wide open with the sensation of so many beautiful women on the streets. He went off on his own.

In Ann Arbor, unfortunately, he did the same, disappearing with an old college girlfriend for hours at a time. I gave him an ultimatum: either get on with the photocopying job, or I'd put him on the next plane back to Iraq. But the job, he told me, gave him the jitters; he was paranoid the FBI was watching and would tap him on the shoulder and ask why he was copying so many technical documents about uranium enrichment (all borrowed from the university library's shelves). After a couple of days he came to me with an idea. He knew an Iraqi graduate student at the University of Wisconsin whose ID could get him into the stacks to do all the photocopying we needed. I gave him some money and sent him on his way.

The Michigan space conference was a good place to throw off any interest the FBI might have in me, since they'd see I was engaged only in the most innocuous rounds of sleep-inducing technical seminars. But in a short time I found myself drifting into a disaster anyway, one of my own making.

It began when I met a staff member from the House Committee on Science and Technology, in Washington, D.C. He saw on my name tag that I was from Iraq, and introduced himself. He said he was curious to know how the Reagan administration's new export controls on technology were affecting us.

I put an Iraqi spin on the facts, telling him that the new controls were only successful in taking business away from the United States.

"Take computers, for example. IBM couldn't sell us their new mainframe because of the export controls. So we went to Japan and bought an NEC 750, which actually is more powerful than the IBM model we were going to buy."

He was listening with great interest.

"Let me give you another example," I continued. "ArabSat. The Saudi government owns seventy percent of it. Iraq owns only seven percent, but Dr. Ali al-Mashatt, the company's CEO, is an Iraqi friend of mine. He told me the Saudi partners wanted to buy all three of its communication satellites from the United States, but the export controls made it such a pain in the neck they finally went elsewhere. They were presented with all sorts of forms that were ridiculous and insulting. They had to promise that the satellites wouldn't be put to military use, especially in a war with Israel. They had to promise that they wouldn't use the satellites to gather intelligence on Israel. They wanted all sorts of guarantees on how the satellites would be used after they'd been bought and paid for."

The Saudi princes would never accept terms like that, I said.

"So al-Mashatt went to the French, who offered to sell him the satellites without any restrictions. But the Americans wouldn't leave well enough alone. When they got wind of the French deal they complained to King Fahd that my friend had bought the French satellites because there was something in it for him. A bribe, in other words."

I was getting a little steamed over this story myself. I felt al-Mashatt's integrity was beyond question.

"By blaming al-Mashatt instead of their own stupid export laws," I said, "the American companies created a lot of ill will with the ArabSat executives, who all sided with Dr. al-Mashatt. The king was forced to investigate, of course. He sent for al-Mashatt, who brought along the pile of American forms. When the king saw them, he blew up and ordered al-Mashatt to go ahead and buy the first satellite from the French." Unless U.S. controls changed, he'd buy the next two satellites from the French as well, I said.

I smiled. "Those silly forms cost the U.S. companies three hundred million dollars."

The congressional staffer was amazed. He asked me how much I thought the export controls were costing the U.S. economy in the Middle East.

"Billions a year in Iraq alone," I said. "The United States has lost the Iraqi computer market entirely because of export controls. We buy almost all of our technology now from France or Germany."

The man exhaled and excused himself. He said he'd be sure to look me up again.

The next day he buttonholed me with an air of great urgency. He'd talked to his people back in Washington, he said, and they were extremely interested in hearing firsthand what I'd told him. Would I be able to testify at a hearing? Or at least give a statement? A couple of congressmen and their staffers were flying in tomorrow and my testimony could be taken right here.

I stalled. "I'll have to consult with my boss first," I said. That night I was on the first plane out of Ann Arbor.

Route 128, the golden arc of high-tech suburbs around Boston, is an engineer's Sharper Image. Everything's there: super-computers, lasers, missiles, rocket engines. I'd come there to buy something simple but apparently beyond the reach of our Baghdad agencies: air filters. Not the kind you buy for a car, but the same idea: air filters so sophisticated they can prevent microscopic contaminants from fouling top-end computers—or, as I was to discover, block viruses from seeping into a lab devoted to the manufacture of anthrax or biological warfare agents.

At Atomic Energy we'd perfected the art of acquiring sensitive foreign technology by routing purchase orders through universities or ministries such as oil, industry, agriculture, and even health. I should have suspected that an even more secretive agency might use us for the same purposes. But to tell the truth, it didn't occur to me at the time. We were too busy scheming to use everybody else.

It should have been obvious that something especially terrible was going on at Al-Hazen, the sprawling military-industrial complex ten miles south of al-Tuwaitha. Its full name, the Al-Hazen Ibn Al Haytham Institute, named for a tenth-century Arab pioneer in optics, was originally the brainchild of Merwan, the voluble Palestinian who'd lectured us on military innovation a decade earlier. Back then he was Saddam's pet, the personal envoy of PLO chairman Yasser Arafat, given millions of dollars to pursue his scheme of acquiring vast amounts of foreign military technology to get Iraq's own armaments industry off the ground. Merwan had had an impressive rollout, enticing big-time foreign scientists to Al-Hazen, forging an ambitious partnership with the University of Arizona's Optics Science Center, and traveling the world spending millions of dollars. Saddam had given him a long leash, but it was only a matter of time before he yanked. And when he did, as it turned out, nothing was there. Merwan and his brother had ripped off Saddam for very large sums of money and not even come up with a pop gun.

Saddam was in a murderous rage, and wanted Merwan's head on a stick. But Arafat implored Saddam to spare his protégé's life, invoking their longtime solidarity. Saddam, uncharacteristically, relented and merely sent Merwan to jail for a term of thirty-five years. Not long after, however, Arafat repaid this kindness by embracing the Ayatollah Khomeini, Saddam's archenemy. Saddam threw the PLO out of Iraq and, according to the story I heard, had Merwan chopped up and sent back to Arafat in a box.

The idea behind Al-Hazen, however, never died. Mukhabarat relaunched it as a clandestine laboratory for the production of chemical and biological weapons. Al-Hazen would no longer be part of the army, it would be run by the Special Security Organization, Saddam's own Gestapo.

Hints of Al-Hazen's rebirth came when it started borrowing AE's biologists, who were doing secret research on crop diseases and gene mutations induced by radiation. Other signs were more visible.

One day, for example, I was at an auto parts store near Al-Hazen when a man came in with two obvious bodyguards. The shop owner, a friend of mine, nudged me and signaled for caution. The object of the bodyguards' protection himself looked like one of Saddam's executioners, especially with his dead-looking eyes. When his gaze fell on me, I felt as if he were measuring me for a coffin. After he left, my friend said he was one of Saddam's top hit men, and that he'd assassinated the head of the Egyptian parliament the year before.

Al-Hazen was a nest of goons, we were discovering. We had constant run-ins with them. One erupted in road rage, pulling a gun on me for simply honking because he was blocking the road. Two others beat an AE employee to the sidewalk because he didn't get out of their way fast enough. We soon learned to spot their sport utility vehicles and Mercedes and give them a wide berth. Later, when I moved into the presidential palace, I got the full story on Al-Hazen, but at the time I took Jaffar's shopping list to Boston, I was still mostly in the dark.

I'd called ahead to Millipore, a company in Bedford, a suburb northwest of Boston, and reiterated what kind of air filters we wanted. I'd gotten a quote for twelve thousand dollars. "I'll be paying you in cash," I added.

The man on the other end of the line hesitated, but just for a second.

"That would be fine," he said. He asked me no questions about how we planned to use the filters, and also agreed that Millipore could ship the filters directly to Iraq on the Jordanian airline, Alia.

I taxied out to the company's headquarters with a briefcase full of dollars. A young man with a pad of plain paper came down the stairs, ripped a sheet off the top, and handed it to me.

I looked at it. It was a handwritten receipt. I looked back at him.

"I'm very sorry," he said. "We're just not used to dealing in cash and this is the only kind of receipt we can give you."

"You've got to be kidding," I said. Nobody at Atomic Energy would accept that scrap of paper. One man who'd come back to AE with a handwritten receipt for a large purchase was languishing in jail.

"I'm afraid that's all we can do," he said.

I shook my head. The briefcase of cash was between my feet. "But it's not all *I* can do," I said. "Where's the closest bank?"

"Why?"

"Because I'm going to go get a cashier's check made out to Millipore. That will be my receipt, not this."

An hour later I was on my way back to Boston, a copy of the cashier's check and Millipore's shipping order in my pocket.

By the time I called Jaffar from New York a few days later, the filters had already arrived. He was elated.

Somebody in Baghdad had wanted them very, very badly.

CHAPTER NINE

THE INSIDE GAME

SADDAM SAW what he had done, and it was good.

From his office in the presidential palace, the president could survey all he'd built in recent years—the broad new avenues (designed by German engineers), the sparkling new airport (French), the elegant new campus of Baghdad University (Frank Lloyd Wright), new hotels (French, American), and a rudimentary skyline of new, twenty-story government ministries.

The change in Baghdad since I'd returned from America was startling. In 1970, Baghdad was dead. The dusty streets were clogged with exhaust-spewing Citroëns and Russian Ladas. Rush hour sometimes lasted until eleven at night, with people abandoning their vehicles on the side of the road. In the central marketplace, goat carts and camels vied with old trucks. Now the new Saddam Hussein Bridge whisked cars across the Tigris to a new network of freeways bypassing the city, giving Baghdad the look and feel of a modern metropolis.

Saddam was also fond of strumming the chords of ancient grandeur—sponsoring an archaeological dig at Babylon, sixty miles south of Baghdad, for example. Iraq was the "cradle of civilization," he often recalled, where Sumerian writing and even the wheel were born. Indeed, twelve hundred years ago Baghdad was the epicenter of the civilized world, capital of the Abbasid empire. While Europe labored through its Dark Ages, "the city of the Arabian Nights" was a vibrant center of science and law, music and literature. Baghdad was festooned with fountains and parks; marble gardens; sprawling, elaborately gilded mansions and palaces hung with silk and brocade.

Thousands of pennant-flying gondolas plied the elegant waterfronts on both sides of the Tigris, ferrying pleasure-seekers and ordinary citizens around the city.

With his massive rebuilding, Saddam more than hinted at a return to Baghdad's glory. In all this, of course, he had an immediate ulterior motive: hosting the Summit of Nonaligned Nations, which had been scheduled for Baghdad in 1981. He hoped to be named its president. When he invaded Iran, however, the conference was moved.

Now, six years later, the more Saddam built, the more people wondered what it was all about. The fact was, his empire was a brittle shell, an emerging military colossus absent the civilizing attributes of his ancestors. He could build, but his armies were bogged down in a war of attrition with the ancient enemy, Iran. He was not the second coming of Nebuchadnezzar. Or even an Arab Napoleon, people were discovering, he was a Wizard of Oz. The power of the regime rested on fear, not the triumph of culture, or even victories on the battlefield. In mid-1987, Saddam was on the ropes despite all the window dressing.

My own first trip into the presidential inner circle was a nightmare. It began with a summons to the palace from Hussein Kamel, Saddam's volatile son-in-law, on a sizzling-hot morning in May 1987.

Kamel's invitations were not to be taken lightly. A compact man with darting black eyes in a peanut-shaped head, Kamel was the second most powerful man in Iraq. His power flowed not only through blood—he was Saddam's first cousin, a member of the Tikriti clan—but from his marriage to Saddam's most beautiful daughter, Raghad. In the family dictatorship of Iraq, that made him prince of the realm.

Kamel held the regime's two most powerful portfolios, beginning with his command of the Special Security Organization (SSO), Saddam's personal army of spies, bodyguards, hit men, and torturers. He would soon also become the chief of MIMI, the all-powerful Ministry of Industry and Military Industrialization, Iraq's vast complex of domestic arms manufacturing and technological development. He had an immense say in Saddam's budgets and priorities.

MIMI was Saddam's brainchild, born of a prudent but inescapable conclusion, after the wars with Israel in 1967 and 1973, that the Russians were unreliable allies. Before each conflict Moscow was an eager vendor of aircraft, tanks, artillery, radar, bullets, shells, and parts to the Arab entente—Egypt, Syria, and Iraq—but when the shooting began and critical supplies fell short, the Kremlin's phone line always seemed to be busy. Thus Saddam set out to create Iraq's own military industry, giving the country its logistical independence, and handed the job to his cousin Hussein Kamel. Never again, he vowed, would Iraq face its enemies from a standpoint of weakness. And his son-in-law would make sure.

And what better way to move the bomb forward after years of haphazard progress than to give it to Kamel? I'd written three reports on the project for Saddam, at al-Ghafour's direction, and the president made a key decision: No longer would it be run by Atomic Energy. From now on the bomb effort would be run from the presidential palace by Hussein Kamel and his ministry of military industry.

Working for MIMI was like winning the lottery. Half the officials seemed to have been rewarded with a shiny Mercedes-Benz and a posh new house. But this being Iraq, there was always glass in the gravy: Kamel had been known to bludgeon lesser officials to the floor. He ran his own torture center in Taji, a military camp north of Baghdad. The rumors were legend, but as I would eventually find, the truth was even worse. Nobody was immune from being sent to Taji on Kamel's whims, including senior palace personnel and men from Saddam's inner circle.

So it was with a certain trepidation that I parked my Toyota Land Cruiser outside the main palace gate, cleared security, walked to the first reception area inside, and asked to see the powerful man by name.

The guard checked a book, failed to find my name, and looked up with disgust. "No one walks in here without an appointment to see Hussein Kamel. You have to ask through proper channels."

I hated these guys. "Kamel personally summoned me," I declared, giving him my name and title. But he held up his palm and began to give me a lecture.

By now, however, I'd learned a few things about dealing with security. I told him who I was and warned he'd soon be guarding the Iranian border if he didn't pick up that phone and make an inquiry. With that I turned away and privately steamed.

The guard handed me the phone. It was Kamel himself.

"What the hell are you doing going through reception?" he demanded. "This is for ordinary citizens, not for official business." He told me to go out the door and drive around to an adjacent bridge. Underneath it was a guard. Go under the bridge. "Give him my name, nothing else. They'll take you from there." Click.

I put down the phone, smiled thinly at the security guard, and walked out. To my utter astonishment, there was indeed a secret, unmarked entrance under the bridge. I drove through and arrived in front of an elaborate, Moroccan-style building, landscaped by luscious gardens. Impressive, I had to admit. At the entrance I was met by a military guard, who led me down a quiet corridor to Kamel's doorway.

I found the presidential son-in-law sitting on a couch at the far end of a huge office, behind a coffee table stacked with official papers. He barely looked up and told me to sit.

Immediately an orderly appeared with a cup of tea. I took it carefully, noticing the stack of documents he'd been reading. They were my handwritten reports. I studied his oval, mustachioed face and wavy black hair.

Kamel looked up at me with disapproval, then sat back on the couch and stared. Finally, he said quietly, "How long will it take you to make the bomb?"

I answered as calmly as I could. "Well," I said carefully, setting down my cup. "The same as I have written in my reports. Five to eight years."

Kamel moved his head slowly from side to side.

"You have a maximum of two years to finish the project," he said.

I felt my tongue thicken.

"Two years," he said. "You have two years."

By 1989. I scrambled for a response. "But, sir, there will be no bomb-grade uranium available for at least five years. We're five years away from that."

Kamel's eyes narrowed.

"What?" he shot back. "That is not what the chairman and Jaffar are telling the president."

Suddenly I realized what had happened. Al-Ghafour and Jaffar had bought time for themselves by creating a tremendous fiction for Saddam, that a breakthrough in uranium enrichment was imminent, that the real hitch in the program was the design and construction of the bomb.

Constructing the bomb was my job, of course. Once the fuel was ready.

I groped for a response. Kamel waited. Finally I decided to tell the truth, and launched into the project's history, covering all the problems with uranium enrichment, from the French reactor to Jaffar's diddling with magnets, to the technically forbidding challenge of the diffusion process. I told him how Jaffar had put the launch of the Office of Research and Development on my shoulders, which further delayed my moving on to design the bomb itself. It took a while to unravel, but Kamel listened closely. When I finished, he sat back and assessed me anew.

"What kind of car do you drive?" he said suddenly. There was a hint of congeniality in his voice.

When I gave him my answer, he smirked and picked up the phone. Seconds later one of his uniformed staff appeared on the rug. Kamel ordered him to get me a luxury car from the palace fleet, "one of the newer ones."

Then he turned to me again, quite solemn.

"It is time to get Atomic Energy straightened out," he said. The only way for him to do that was to take over the bomb project himself, to take it under the wing of MIMI.

And take its billion-dollar budget, too, I thought. Money always talked in the considerations of Saddam's inner circle. But, of course, I said nothing.

"You are going to be working for me from now on," he added. And a few more things. I'd have a private apartment on the palace grounds. In addition, the twenty-story building adjacent to the palace that previously housed the Iraqi Labor Union was to be my new headquarters and office. The union didn't need it—as we both knew, it had been forced out of business. That was where I would construct the bomb, Kamel declared—and on an accelerated schedule.

I was flabbergasted. The building he'd chosen was right next to the Al-Rashid Hotel, the luxury accommodation for international guests in central Baghdad. It was made of steel and glass. Its design and construction, moreover, were the laughingstock of Baghdad, because its steel girders were so thin that the top of the building swayed ten feet or more in a strong desert wind.

And here we would build our bomb? The scientific ignorance of the regime's top officials was astounding.

With great caution, I explained to Kamel why the building was inappropriate, starting with the conditions needed for sensitive electronics and nuclear instrumentation.

I left unsaid what a nuclear accident could do to Baghdad, but I could tell he eventually got the point. At the end of my discourse, he shrugged and told me to use the building temporarily—for administration, design, and nonexplosive experiments. He'd get me a helicopter to scout the desert for other sites, he said. With that, he picked up the phone and barked an order. Someone would show me to my new car, he said.

I started to get up. But there was one more thing, he said.

"You'll need a new rank."

He feigned weary collegiality. Not only did he have responsibility for military industry, he sighed, but the president's personal security. He shook his head slowly. To make things work smoothly, he said, I'd have to have a title in the Special Security Organization as well.

And a new name.

I froze. The function of the SSO was to make unpopular people disappear, among other things. I did not want any part of it.

"You will be a director general," Kamel declared, as if he were casting a play. "But don't worry"—he must have seen me blanch—"you won't have any responsibilities." My new rank and title were merely to tell people I belonged to him.

Me, a general.

As for a cover name, he said, that would help camouflage our new project as well. It would put another firewall between the bomb program and prying eyes. All my staff would also have to take on cover names, he added.

He had already chosen a name for me: "Mohammed Hazim." That's how I would be known to the outside world from now on.

What about a family name, though. Did I have any preferences for that?

I was in a daze. "Hussein" popped into my head.

Kamel's smile evaporated. "That is unacceptable," he said. "You'll have to think of something else."

Only later did I learn why "Hussein" was a bad choice. Saddam hated his father and bristled at the sound of his name.

"That's it," Kamel said, his amiability quickly returning. I got up to leave. When I stopped at the door, he waved from his seat on the couch.

"Enjoy your new car," he said.

In the years since Saddam had taken over in 1979, the grounds of the Republican Palace had spread like an inkblot, swallowing up Baghdad real estate. The palace had enveloped nearby office buildings, homes, shops, restaurants, gas stations, and even a hospital, turning the palace grounds into a small city. Its unmistakable centerpiece was Saddam's own two-story, columned, white marble headquarters. Scattered around it over the two-square-mile redoubt were about a hundred administrative office buildings.

It was an armed fortress. Checkpoints began several blocks from the presidential grounds, increasing in rigor as the visitor approached. At the main gate, heavily armed soldiers closely studied my face and my identification cards as a director general of the SSO.

Then I pulled forward. I was directed to drive my new Mercedes onto concrete tracks over an open pit and ordered to step out. Security men checked under the car, opened the hood and trunk, looked under the seats, and rifled the glove compartment. After a thorough search, I was ordered back into the car and cleared to drive forward. Behind several windows in the surrounding buildings, I was told, sharpshooters fingered sniper rifles.

The security checks would slack off only slightly in the ensuing weeks, as the guards began to recognize my face. Yet knowing that their jobs, not to mention their lives, were on the line if an assassin or terrorist gained entrance to the grounds, they never completely relaxed. I soon heard that in the early days a few arrogant officials had tried to bull their way through and had been quickly cut down with a few bursts of automatic-rifle fire. Far from being upset, Saddam awarded the guards medals.

Meanwhile, I quickly took advantage of one of the perks of the palace, free high-quality gas for my car. Only top officials could get fuel that was up to U.S. standards with high octane and antiknock additives. The ordinary citizen's car coughed along on subpar gas—this in a country that was the world's second largest exporter of oil.

The Al-Hayat was a beige concrete and mortar affair, about five or six stories high, with four apartments on each floor. About twenty of Saddam's senior aides had apartments there, including Hussein Kamel's brother, Saddam Kamel. My own unit was more functional than luxurious, with a bedroom, a living room, an office, and a small kitchen. It also had a safe where I could stash classified documents I was working with. The idea was for officials to use the apartments when they were working late. But for many, of course, the apartments amounted to no more than well-appointed bachelor pads. High-quality food and drink was available around the clock with just a call down to the palace kitchen. All-night poker games were common, as were dalliances with the pretty palace staffers. Needless to say, Saddam knew everything that was going on.

Admittance to the inner circle unquestionably had its thrills. Here I would rub elbows with the men who ran Iraq. Of course, in Saddam's world, there were always trapdoors. My companions here were the men who controlled Iraq's vast military-industrial complex. Within a few weeks I'd learn of a sprawling network of facilities I'd only imagined, industrial operations turning out advanced missiles, bombs, and munitions of all kinds, including chemical and biological weapons.

My education in presidential protocol began right away, with the arrival of my new cleaning ladies, one for my office, one for my apartment. Both were far from ordinary. In fact, they were young, beautiful, and flirtatious. The first one floored me when she announced she wouldn't be in the next day because she'd be off "picking up my new car." She got one every year—free. "It's a gift from the president," she smiled. I put the same question to the woman who cleaned my apartment. Same answer. "A gift from the president."

It didn't take much digging to get the story behind these women. One night at the Hunting Club, I ran into another official who lived in the building. Over drinks, I asked him about it.

The women were all "hired personally, by the boss," he whispered, meaning, of course, Saddam. Some had been his mistresses, some he just liked to keep around. As he tired of them, they were removed from his inner sanctum and made available to others.

"If you're thinking of taking a fling," my confidant warned, "be careful. If you do her wrong, you know who she'll complain to. Unlike the ordinary ex-mistress, these girls have protection."

Saddam's women were everywhere in the palace, he whispered. They were Saddam's eyes and ears—in addition to the microphones hidden in the lamps and walls of our apartments. Some of them were given clerical or administrative titles, though they were basically no-show or make-work jobs. Saddam had other mistresses as well among the wives of cabinet members to whom he'd taken a fancy.

"How do you think Hamid Hummadi got his job?" my friend said, speaking of the portly cabinet secretary. "That, and his huge bonuses, and the very nice ranches he has along the Tigris?" He raised his eyebrows.

"His wife is Saddam's anytime he wants her," he said. Which led to an amusing conflict. One day Saddam assigned another of his young mistresses to Hummadi's wife as an administrative assistant. Neither knew the other was sleeping with Saddam. It didn't take long for the two women to clash, and soon they had to be pried apart, fingernails at each other's throats, in one of the offices. The younger woman, Latifa, was transferred out the next day, to the Ministry of Information.

I chuckled at the story. Over the coming weeks, however, I began to hear darker rumors about Saddam and his women.

It was well known among the inner circle, for example, that Saddam was extremely aggressive, culling women from the crowd, coercing them into sex, and then discarding them after he was through. He used them like towels, passing them on to aides and other senior officials—generously, he thought. Of course, Saddam had other considerations. A mistress to one of his underlings was less likely to spread rumors beyond the palace. Likewise, the people who inherited the women were less likely to talk outside. A hand-me-down from Saddam was a fringe benefit, the aides thought, one of the perks of palace living.

Saddam's favorites, by far, I was told, were virgins, probably because of his well-known fear of disease. He'd spot a young woman in a hotel or on his travels and instruct his security detail to procure her. But the saddest story I heard concerned women who'd come to the palace gates to petition for information on fathers, brothers, or husbands missing at the front. Some were war widows seeking benefits. If Saddam liked their looks, a signal went out to a security agent to follow up.

Most of the time these were one-shot affairs. One woman I met later told me how she went to see Saddam early in the Iranian war, after her father was killed. She was destitute and begging for help. Two weeks later, she was called to come back for some formality concerning her benefits, but instead of an appointment at the palace, she was directed to one of Saddam's secluded downtown facilities.

When she arrived, two women who looked like beauticians were waiting for her with hairbrushes and makeup kits. They immediately began criticizing her looks, asking her how she expected to interest Saddam looking so wan. As she stood in a confused daze, they began to laugh and tease her. What did she think this was all about? they asked. Don't play dumb. As the situation dawned on her, she was mortified. If she refused Saddam, she feared her fate would be the same as that of other women she'd heard about, found dead on a side road on the outskirts of Baghdad. Most times it would be made to look like a car accident.

So she submitted to the makeover. It felt like sitting for a death mask. The women washed and styled her hair, applied bright lipstick, and outfitted her in a new, tight dress. Then the guards came and took her to a waiting car. The Mercedes delivered her to a side door at the presidential palace. An armed guard led her through the corridors to a room upstairs. She was told to undress and lie on the bed. She looked around. The room was furnished like a hotel, with one large bed and a side table with a reading lamp. The guard waited until she was naked on the bed, then he left, locking the door behind him.

The minutes passed like eternity, she said. Finally, Saddam appeared from an adjoining room, naked. He looked at her as if he was in a trance, with glazed eyes and a wooden face. Without a word, he immediately came to the bed, got on top of her, and satisfied himself. Finished, he went back into the adjoining room and shut the door behind him. He had not spoken a word.

A few minutes later, as she lay crying, a guard came into the room, placed an envelope on the bedside table, and ordered her to get dressed. Inside the envelope was five thousand Iraqi dinars (about fifteen thousand dollars).

The payoff was enough of a crude insult. But what disturbed her more was losing her virginity in such a cold and impersonal way. Another thing she would always remember: Saddam's yellow, lifeless eyes.

"They were the eyes of death," she told me. "He looked at me as if I were a corpse. There was not a hint of humanity or warmth in them."

I heard other darkly disturbing stories over the ensuing weeks—tales of Saddam's volcanic temper, of his pulling a pistol from his holster and waving it around in a fit of rage. Most were explained as a product of the stress of the war with Iran, now in its seventh year with no good end in sight. Others said years of heavy drinking and painkillers had taken their toll.

The war had revealed a major weakness in the Iraqi officer corps, which Saddam was determined to fix. Like everything else in Iraq, the army was ruled by connections. Officers didn't always obey orders. In the early days of the war it was common for an officer facing battle or hazardous duty to leave his post and lobby for a change of assignment. Thus the army's old boy network took care of itself.

It was only a matter of time, of course, before Saddam got wind of what was happening. He dealt with it in his usual manner, putting military intelligence agents, augmented by Baath Party informants, into the ranks to tell him what was going on. Meanwhile, the elite Republican Guards were mobilized to check the papers of officers supposedly on leave. Several trials and executions for desertion swiftly followed, and the widespread dereliction of duty subsided.

Command and control, however, remained a problem. Units tasked to support various battle plans frequently failed to follow orders—usually because they were afraid of heavy casualties. Excuses and finger-pointing followed, with senior officers blaming subordinates and vice versa. Saddam ordered his SSO to monitor all planning sessions and military communications. As a result, a number of officers' lives were spared when the record showed they'd been falsely blamed for defeats. Plenty more, however, were executed when their incompetence or cowardice was exposed. The troops, meanwhile—facing human-wave assaults on one side and roving squads executing deserters on the other—were surrendering to the Iranians in droves. Whole divisions began to disappear. Finally, Saddam came to the front to take over the battle himself.

The issue at hand was the Iranian occupation of Majnoon, an oil-soaked island at the edge of Iraq's southern marshes. Iraqi attempts to dislodge the Iranians had twice failed, and now the Iranians were talking about pumping oil out of the island. Saddam decided to take the matter into his own hands.

As was his habit, he showed up at the front unexpectedly, having ditched his motorcade, sending it on to another destination while he traveled to divisional headquarters in a simple army truck. The commanders immediately stepped aside when Saddam entered the room, according to a close friend of mine who was present; there was no question he was taking over. After going over the maps and making his assignments, which called for a brutal frontal assault on the Iranian positions, Saddam asked if anyone had any questions or suggestions.

No one spoke. Old hands knew that Saddam invited comment only to ferret out any "defeatism" in the group. But a young, inexperienced officer raised his hand. Saddam smiled and invited him to speak.

The officer unspooled what he thought was an objective analysis of Saddam's plan. The frontal attacks on Majnoon, he said, had cost thousands of lives without attaining the objective. Why not pound it with artillery and hit at Iranian supply lines until the cost of holding the island became too great for them? By the time the Iranians were forced to withdraw, their losses would be overwhelming, the officer suggested. Meanwhile, they'd be tied down.

Little did the upstart know that his lecture was exactly the kind of cool, rational, patient—and impertinent—thinking that enraged Saddam. To the commander in chief, Iran's occupation of one inch of Iraqi territory for a day, not to mention a few years, was an insult. Saddam wanted the Iranians out *now*. Forever. Anything less was an excuse, or cowardice. And here was a young officer prattling on to him about casualties and patience—just another excuse to avoid a fight, to Saddam's way of thinking. He listened to the officer quietly, without interruption, until the young man came to an end. Then he asked politely whether that was all.

Yes, the officer said, he had nothing to add.

Did anyone else have a comment? Saddam asked, reaching for his holster.

No.

Saddam drew his gun and shot the young officer in the head. He fell in a heap.

"Coward," he spat.

The assault went ahead—and was a disaster. The Iraqis were repulsed.

As I was learning, even life-and-death decisions on the war were driven by greed and corruption. In July 1987, Kamel asked me to attend a meeting at the Republican Palace to discuss military munitions. Iraq had its back to the wall at that point, and we'd been directed to explore making a radiation weapon that we could set off on the Iranian frontier to stop the ayatollah's incessant human-wave attacks. But first, Kamel wanted me to attend to become familiar with the battleground and the status of the war.

The idea of irradiating the border to create a buffer zone against the Iranians had become an obsession with Kamel and his chief weapons adviser, General Amir al-Saadi, the genial technical director of military industry. I'd explained that even the United States had abandoned the "radiation bomb" as impractical and unwieldy, if only because a wind shift could blow radioactive material back on our own troops. But they weren't deterred. They were terrified of the Iranians and desperate for any weapon that would repel them. So I took another tack. I brought in two experts from the reactor division at AE and presented them with the problem: Could they manufacture enough radioactive material to contaminate a ten-to-twenty-mile strip of land one mile deep on the Iranian side of Shatt-al-Arab, the river dividing Iraq and Iran? After a week of discussion and argument, we finally persuaded al-Saadi's people that the AE reactor did not have the capacity to produce the required material. They dropped the idea.

The first meeting was convened around a long table in a high-ceilinged, Moroccan-style room adjacent to Saddam's office in his headquarters building on the Republican Palace grounds. Around the table were Kamel; General al-Saadi; Dhaif al-Tikriti, the intense head of the Al-Qaqaa explosives factory; and about a half dozen senior military officers. I took a seat near the end of the table, farthest from the empty chair where the president would sit.

Suddenly there was a stir and Saddam entered from his office. He was clearly in a bad mood. His eyes were swollen and puffy. He took a seat at the head of the long table. Scowling, he turned to the air force general in charge of the air war munitions, which had not been going well.

"What have you got for us today?" Saddam asked.

Most senior officials knew it was always best to start Saddam off with the good news, calming the president with rosy details, engaging him in minor problems, before plunging into serious or even dire developments.

But this particular general was not in the mood. He had just lost two more planes and their crews over Iran. Their bombs hadn't gone off. Many of the bombs the air force was dropping on Iran, in fact, were not exploding, the general sputtered at Saddam.

The rest of the cabinet members shifted in their seats or stared at the table. They all knew who was responsible for the bombs: Saddam's cousin and son-in-law, Hussein Kamel, sitting at the president's right hand. Everyone also knew that Saddam brooked no criticism of his family. Kamel sat quietly, observing the general.

The general continued with his tirade about the risks his pilots were taking to drop bombs that didn't work. Saddam started to speak, but the general ignored him. Now everyone was on alert, as if sensing a barometer dropping before a terrible storm. But the general continued to prattle on about the worthless bombs. Saddam then sat back, allowing the general to continue with his little speech. On and on the general went, building into a fury about his pilots' sacrifice.

Then, suddenly, the door opened and a pair of guards walked in, stopping behind the general's chair. Perhaps Saddam had summoned them with a button under the table. The general looked up at them, bewildered. The guards lifted him out of his chair and marched him out of the room.

The door closed. Saddam smiled, then turned to us. "What else is on the agenda?" he asked.

We went on to other topics. Not a word was mentioned of the extraordinary event we had just witnessed.

Two days later I ran into Kamel and asked tentatively what had happened to the general.

"Oh, he became our guest at Taji," he said casually, referring to his torture chamber outside Baghdad.

I dropped the subject. Two months later, I was talking to my administrative assistant, a sergeant in the SSO, and wondered aloud what had become of the man.

The sergeant beamed. "The general hit the jackpot," he said. After a week or so of torture, the general had been hospitalized and sent home. A few days later a messenger from Saddam delivered a handful of envelopes to his house. One contained his new assignment. Another was a gift certificate for a couple of Mercedes. Another was the deed to a country ranch. The last envelope contained a check for a huge sum of money. All gifts from Saddam.

"He's elated now," the sergeant quipped. "People are congratulating him for his good fortune."

I thought I'd lost the capacity to be surprised by anything Saddam did, but I was astonished. Of course, the only reason the air force general survived while the young officer at the front got a bullet in his head was that Saddam needed the general; the young officer was expendable. Still, the message was the same: Saddam giveth, Saddam taketh away. For every stick, there was a carrot. Except for the expendables.

Meanwhile, huge fortunes were being made on the war. Outside of Saddam and his family, arguably the richest man in Iraq was Mahmoud Bunnia, a rotund little merchant with a pencil-thin mustache who'd parlayed his connections into a tidy empire of manufacturing and imports, from candy to shoes. Early in the war he'd endeared himself to Saddam by supplying food to the troops without advance payment. Gradually, Bunnia started making deals with Uday, Saddam's eldest son, his second mistake.

Uday, a rangy youth with a murderous temper, was a chip off the old block, a dart-eyed boy who favored black leather jackets and bounced from one brawl to another. He was known simply as "the prince." People soon learned to give him a wide berth. Early in the war he'd taken pilot flight training, but no one thought seriously of giving him an aircraft, much less a command. Instead, his father appointed him director of the Iraqi Olympics Committee, which he turned into the Ministry of Youth. Right away, following family tradition, he figured out how to make money out of the deal, letting contracts that fattened his personal coffers.

Uday was incensed that Bunnia was making a fortune from the government, so he alerted the treasury department that the merchant had ducked some thirty million dinars (about a hundred million dollars at the official rate) in taxes. Bunnia was promptly told to pay up immediately or risk his accounts being frozen.

Then Bunnia made his third mistake: He took his complaint to Uday's father. Not finding Saddam at the Republican Palace, he asked a familiar guard where he was. At the homestead in Tikrit, the guard said. Bunnia jumped into his Mercedes and sped up the highway—his last mistake, it would turn out. Two hours later, he arrived at the country palace and asked the receptionist to fetch the president.

"Who told you where I was?" Saddam demanded, coming out of his office after being alerted by an aide.

Bunnia's face drooped. "One of your guards, sir."

Saddam fumed. "Wait here." He disappeared behind the door

Two hours passed. Finally, Saddam came out with a security detail and a couple of quivering palace guards in tow.

"Which one did you talk to?" he asked.

Bunnia hesitated, then gestured at one of the hapless men. Saddam nodded to a security agent, and the guard was trundled away.

The president locked his eyes on Bunnia, waiting. Then suddenly, from outside, came the report of a pistol. Saddam led Bunnia to the lawn. The guard was lying on the ground, a pool of blood around his head.

"See that?" Saddam said. "If you pull a stunt like that again you'll end up like him."

Bunnia froze. The president wasn't through.

"What did Uday assess you?" Saddam demanded.

"Thirty million, sir," Bunnia murmured.

"It's fifty million now." With that, Saddam hailed two agents and told them to get Bunnia off the palace grounds. He walked away without another word. Bunnia's legs were so wobbly he needed help getting into his car.

Saddam's temper was legendary, but he rarely made a far-reaching decision when he was in a rage. Or drunk.

In the early years, Saddam was a heavy drinker, but as he climbed the party rungs, he began to cut back. A couple of scotches from his personal preserve of Johnnie Walker Blue at the Hunting Club was all we saw in public. Behind closed doors, however, he continued to indulge, and was eventually forced to abstain altogether. Then, according to one of his personal doctors, the withdrawal symptoms kicked in. He required shots of a strong sedative. But then he started demanding more and bigger doses. His personality grew more erratic with the ups and downs of the drugs, the liquor, and the pressures of command.

One of his doctors, who later defected to Britain, told the story about being summoned to deal with one of Saddam's explosions one night and finding him out of control, stomping around his palace bedroom in a blood-splotched shirt. With the help of a bodyguard, the doctor managed to get Saddam onto his bed so he could administer a sedative. When he went to the bathroom to wash his hands, however, he discovered a woman in the bathtub with her throat slit. He quickly fled the country.

Late one night the telephone rang at our house, only a couple of days after I'd been transferred to the presidential palace. Most nights I was still sleeping at home.

Kamel was on the line.

"Come over here right now," he said, and clicked off.

I was in bed, but there was no question I would go. The second most powerful man in Iraq had ordered my presence. And by now, Souham was long used to my abrupt departures and extended absences. I sighed and got out of bed.

There could be any number of reasons why I'd been summoned like this, but most of them were bad. In a little while I was in Kamel's office. He was full of noontime energy, even though it was the middle of the night.

"Good," he said. "You're here." He picked up the telephone and ordered a car brought around.

"So you think you won't get any support over here with us?" he asked, a joke crinkling his eyes.

I didn't get a chance to answer.

"Come," he said, rounding his desk. "Let me take you on a little tour. I think you'll see the kind of support we can give you." I followed him out the door.

Outside, a shiny new Mercedes 280S was waiting, engine purring. Security guards sealed us inside. Kamel yanked the car into gear and peeled off. At the palace gates a squad of security guards ran up, but he barely slowed. "Al-Nassr," he shouted out the window, then sped off. In a few minutes we were swerving up the ramp of a bridge, past a dirty, ragged-looking man on the side of the road.

"He works for us," Kamel grinned. That explained all the "homeless" men who'd suddenly showed up in Baghdad, camping around the bridges and highways. I'd vaguely wondered why they hadn't been swept up. Now I knew they were Kamel's eyes, his response to a recent outbreak of Iranian sabotage in the capital.

Kamel was in an expansive mood, relaxing behind the wheel. I watched the speedometer needle tick past a hundred, then beyond, as we hummed down the German-built blacktop. The lights of Baghdad disappeared behind us. "This size is very nice," he said, patting the dashboard. "Also not so conspicuous." He glanced in the rearview mirror. "Speed is my security," he said. The Mercedes rocketed into the blackness.

We rode in silence for a few minutes, then Kamel glanced over to me.

"I talked to Hummadi," he said, referring to Saddam's secretary, "about what you told me. He doesn't believe that Jaffar and al-Ghafour would lie to him about the uranium. So before I go to the president about this, I need to verify their claims. Or not verify them, whatever the case may be."

"What claims?" I asked.

"That they've succeeded in enriching uranium by diffusion," he said.

I nearly lost my breath. My quality-control man at AE, Saleh Majid, had just told me that the alumina barriers weren't working, they were getting clogged by uranium gas. So this was distressing. If Jaffar and al-Ghafour were actually claiming a breakthrough in diffusion . . . well, I was incredulous. More than incredulous, alarmed. This was proof that those two were trying to move the knife from their throats back to mine. I had to defend myself.

"It's not true," I told Kamel. "I should know. The last time I checked, they had failed the tests."

Kamel didn't skip a beat. Here was his chance to take control of another big chunk of Atomic Energy and its budget. He pounced on it.

"What do you suggest we do?" he asked.

I was resolute. The games were over. "Take some experts out there with you," I said. "Ask for a test in your presence."

Kamel smiled like the cat who'd swallowed the canary. He nodded and pressed the accelerator to the floor. Billions more in the arms budgets would be coming his way. The Mercedes roared down the dark highway. Little did I know it was carrying me into Kamel's underground empire of missiles, rockets, gas, and germ warfare.

CHAPTER TEN

———

THE INVISIBLE EMPIRE

THERE WAS A BOUNCE to Kamel's voice when he telephoned me a few weeks later.

"I want you to stay in your office tonight and wait for my call," he said jovially, clicking off.

I had a good idea why he wanted to see me: The uranium diffusion demonstration I'd suggested on our midnight ride to the munitions center at Al-Nassr. Of course the test showed I was right: Jaffar and al-Ghafour were exposed as liars and frauds. Now, like a vulture in a jacaranda tree, Kamel hungrily eyed the struggling enrichment program and its multimillion-dollar budget. He'd gone to Saddam and, within a few short days, convinced him that Atomic Energy was incapable of getting the job done. A presidential decree was issued, transferring the diffusion group and its assets to him.

It was only Kamel's first bite of Atomic Energy, but I could tell he liked it. Billions more of AE's program dollars could be his if he could make the case to Saddam, and apparently, I was to be his star witness. After the flop with the diffusion test, Kamel had intimated that he wanted me in a bigger, more official role in his office.

I held the telephone in my hand for a few seconds after Kamel rang off. I'd learned never to press him for details on the phone: We'd uncovered a sophisticated Israeli tap on our lines, and we assumed there were others.

As often happens in these things, the discovery of the listening device was a lucky accident. A shepherd watching over his flock in the Iraqi desert three hundred miles west of Baghdad was sitting on a hillock one night in 1985 when he noticed something strange.

Although it was winter and the ground around him was cold, the very top of the hill where he sat was not. Curious, he began to scratch at the earth. Soon, he uncovered a metal tip. He touched it. It was warm. He dug farther. It looked like it was connected to some sort of machine. The shepherd bolted from the hill and alerted the authorities, who sent a military engineering team to investigate. They dug it up and discovered a nuclear-powered communications intercept on our main telephone trunk to Jordan.

Of course, the device didn't have any identifying markings, but we didn't need to find a Star of David stamped on it to know where it came from. Only one country had the technical sophistication, daring, and motivation to plant the tap right on Iraqi soil: the Israelis (perhaps helped by their American friends). And they were clever. According to interviews the security people conducted with other shepherds and Bedouins in the area, helicopters with Iraqi markings had unloaded soldiers on the hill a few months earlier. They'd seen the soldiers digging on the hill, and even heard them talking in Iraqi slang.

The device was carefully dug out of the hill, crated up, and, under tight security, trucked to AE headquarters at al-Tuwaitha. That's when the second, lethal surprise occurred. The actual communication apparatus had been booby-trapped. It exploded, killing two demolition experts. Thankfully the Israeli designer did allow the nuclear-powered battery to be separated easily from the rest of the equipment without triggering an explosion. A similar device had been discovered in Syria in the 1970s, I would later learn.

I waited at my palace apartment for Kamel's call, along with two of my assistants, and ordered dinner from the palace kitchen. Around six P.M. a bevy of waiters arrived with enough food for twenty, including a whole roasted lamb on a bed of saffron rice. Stews, sweets, and other Iraqi dishes filled the rest of the table. Outside in the city, poor Iraqis were struggling to find fresh milk for their babies.

At about eight, Kamel called and summoned me to his office, alone. When I arrived, he briskly informed me that we had an appointment with Saddam. We left immediately.

The president's headquarters was unmistakable among the drab, rectangular concrete buildings that made up the bulk of the structures in the palace complex. Encased in beige Italian marble and fronted by majestic Corinthian columns, it trumpeted power and authority. Mussolini would have loved it.

Underneath was a labyrinth of offices, supply rooms, medical facilities, kitchens, bedrooms, and bomb shelters, plus a tunnel big enough for a car that led to an airfield two or three miles away where a plane was kept ready for Saddam around the clock. When the *New Scientist* published a map of the presidential complex in the late 1970s, it was estimated that the underground construction work alone cost three billion dollars. It was said to be sturdy enough to withstand a modest nuclear bomb.

Two SSO guards at the door clicked to attention when they saw us coming and smartly saluted. Kamel and I went directly to the office of Hamid Hummadi, Saddam's secretary, who was reading an American paperback when we entered. He put it down and greeted us pleasantly. After some idle chitchat, Kamel told me to wait and disappeared into Saddam's adjacent office.

I took the moment to look around. The top of the white stucco walls were festooned in a complex Arabian pattern sprinkled with gold fleck. A large, oval, richly textured Persian rug lay on the floor. Hummadi's sleek desk was made of heavy oak, as were the chairs and side tables around the office. Fluted lights gave the room a soft, opulent feeling.

Hummadi and I passed the time in light gossip about AE. But I was careful: The scheming, highly powerful bureaucrat was the ultimate insider. Tight-mouthed and deceptively mild-mannered, with folds of skin drooping off his jowls, Hummadi had amassed a fortune by trading favors with supplicants for juicy pieces of land along the Tigris. Whether it was to reinstate someone who had been blacklisted or steer a government contract a certain way made no difference: Hummadi's menu of favors was prix fixe. Everybody knew it.

"How do you like your new accommodations?" he inquired with an amphibian-like smile. He clearly meant my apartment, not my new office downtown. Before I could answer, Kamel opened the door and signaled for me to come in. I politely took my leave.

Saddam's large office was simply a larger, more opulent version of Hummadi's. It was longer, the ceiling higher, the oval rug bigger and more elaborate, with swirling colors and thick silky tufts. A bookshelf along one wall was stacked with political and historical biographies, including the lives of Stalin and Hitler. A few paintings of archetypal Iraqi scenes were hung on the white walls, along with a few rich tapestries. His large, engraved oak desk was fit for a chief executive.

Saddam was sitting at his desk in his olive-drab military uniform, his thick brows deeply furrowed. He did not look up or acknowledge our presence. We waited at mid-room as the president flipped through some files. After seven years' fighting, his army had failed to dislodge the Iranians from the border. The waterway at al-Fao, Iraq's primary access to the Persian Gulf, was practically cut off. Casualties were heavy and debt was mounting at an alarming rate. The Gulf states Arabs had loaned him billions, fearing the fanatical Iranians and happy to hold Saddam's coat for the fight. But no amount of Iraqi sacrifice seemed sufficient. Saddam's only hope now was America's tilt toward Baghdad, the lesser evil. Beginning in 1985, Washington had extended billions of dollars in agricultural and other financial credits, an untold percentage of which was being secretly funneled into chemical and biological warfare programs. U.S. naval units were attacking Iranian shore installations and gunboats for Saddam. Top-secret satellite data was being covertly provided to Iraq. For now, the Reagan-Bush team had closed its eyes to Saddam's excesses in order to block Iran. Nothing Saddam did could be worse than the ayatollah's fanatical minions, they decided, who had now planted their revolutionary flag in Lebanon and the Gaza Strip.

Saddam continued to study the files, oblivious to our presence. Finally, Kamel left my side and talked to Saddam in a whisper. The president nodded, and then looked up at me. His infamous, brooding eyes gave away nothing.

"That was good advice you passed to us through Hussein," Saddam said without any prelude, referring to his son-in-law by his first name. I assumed he meant my report that the diffusion process was not working. "We need to get a better understanding of what's going on inside this expensive AE program," the president added. I waited for the other shoe to drop, expecting that he was going to hand over the entire AE weapons program to Kamel. But it didn't come.

Suddenly, he sat back and turned philosophical. "Sometimes people get carried away," he mused. "Sometimes people overstate things. They think they've achieved things that they haven't, they claim results that aren't really justified, they see things that aren't there." He gazed around the room, seemingly distracted.

I hadn't seen this side of Saddam before. "Reflective" just wasn't a word that came up when people talked about Saddam. But it was clear he'd not only read my report thoroughly, he'd completely digested it. I'd written that Dr. al-Obeidi, under Jaffar's direction, had managed to separate neon and argon gasses, but that the uranium itself had gotten clogged in the aluminum barriers. I'd bent over backward to explain that diffusion was working in a limited fashion, but the end zone of sufficient uranium enrichment through that method was nowhere in sight.

To me, Jaffar had been disingenuous, and had been caught out. But from what Saddam was saying, Jaffar and his team had merely overstated their results from an excess of zeal.

Amazing. It was certainly a benign interpretation of events, especially coming from Saddam. I guessed that the bottom line was that the president was not ready to hand over the rest of AE to his impetuous son-in-law, as I'd expected. As I pondered what else he had in mind, the president addressed me again.

"As my adviser, Khidhir, you would be in a good position to investigate what's going on at AE," Saddam said. "We'd like you to continue in this advisory capacity by making a detailed study of the situation at AE."

"Yes, sir," I said, nodding, but my mouth was going dry. The enormity and delicacy of the task hit me like a hammer. Now I'd be judging the performance of my former bosses. Put differently, I'd be Saddam's chief snitch at AE.

"We expect a report from you in a month's time," he declared. "Don't hesitate to give your expert opinion, even if it displeases some people. But be factual, as you were this time." He tapped the report I'd written.

Then he looked at Kamel and nodded curtly. The meeting was over. Kamel immediately came to my side, thanked the president for us both, and then led the way out of Saddam's office.

Outside, I could feel the still-warm pavement through the soles of my shoes. It must have been a hundred and twenty that day. But a clammy chill spread over my face. Now I was under the thumb of a man who could squash me and my family like bugs. And what about my position at AE? By reporting truthfully on my friends and colleagues, I could create murderous lifelong enemies. And I'd be helping Kamel in his drive to acquire the rest of the nuclear program. Money would disappear. By the time he was through, AE would be as bankrupt as it was when al-Mallah and Sharif first approached me about building a bomb in 1972.

Those two had been ridiculously naive about how things worked at the palace. The idea that we could keep control of things, soft-pedaling the bomb program while diverting billions of dollars into our own pet projects, was silly. How could we have believed that Saddam and clan would give us billions of dollars for our atomic playpen and never ask for anything in return?

I couldn't afford any more illusions. Ambition had clouded my moral judgments, fear had immobilized my better instincts, creature comforts had paralyzed my courage. I stood outside the palace stripped of my pretenses. I had cared more about splitting atoms than about nuclear sanity. I had sold out for a Mercedes. I was a coward. I had sleepwalked into a cage of my own making.

I couldn't kid myself any longer: I was an important cog in an evil machine. The killings and torture by Saddam and his agents were just the starting point. I'd heard rumors of sinister new things—experiments on humans in the Salman Pak biological warfare labs, where truckloads of political prisoners were being dumped. One of my assistants was questioned for a whole day by the SSO on the potential for using radiation to kill political adversaries without a trace. The deportations of Shiites and the massacres of Kurds were being stepped up. Soon enough, I would learn firsthand about a vast, clandestine apparatus for the creation of weapons of mass destruction, far beyond our bomb. What had started out, for me, as a rational plan for national defense and a "balance of terror" with the Israelis had become just a cog in a Baghdad-based Murder, Inc.

As I stood outside the presidential palace, the scales fell from my eyes. I had little confidence now that any bomb we developed would be used "responsibly"—that is, just for diplomatic leverage. Who would say no to Saddam? He'd drop it on anybody if the regime were threatened—Iran in the near term, Israel perhaps in the future.

The fact was that Saddam was incalculably cruel. Thousands of men were dying weekly at the front, but their widows were waiting a year or more for death certificates that would allow them to collect their benefits. Hospitals and pharmacies were running out of basic medicines, including those for heart ailments and diabetes, while no one could leave for medical care abroad. The quality and availability of basic foodstuffs were dramatically declining; at the same time, officials like Jaffar were importing millions of dollars' worth of luxury furniture from West Germany.

The regime had produced a general coarsening of Iraqi society, which had once been the Arab world's most cultured and humane. Public executions were becoming more common. One day checkpoint guards outside AE caught an army deserter. Soon thereafter, all party members at AE were summoned to participate in the "celebration" of the deserter being shot. To keep their standing in the party, everyone had to pretend he was enthusiastic. Women were encouraged to cheer. This, for the death of a young man they'd never known or seen—some bitter mother's son. A similar event happened in my own neighborhood when a sixteen-year-old boy was arrested for scrawling some anti-Saddam graffiti in a book. Everyone was drummed into the street to "celebrate" his execution.

And where was I in this sinister pantheon? Right at the center. Yes, I was hostage to the regime. Any hesitation on my part could lead to my own execution and the jailing of my family. But facts were facts. No longer would I be remembered as a scientist, the developer of an Arab bomb who checkmated the aggressive Israelis. I would be remembered as one of the regime's evil hands. What would I tell my sons when they grew up?

I had to get out. The question was how.

My first plunge into the labyrinth of Saddam's secret weapons programs came the night Kamel drove me to the Al-Nassr industrial plant, fifty miles north of Baghdad. Its main building was the size of a Boeing hangar, perhaps ten thousand square feet. Inside, even though it was the middle of the night, the factory was humming under bright lights, with hundreds of workers laboring at machine tools, computer-controlled lathes, and high-tech vacuum furnaces, spinning, twisting, and hammering metal sheets and steel parts into Iraqi missiles. It reminded me of a scene out of *Dr. No.*

We arrived unannounced, but word quickly spread that Kamel was on the premises. A slight commotion broke out and a foreman quickly appeared to tell us that the plant director, Safa al-Haboby, was on his way.

Al-Haboby was the man to talk to for high-tech acquisitions abroad, Kamel had explained en route. A deal was in the works, he said, to buy a British machine-tool manufacturer, Matrix Churchill, which al-Haboby was slotted to run in London. Putting him there, Kamel hardly needed to point out, would facilitate the purchase of all kinds of restricted equipment.

Al-Haboby materialized within fifteen minutes, a deferential but self-confident man in his late forties. His face was darkly serious. After a few introductory exchanges with Kamel, he offered to show us around.

Apparently he had been briefed about me, because he immediately headed to the high-tech part of the facility. "We machine and cast parts for missiles, such as second-stage extensions of the Scuds," he explained along the way. "But we don't just handle metals, we also handle materials like graphite." We stopped in front of a machine processing a graphite piece. Apparently he thought I was interested in building a graphite reactor, because he pointedly waited for my reaction. When I had none, he moved on. By the smile on Kamel's face, however, I could tell he thought al-Haboby was quite a showman. The main point Kamel was trying to get across to me, however, was that these facilities could meet any need I had—if I worked under his direction.

Later, on the drive back, Kamel unburdened himself of his management philosophy. When he first took over military industries, he said, most machine workers were producing only a hundred or two hundred bomb parts a day. Since each bomb required about twenty parts, that meant the average worker was producing only five to ten bombs a day. With the war raging, it was unacceptable, he said. Despite its huge cost, MIMI's contribution to the war effort was minuscule. So one night he went to the Badr industrial center, thirty miles southwest of Baghdad, where bomb parts were made. He gathered the workers around him and announced that anyone who could double or quadruple their output would be richly rewarded. The workers should call him personally, he said, leaving their name, production totals, and telephone number, and he'd get right back to them. "Big rewards," he emphasized. Something they'd really like.

Well, Kamel continued, cruising along the highway in the darkness, a worker called him that very night. "He asked to have a special supervisor assigned to him so that he could prove it when he exceeded the quota. I made arrangements, the man made his mark, and the next day I gave him a brand-new Mercedes. I also made him a foreman." Kamel smiled. "I repeated the same process at every bomb parts factory. It worked. The production levels rose to more than a thousand, then two thousand parts per machine per day."

Kamel smiled in self-satisfaction. What went unsaid, of course, were the complaints of air force pilots and artillery crews that many of the bombs and shells they were using were duds. They might as well have been throwing iron skillets at the marauding Iranians. Kamel's triumph was strictly an illusion—a profitable illusion. To hell with the troops.

My next lesson in the palace economics of military procurement took place at the al-Qaqaa explosives factory, in the scrub-pocked desert about thirty miles south of Baghdad. We arrived around noon under a blistering sun, sweat glazing our faces within steps of Kamel's air-conditioned Mercedes.

The sprawling, Yugoslav-built factory reminded me of an aging auto-assembly plant. It was meant to supply Iraq with enough explosives for a large-scale ground and air war, like the one we were fighting. But not long after our tour began, I found new reasons to understand why Kamel's magnificent war machine didn't work quite right.

Whereas even mid-level people at AE were now fluent with international technical developments, the floor stewards here hardly seemed able to read, much less understand a technical manual. The workers also displayed a careless attitude toward safety—a fatal extravagance in an explosives factory. Laborers hauled TNT in wheelbarrows around a huge yard surrounded by a concrete wall. Under the Iraqi noontime sun, where temperatures commonly exceeded a hundred and twenty degrees, a disaster was only a matter of time. True enough, near the end of July 1987, it happened. A wheelbarrow may have tipped over—we don't know for sure—but several thousand pounds of uncovered TNT in the yard blew up, sending shock waves as far away as Baghdad. Needless to say, the yard workers were vaporized.

On this particular visit, Kamel and I were accompanied by General al-Saadi, the avuncular father of Iraq's missile and chemical weapons programs, MIMI's only successes to date. Mild-mannered and smooth-talking, the general was Kamel's righthand man and chief technical adviser. He laughed when I asked him why the factory library's bookshelves were empty, with only a couple of popular scientific journals scattered about.

"These guys barely have the time to produce their quotas of explosives," he chortled. "You think they have time to read?"

It was a stunning response from a man with a master's degree in chemistry from Oxford. Later, when we were alone, I brought up the subject again.

"How can I expect a plant like this to produce the very, very sophisticated explosives we'll need for the bomb?" I asked him. I wasn't sure he really understood the strict tolerances required for the shaped charges that triggered the chain reaction in a nuclear bomb.

"You can train a bunch of them and we'll form a special team for the project," he replied breezily. It wasn't an answer that inspired confidence, not that I was surprised. I'd gotten a sample of al-Saadi's skepticism toward Atomic Energy when I was introduced to him at MIMI headquarters weeks before. He'd kindly pledged his help to me, but he couldn't disguise his opinion that the bomb project was a huge waste of money. The same level of destruction could be achieved more cheaply by conventional and other means, he said, and I agreed. "But that's not the point, is it?"

He smiled genially and sighed. "Yes, I know. It's all about the status and the aura of being a nuclear power. But that's the only thing you have on your side to justify your costs, you know. And God knows, it is huge." He shook his head and chuckled softly.

Meanwhile, I had to work with what I found at the explosives factory. The plant was run by Dhaif al-Tikriti, a confused and uncommunicative man from Saddam's hometown. I would have to rely on him and his team to manufacture the very powerful explosives we needed for the bomb. Yet to my utter shock, he wasn't even familiar with lenses, a common class of shaped explosives widely advertised in professional journals and used for such projects as excavating tunnels. I needed him to modify the lenses to produce the pressure required to compress uranium to supercritical size and kick off a nuclear explosion. Yet the man in charge of the largest explosives factory in the Arab world had never even heard of them.

Kamel's solution when I complained: Teach him.

I felt like I was back at Fort Valley State College in Georgia, teaching arithmetic to college students. In this case, I'd be teaching people basics in explosives so they could carry out critical responsibilities in a multibillion-dollar nuclear bomb project. Big difference.

Fortunately, a conference on high-tech explosives was scheduled for the United States in 1989, sponsored by none other than the major U.S. nuclear weapons labs, Los Alamos and Lawrence Livermore. It was open and unclassified (its program guide even included advertisements for nuclear triggers, which would put us on the path to getting them). We decided to send some people from the plant to America to learn about lenses.

Day by day, I was learning more about the secret foreign arrangements Saddam made to acquire what he needed for his weapons programs. One was with the Yugoslavian Serbs. Another was with the West Germans, in a chapter right out of *The Odessa File*. Both connections were designed to provide Iraq with ballistic missiles and warheads—nuclear, chemical, and biological—which Saddam could use not only to destroy his immediate enemies but to become the unrivaled leader of the Arab world.

The Serb connection, I learned, had opened in 1975, when Saddam sent General al-Saadi and four of his engineers to Yugoslavia for training in ballistic missiles, ranging from the assembly of Russian-style Scuds to configuring warheads and calculating trajectories for our own missiles. After another humiliating defeat at the hands of the Israelis in 1973, Saddam was determined to build an arsenal independent of Moscow, up to then Iraq's principal, but unreliable, weapons supplier. Yugoslavian strongman Josef Tito, who'd broken out of the Soviet orbit in 1948, was a natural partner for Saddam. Both men were ruthless leaders obsessed with secrecy and independence.

Saddam's alliances sometimes surprised outsiders, but they conformed to the peculiar logic of the Middle East. For Saddam, self-interest always came before religious or other considerations. In the Lebanese civil war, for example, he'd supported General Aun, a Maronite Christian. The reason was simple, beyond the fact that the Maronites, who controlled the army and government, were resolutely opposed to Syria, Saddam's main rival for Arab hegemony: The revolutionary Islamic Hezbollah guerrillas, whom Saddam might've been expected to support for their fanatical attacks on Israel, were backed by Iran.

A similar factor was at work in Yugoslavia. Saddam preferred to deal specifically with Serbian, as opposed to Bosnian Muslim, firms, because the Serbs were reliable suppliers with a record of keeping their mouths shut. Around 1984, Iraq contracted with the Serbs for two chemical processing plants, one to leech uranium from ore, another to make rocket fuel, which al-Saadi arranged to be smuggled across Jordan in a specially built trailer. The Serbs had also been hired to build the Baghdad headquarters of the ruling Revolutionary Command Council.

But the shocker came in 1987 when al-Saadi told me that the Serbs had been given a six-hundred-million-dollar contract to build a magnetic uranium–enrichment factory for Jaffar. I'm sure my jaw nearly hit the floor.

"You know, they never reveal the location of the sites they work at," al-Saadi said of the Serbs. "Also, they are about the only foreigners left who will take on projects inside Iraq without demanding payment up front. Our credit is good with them."

I wondered if al-Saadi really believed such claptrap? Serb generosity was directly related to the fact that Iraq sold oil to them at a discount and paid for Serb goods and services with cash. Whatever the case, al-Saadi was proud of what the Serb connection had done for his rocket program.

"Nobody believed we could develop our own missile technology," he related to me one day in his twentieth-story office at MIMI headquarters in Baghdad. Below his window was the Unknown Soldier Memorial, a large cracked sphere in a sculpted lake. In the basement was a secret prison.

"It took some time before we had a solid core group to carry out the rocket work," with the help of Serb-supplied technology, to modify the Russian Scuds, al-Saadi continued. In time the missile group grew to a few hundred engineers, designers, and technicians—tiny by AE standards. "We use people efficiently here," the general jibed, "unlike you at AE, with your huge research and development teams. We are more product-oriented, more attuned to actually delivering a product." He chuckled.

I smiled weakly, going along with the general's boast. Indeed, Iraqi missiles were being flung at Iran. But the fact was that they usually couldn't hit Teheran in a strong wind, often missing the city completely or vibrating so violently that they broke up in mid-flight. I knew they were working hard to produce enough modified Scuds to hit Teheran, because our people at AE were helping them calculate trajectories. But just like Kamel's bomb factory and the pathetic TNT plant, al-Saadi's missile group hadn't devoted time to mastering the science and technology of their product. He seemed to sense my disdain, because he suddenly invited me to visit his new research and development complex, called Saad-16.

We flew there in one of the two aging, eight-seater executive jets available to senior officials, landing at Mosul, about two hundred and fifty miles north of Baghdad. I was interested in seeing what al-Saadi had going, but my main reason was to get my hands on a highly sensitive ultrafrequency German oscilloscope, which Saad-16's director, Dr. Basil al-Tai, had promised to loan me so we could calibrate the explosions that would set off our nuclear core. In any event, I had to start forming a good working relationship with Saad-16, since its engineers and ours would have to match specifications to mount our bomb on their ballistic missile.

When we arrived at Saad-16, I was struck by the installation's size, organization, and up-to-date facilities. The thousand-acre complex was buzzing with activity and much more impressive than the other MIMI operations I'd visited. The reason was immediately apparent: The billion-dollar facility was constructed by a German consortium to current standards of missile technology. It had a huge wind tunnel, pristine electronics labs, new missile-assembly buildings, and humming machine shops. In addition the Germans had not only built Saad-16 and supplied its equipment, they had stayed on to train the Iraqis thoroughly. As I toured the facility, I saw Germans in crisp white lab coats in nearly every department.

I was surprised at the extent of the collaboration, but the German connection went back a long way. During World War II, pro-Nazi Iraqi nationalists (including Saddam's uncle, Khairallah Tilfah) attempted a coup d'état that was thwarted by British intervention. King Ghazi, who'd had a radio station broadcasting Nazi propaganda from the royal palace, died in a mysterious car accident.

The Arab love affair with the Nazis continued after the war, when Egyptian president Gamal Abdel Nasser, Saddam's mentor and idol during his 1960s exile, recruited German scientists to develop his rockets. German know-how and technology would enable Nasser to develop missiles capable of hitting Israel with reasonable accuracy. It came too late for the 1956 Suez War, but Saddam never forgot the German assistance, and the Germans did not disappoint him.

"We'll have you up to your ear in Germans if you want," al-Saadi cracked to me as we toured the installation. "You just have to make up your mind what is it you want." Obviously, he'd be delighted to grab more of AE's budget for himself.

"We don't waste time developing technology, like you people at AE," he said. "We simply buy it. It's cheaper and faster. It takes guts to build a network of foreign purchasing agents, you know, and the risk can be pretty great. But so far we've been successful, both with chemicals and missiles. The Iranians are going to be surprised when they see what we have in store for them."

Then he let me in on a surprising development.

"After your friend al-Obeidi failed the barrier test for uranium enrichment, he was a broken man," al-Saadi said. "He was transferred here on the president's orders, as you know. So I encouraged him to try enriching uranium by centrifuge, which is more complex but has a higher chance of succeeding."

But then he dropped the bombshell.

"Kamel also promised to get him German help. And now he has it. Two German scientists are helping him full-time. They've provided him with classified reports, and now they're going to get him

restricted parts for a centrifuge. Their plan is to install a full working machine that he can then duplicate."

Al-Saadi waited for my reaction. If he hoped I'd be impressed,
he got his wish. I was. Actually, "stunned" would be more accurate. Getting Germans to work in Iraq was as clear a demonstration of the regime's power as it could be. "I'll tell you something
else," al-Saadi continued. "With German help, we'll get you the
uranium you need—long before Jaffar supplies you with uranium
from using magnets. And we will do it cheaper, not at the cost of
the billions that Jaffar's thrown away. The German centrifuges
won't cost us more than ten million, installed. Then all we have to
do is duplicate them." He laughed. "And you know that we are
very good at that."

One area al-Saadi was not eager to talk about was the chemical and
biological weapons development under his purview. Here, too, the
Germans were deeply involved, I began to learn. Iraq's cover story
with the Germans—of buying pesticide plants—was so thin as to be
transparent. But German officials not only went along with it, they
pretended not to understand the significance of the animal pens at
the plant in Samara. They even helped make the technical adjust-
ments needed to turn the plant into a full-production chemical
weapons facility, and covered up for a couple of accidents in which
some workers were poisoned from chemical leaks.

There was also an American connection to the chem-bio programs, I discovered. Starting in 1985, American Type Culture Collection, in the suburbs of Washington, D.C., had shipped to Iraq
various strains of toxins and bacteria for "research" purposes.
Most were obtained by the Ministry of Higher Education, but others were handled by the biological section at AE.

I'd suspected that an aggressive chemical and biological program
was going on, of course, going back to the time Jaffar assigned me
to buy special air filters in Massachusetts. AE's engineers had also
been borrowed to boost electrical capacity at the rejuvenated Al-
Hazen Institute in Salman Pak, ten miles south of al-Tuwaitha,
where biological research was being conducted. Each biological
agent was tested for its lethality and dispersal properties and, as we
would learn, its effectiveness in the field.

Saddam's use of chemical weapons on humans began with Iraq's own Shiites, not, as is commonly believed, the Kurds.

With the onset of the war with Iran, Saddam saw every Iraqi Shiite as a potential fifth columnist, a potential recruit to the Ayatollah Khomeini's Islamic crusade. Deportations began even before the first shots were fired in September 1980. Later, realizing that he was inadvertently stocking the enemy army with Iraqi recruits, Saddam had second thoughts. He continued to deport women and children, but began locking up fighting-age men in prison camps. Inevitably, the prisoners developed a murderous hatred for the regime. Like my former colleague al-Shahristani, who went to prison clean-shaven and turned into a bearded zealot, they formed militant cells inside the camps and vowed vengeance if released.

That, at least, is what Saddam was hearing from his prison sources. His problem was that there were still tens of thousands of Shiite conscripts in his army, most at the front. The question was what to do with them. One solution was to start using them as mine detectors, or more accurately mine detonators. Commanders began marching the Shiite soldiers to the front of the line, backed by execution squads, and sending them into the minefields in advance of the troops. It was how I lost one of my brothers-in-law.

But that just created another problem for Saddam. News of the slaughter spread to the prisons, which erupted in protests. Issam al-Douri, the deputy chief of the Ministry of Social Welfare, which was responsible for running the prisons, told me what happened next.

"Every day I got a call to execute this prisoner or that prisoner," he said. "But they didn't send me written orders, they merely ordered me by phone. That started to worry me. Who was to say that these guys were killed on government orders? I was afraid people would think I killed them for personal reasons, and when it came out, somebody might seek revenge on me."

After carrying out a few of the killings, al-Douri managed to transfer to another job and years later eventually fled to Libya (one of the few places to honor an Iraqi passport after Desert Storm). But the systematic murder of prisoners was just beginning.

I heard another story from Rabah Khafaji, a onetime psychology professor. In 1973, Khafaji told me, the Mukhabarat sent him to communist East Germany for training in intelligence work. Upon return, he was ordered to launch an import company as a front for secret operations. After a while, he discovered that his principal business was importing poisons, which were being administered by injection to Shiite prisoners before they were released. After several days the victims would fall fatally ill with flulike symptoms (characteristic of anthrax). Even the East Germans balked at the number of injections, Khafaji said, which cost five hundred dollars per victim. As soon as he could, Khafaji also escaped to Libya.

But al-Saadi and his scientists weren't finished with the prisoners. They wanted to confirm the efficacy of their chemical and biological weapons in the field, as well as test various vaccines and treatments for Iraqi soldiers assigned to handle the weapons. Thus began one of the most grisly episodes of these awful weapons in history—and a story that has never been told.

Initially, the experiments were designed to test the effectiveness of defense measures, such as gas masks, antidotes to chemical agents, and vaccines against biological weapons. During the initial phase in 1984, about a hundred Shiite prisoners were taken to the German-built "pesticide factory" at Samara and subjected to chemical agents. None returned. In 1985, about fifty prisoners were shipped to Salman Pak for biological experiments. None returned from there, either.

The next phase was to test the effectiveness of doses. At Salman Pak, fear of losing control of the germs restricted the biological experiments to cell samples. In contrast, the chemical program moved quickly from petri dishes to experiments on humans.

Shiite prisoners were trucked to the border area near Khanaqin, in Iraqi Kurdistan, and placed in trenches. Careful notes were taken on wind conditions and terrain by al-Saadi's scientists. Then, Iraqi aircraft flew over and dropped canisters with chemical agents on them. Studies, of course, were made of the results. The experiments were repeated again and again with different agents, with varying doses, and under different weather conditions. Several hundred prisoners were said to have perished.

Disposing of prisoners' corpses from biological experiments at Salman Pak presented another problem. The prevention of infection was paramount. Special disinfectants were developed to use on the cadavers, as well as the mass burial grounds in Salman Pak. Cremation was used in a limited number of cases when the danger of contamination was thought to be too high.

By the time I arrived at the Republican Palace in 1987, the basic experiments were over. Now it was time to put the results to use. One of the targets was Iranian troops. But the worst dose was reserved for the rebellious Kurds.

The regime had nearly lost control of the Kurdish north because of the war with Iran. Iraqi soldiers were no longer safe in their bivouacs adjacent to Kurdish villages. Snipers were picking them off when they left their camps for food or water. Some of the Kurds were even helping the Iranians. Enraged, Saddam designed a special hell for the "back stabbers": He assigned his infamous cousin, Ali Hassan al-Majid, aka "Ali the Chemist," to take care of them.

One of al-Majid's ideas was to test the effect of certain natural disease spores on water supplies, part of a long-range scheme to use biowarfare agents with complete deniability. Typhoid fever had been tested in a limited program, but al-Majid wanted to practice on live human subjects. Kurdish mountain people, who were used to getting their water from clean wells and waterfalls, were easy targets. In late 1987, typhoid spores were dumped into their water supplies, especially around the city of Sulaimanya, in the remotest part of the Kurdish area. The number of deaths ranged from a hundred to three or four hundred people. The survivors, however, unwittingly revealed the operation. A forensic medical probe of the epidemic in England revealed that the typhoid victims were all infected with one strain of the disease, unlike a natural outbreak that would consist of many typhoid strains, including cholera. Word also leaked from Turkish hospitals where victims sought treatment. Interestingly, the world greeted this gruesome news with a deafening silence. Saddam was the West's dog in the fight against Iran.

Then, in late 1987, Kurdish villages in the Balasan Valley near Arbil were targeted by a gas attack. The estimates of dead and injured ran from the tens to a few hundred. But it was not a controlled experiment. The Iraqi army wasn't on hand to evaluate the effects. When survivors tried to escape to nearby Arbil for treatment, troops intercepted and shot them—men, women, and children. After that experience, officials decided that their next target shouldn't be so close to a city. The experiments were supposed to be secret. Things could get messy.

By March 1988, the stage was set for a major gas experiment. The target was Halabjah, a name that would join Guernica, My Lai, and Srbrenica in the pantheon of history's infamous war crimes. Yet the full story of what happened there has never been told.

Other targets had been considered, I found out from a close friend, but Halabjah was chosen to be the first, full-scale recipient of a nerve-agent attack. A town of forty thousand people, Halabjah was nestled in the mountains of the north, and as such, presented a totally new environment for chemical warfare (the French and German gas attacks in World War I having been conducted on plains where wind currents were relatively predictable).

As it turned out, an Iraqi army doctor I knew quite well entered Halabjah shortly after the attack. Later, he described to me what happened.

"Late on the afternoon of March 17 our unit was ordered to surround the town about a mile from the nearest house," he recalled. "It was a mostly clear, cool day, with very few clouds." The late hour was chosen to avoid moisture in the air, he said, which absorbs chemical agents and generally impedes their effectiveness. "Around three P.M. we were told to don gas masks," he continued. "The agents to be tested were nerve gasses—tabun, sarin, and soman—plus mustard gas, which is easy to evaluate because it blisters the skin and lungs."

Soon, Iraqi airplanes flew over and dropped the canisters on the village.

"We heard some people shout and saw people running to their houses from the edge of the village," the doctor said. "After about a half hour, we were ordered to go in. Our orders were to count the number of dead around each canister, plus describe the number of sick and their symptoms." The reports were designed to help the scientists at Salman Pak determine if the gasses penetrated windows and doorways, and so forth.

"I was assigned the center of town, the area adjoining the market," the doctor went on, grim with the memory. He had been conscripted into the army against his will.

"Walking among the dead and dying, I heard the crying of a small child. But I could not see it. Then I noticed a dead woman, facedown.

201

The crying seemed to be coming from her. I went to her body and rolled her over. Beneath her, miraculously alive, was a beautiful, blue-eyed Kurdish girl, about a year old." The doctor cleared his throat as he told me the story, struggling with the memory.

"I picked her up and cleaned her face with a damp cloth," he said. "Not knowing what else to do, I took her out of the danger area, and handed her to a soldier to hold for me while I finished filling out my sheets."

He planned to adopt the baby girl, he said. When he went to retrieve the infant, she was gone. He was told that a member of a pro-Saddam Kurdish militia group had whisked her away. Her fate was unknown.

"It was the worst day of my life," he said, starting to weep. "I never saw so much death and suffering, and for absolutely no reason. These were peaceful villagers, minding their own business. At least five thousand were killed and probably twice that many will suffer for life. The village's soil will be contaminated for years."

Later, he told me, a deputy to "Chemical Ali" came by and personally collected the data sheets from the doctors. "He said that anybody who talked about what happened at Halabjah would be shot."

The Kurdish rebellions promptly stopped. Emboldened by his success at Halabjah, Saddam now unleashed chemical weapons on the Iranians, finally ousting them from Majnoon Island and other positions they'd held for years. The ayatollah soon sued for peace.

Eventually the news about Halabjah did get out, of course. Along with reports that a half dozen nearby villages had been gassed. But people would always remember Halabjah, mostly because of the grotesque pictures of dead mothers holding their children that were published widely in the West. Iraq's deputy prime minister, Taha Yasin Ramadan, blamed the Iranians for the attack, but no one believed him. Everybody knew that if the Iranians were really responsible, Saddam would have made Halabjah a household word. But in March 1988, he was silent.

My visits to the far-flung outposts of military industry were opening my eyes, but no more so than when I began learning about Kamel's international operations.

Kamel ran his foreign purchasing agents like terrorist cells. No one knew what the others were doing. His major European base was West Germany, where a diminutive man named Ali Abdul-Muttalib did his bidding. Officially, Abdul-Muttalib was the Iraqi trade attaché in Bonn, but that was the least of his duties. Weekly bank transfers from Baghdad to his accounts were averaging a hundred million dollars a week. In two years he'd spent ten billion dollars, a huge chunk of it on German technology. With that kind of money flowing through his hands, every major German company was at his beck and call, along with his network of black marketeers, smugglers, and front companies. In 1988, Abdul-Muttalib was handling final transfers for the purchase of Matrix Churchill, a manufacturer of computer-controlled machining equipment, when word spread that a lot of money was disappearing into the numbered accounts of front men who were handpicked for the deals.

Presumably, Kamel's system was airtight. His front men all had family living in Iraq as virtual hostages. Often they posed as political refugees in Germany or other Western countries, in some cases arriving with certificates manufactured by Iraqi intelligence saying a father or brother had been executed by the government. Once settled, the front men would start getting bank transfers from Baghdad to buy equipment and companies or just to invest in brokerages or various investment funds.

In this manner, it was said, Minister of Defense Adnan Khairallah, Saddam's cousin and brother-in-law, squirreled away about five billion dollars. Of course, the regime eventually caught on, but after "an accident" was arranged for Khairallah in 1988, the regime was at a loss to identify his helpers. Many of his associates were interrogated, to no avail. Apparently, Khairallah had been so tight-lipped, even Saddam couldn't find all the loot.

Saddam apparently did manage, however, to get his tentacles into Jaffar's family fortunes.

I'd wondered why we suddenly started seeing so much of Jaffar's brother Hamid shaking hands and exchanging gifts with Saddam on TV. I figured there had to be some connection between Hamid's successful oil business and Jaffar's continued survival outside of jail, especially considering his lack of progress, even dissembling, about his uranium enrichment schemes. It took a little poking around, but eventually I found some clues.

Hamid was the family pride and joy, Jaffar told me when we first met. Their father was a finance minister under the king and had extensive contacts with the Persian Gulf states. So Hamid, young and ambitious, used the family connections to make his own fortune in the oil business. When Jaffar came back from Switzerland in 1974, he told me that his brother's share of the company Crescent Petroleum was probably worth sixty-five million dollars. In 1987, it could have been at least a hundred million. Saddam's clan could hardly allow that kind of treasure to go untouched. In 1989, Kamel's military industries empire, or MIMI, signed a joint venture agreement with Crescent.

Now, at last, there was no mystery to me about Jaffar's survival, despite his lies about the diffusion program and the hundreds of millions he'd spent on magnetic enrichment with a decided lack of progress. The old rule held: Money talked. Money had probably saved Jaffar's life.

After a few months around Kamel and al-Saadi, I didn't need a picture drawn for me. I knew what I had to do. The way to leapfrog forward on the bomb, which was exactly what I was put in the palace to do, was to buy foreign technology. Forget doing the bulk of research and experiments from scratch. Just go out and buy what I needed.

I could do that, although getting involved in illegal deals made me queasy. I didn't think I was cut out to be a secret agent. But then a light clicked on in a recess of my mind. What if MIMI's German connections could get me out of Iraq for good? From the sound of it, Ali Abdul-Muttalib's web of front men in Germany didn't sound like Boy Scouts. One of them had to be for sale.

I became obsessed with the idea. I envisioned the whole family somewhere in the West—I didn't care where. I thought of what I could tell the United States about Saddam's nuclear bomb and his chemical and biological weapons. Surely that would be enough to get us residency. The vision of it seized me. It became the first thing I thought about when I woke up in the morning and the last thing when I went to sleep. I thought about it as I drove the desert for hours alone, scouting for a remote site to construct the bomb. It was such an exciting—and dangerous—prospect that I tried to hammer it from my brain, lest I talk in my sleep or utter it unconsciously in some other fatal misstep. Nobody, not even my wife, could be told.

Finally, I came up with a plan to get to Europe. Screwing up my courage, I went to General al-Saadi. I told him I had to go to Germany to buy a foundry that could manufacture high-precision bomb components. Without the foundry, the bomb was still years off, I said. Al-Saadi said he'd think about it and take it to Kamel.

As they deliberated, I found a suitable site to build the bomb in the desert near Musseib, about fifty miles south of Baghdad. It was near an artillery and munitions range whose continual booming would mask the controlled explosions I needed to conduct for my own tests. With nearly a thousand acres, we could also annex the adjoining land for housing and other requirements.

I called Kamel about it right away. He told me it sounded good, but since the land belonged to the Ministry of Defense, he needed the president's personal approval. I drove back to Baghdad. By the time I arrived at my office, my secretary said Kamel had called. I phoned him back right away.

"Congratulations, my friend, you're in business," he announced. "The president has approved your plan for the bomb-making site."

He chuckled. There was something more. I waited, nervously drumming my fingers.

"And you can pack your bags," he added. "You're going off to Germany."

CHAPTER ELEVEN

GETTING THE GOODS

THE SKY was a gun gray with a chilly wind out of the north when I landed in Bonn in late August 1987. As usual, a security type from the embassy was waiting when I walked out of the airport with two assistants. A dark, thin man, he quickly put me in a bad mood by trying to chat me up as soon as we got into the car. I'd long ago tired of these low-level agents trying to learn what we were up to. Unprofessional, habitual liars with bad breath and worse Arabic, they were nothing but trouble. I finally told the agent point-blank to shut up because we were too tired for his questions. My two assistants smiled approvingly. When we arrived at the hotel, I dismissed the agent and said we'd catch a cab to the embassy on our own. He sullenly obeyed.

I was exhausted. I'd slept little on the flight, whiling away the hours staring out the window, nursing drinks and picking at my food, contemplating an escape. I hadn't a clue as to how I was going to pull it off, of course, since I had no trusted contacts, or even a name to look up. Few Iraqi officials had defected and lived to tell about it. All I had were my survival instincts from nearly twenty years inside the regime. I decided I'd just have to stay alert to the odd inflection in a voice, the curious expression in a contact's eyes, the hint of corruptibility that told me it was safe to go forward. Ironically, in this hall of mirrors, the people I'd have to keep my guard up with would be Iraqis who encouraged me to grouse about Saddam. It could be a trap.

First off, however, I had to check in with Ali Abdul-Muttalib, the greasy entrepreneur who headed Kamel's clandestine arms-purchasing network in Europe. Apparently he was still in good graces, though Kamel had curtailed his activities in the technical domain. While Abdul-Muttalib dealt with high-tech companies all the time, he was technically illiterate. So Kamel had split my mission in two, ordering me to do as much purchasing as possible with Abdul-Muttalib, but leave the information-gathering and computer requirements to Anees Wadi, his partner at Meed International in London. In addition, since my trip to Germany was budgeted for less than two weeks, I decided to leave the negotiations for a foundry to my assistants and concentrate on trying to fill the other, more sensitive requirements directly with Abdul-Muttalib's many black marketeers. Right away, though, I had to make clear who was in charge. When Abdul-Muttalib started grilling me on the purpose of my purchases and what project we were working on, I put down my pen and locked eyes with him.

"Look," I said, "stop asking questions. Your job is to make arrangements to help me get what I need. If you have any doubts, you can pick up that phone and call Kamel yourself." I waited for him to make a move.

Abdul-Muttalib swallowed sullenly, then quickly morphed into an unctuous servant.

"Of course, sir, I will do as you ask," he said, a degree too eager. I ignored his tone and we went back to work.

My distrust of Abdul-Muttalib only deepened when we got around to discussing finances. Kamel had instructed him to give me forty thousand dollars' worth of German marks in cash, and to transfer a million dollars to an account in my name at the Deutsche Bank. This was on top of a hundred and fifty million transferred to Abdul-Muttalib's own account, some of which was to be used for my purchases. Yet even then, old habits impelled him to double-deal. When he gave me the marks, I discovered I had been shorted. He calculated the exchange at a rate lower than the bank's, amounting to a few hundred dollars. When he insisted I sign for forty thousand anyway, I refused, scratching out his sum on the receipt and writing the true amount in, all the while shaking my head at his petty scam. I could only wonder at the cash he was skimming off arms deals worth billions.

But he did have his contacts. Shortly after word hit the street that the Iraqis were buying, our phone started ringing off the hook. Two rooms at the embassy were reserved for our team, one for my assistants working on the foundry deal with the German firms Degussa and Leybold, another for my own meetings with black marketeers for items that were unquestionably off-limits. Before putting in my orders, I wanted to get a feel for these guys, how much they knew, how good their technical expertise was, and how much I could expect of them.

I had another consideration. Since I was using my real name, I couldn't have any connection to the foundry deal, which my assistants were representing as a commercial purchase to purify tungsten and other metals for machine tools, definitely not anything linked to our nuclear program. Tungsten, we thought, was a useful cover because the temperatures required to purify it were about the same as for uranium. (Uranium has to be purified because impurities in it can cause a premature nuclear reaction.) Since I'd represented Iraq at the meetings of the International Atomic Energy Agency, any papers with my name on them could set off German export controls.

Meanwhile, for just a moment, all the cash I had at hand made it tempting to run. But I quickly banished it from my mind. I couldn't leave my family behind. Ever since the war with Iran began in 1980, the dependents of all AE and MIMI employees were forbidden to leave the country. (Two years later, *all* Iraqis were restricted.) My defection would be a death sentence for them. So I calmed down and made up my mind to probe carefully in the circles of Abdul-Muttalib's acquaintances for an opening. If nothing developed, perhaps something might pop up at my next stop, London, where a large number of Iraqi expatriates lived. Before I did anything, however, I had to be certain I wasn't being watched.

Representatives of Degussa and Leybold arrived early the next day. My assistants, Ghazi and Hamid, conducted the negotiations in the room next to mine. By early afternoon, Hamid reported that the Germans were eager to make the foundry sale but that our cover story was a bust. In fact, he said, the Germans had burst out laughing when they heard the story about tungsten. Hamid said he was shaken up a little initially, but when the Germans kept making jokes about it, he realized they were letting us know they understood what was going on—and didn't care. Over the next few days they worked out the details and took my assistants on a factory tour. They said we could expect an offer before we went back to Iraq.

To my shock, meanwhile, Abdul-Muttalib delivered the first black market agent right into the embassy. A stocky German with shaggy, reddish-blond hair, he introduced himself with a name that we both knew was fake. (Subsequently, I began to refer to all these contacts as Heinz One, Heinz Two, etc.)

I looked him over with some trepidation. Abdul-Muttalib had told me that Heinz One was his very best agent, somebody who could put his hands on the most difficult to obtain items. But his tattered old sports jacket, spotted gray pants, suede shoes, and unkempt hair gave me pause. Heinz looked more like a down-at-the heels college professor than a businessman. And maybe he was. At first I found it hard to divulge the telltale list of items I wanted to buy. But Kamel had told me to trust Abdul-Muttalib's agents, so eventually I relented.

Making an atomic bomb from scratch without a reliable design is, needless to say, tricky. We'd decided to replicate every step taken by the bomb's original fathers in the Manhattan Project. Each stage in the device's construction would have to be tested and perfected, the most critical being the arrangement and timing of explosions that compress a uranium ball to a fraction of its mass, triggering the nuclear blast. Without succeeding at that, we'd have nothing but a very expensive firecracker.

The way explosive charges are observed and tested is likewise expensive. It's done by photographing the explosive sequence with very fast cameras capable of taking pictures at a nanosecond—a billionth of a second. Two cameras could do that, one to photograph the explosion in frames, the other, known as a streak camera, to take continuous images of the explosion with an open lens. I wanted both, if I could get them, although I'd settle for one. But neither of those cameras could tell me what was going on *inside* the explosion. For that, I needed a flash X-ray camera, which could penetrate the explosive plume. The more powerful the X ray (i.e., the higher the voltage behind it), the better the image. I wanted the best camera, of course, but I would settle for less. After all, we were not much different from crack addicts. We'd take what we could get.

Finally, I needed a very powerful, high-frequency analyzer, which would receive signals from sensors that measured pressure on the uranium ball from the explosives. All of these items, of course, had only one purpose: to help us make a nuclear bomb. That's why they were on the proscribed list of exports. Which brought me back to Heinz One.

I studied the rough, ragged-looking man across the table. Heinz would know, of course, exactly what we were doing if I laid out my shopping list. And he'd know I was a key player in the transaction. If he had intelligence ties, which I had to consider, then I'd be putting myself at risk: His reports might make their way into the hands of the Israelis, which would make me a marked man. So I hesitated before going any further with him, and called for a break to talk to Abdul-Muttalib alone.

It was a little late in the game, but I told Abdul-Muttalib I'd prefer that he give the list to Heinz instead of me. He demurred. First, he said, he didn't know anything about nuclear technology. Anyway, hadn't I told him to stay out of my business? He glued on his smarmiest smile.

"Look," he said soothingly, "I've been in this business for years now. We've smuggled all sorts of German technology and arms to Iraq. Don't you think the Germans, and for that matter, every Western government, knows what's going on? Not only going on, but are even encouraging it? Billions of dollars from Baghdad are going through German banks. If we don't have ready cash, the Germans want to loan it to us. Don't you think the intelligence agencies know about that?"

He chuckled. I had to agree. The same thing was happening in the States, I knew. Washington was giving Iraq money under all kinds of programs and guises, all part of a covert campaign to help us against Iran. As for smugglers and black marketeers coming directly to the embassy, Abdul-Muttalib said, it's because they had the approval of their governments. Then he paused.

"Every weapon merchant and technology dealer knows how far he can go, for the very fact that they are all connected to their country's intelligence. If you think these merchants are just smart guys who know how to get around the authorities, then you don't know anything about this business. Why do you think the Israelis are allowed to get away with so much? It's because they're allies of the West; so are we, these days. We're doing the West's dirty work against Iran. So a smuggled piece of equipment here, a purchase without a proper license there, is no big deal, as long as we're keeping Iran away from the Gulf states and the Saudis."

That was the truth. I'd merely forgotten it in all my worries about the trip. Plus I had never made any purchases that were unquestionably illegal. Everything I'd bought fell into the dual-use category. This was new territory, criminal territory.

"In all the deals I've done here," Abdul-Muttalib continued, "none of my contacts has reported any suspicion or harassment by their governments. And I've had deals in almost every country in Europe. There won't be any leak of this to the Israelis. Not from the Germans, I assure you—they'd lose billions of dollars if they let the cat out of the bag." He smiled again, a hard glint in his eyes.

I returned to Heinz and took my seat across the table. He looked bored enough to be picking up laundry. We chatted for a while, then my sense of caution returned. Something just didn't feel right. I decided I'd postpone my requests directly related to bomb-assembly experiments and just ask him for explosive lenses and sensors. Leaving the impression that I worked for the explosives factory at Al-Qaqaa, I told him to come back for the other orders next week. As it turned out, my concerns were probably pointless. Heinz showed no comprehension whatsoever about the bomb-testing components. He merely recorded my orders, told Abdul-Muttalib that he would see what he could do, and left.

At the end of the day, back at the hotel, I met my two assistants at the bar and bought them a drink. They hadn't been to Germany before and wanted to take a tour of the town. I begged off and wished them a good time. When they left, I bent over my drink, exhausted from the day.

Suddenly, a man sitting at the other end of the bar got up and approached my seat. He looked like an Arab but was dressed like a German, in slacks, turtleneck jersey, and a nicely cut sports jacket. He ordered a beer from the bartender in German, then genially turned to me.

"You're an Iraqi, aren't you?" he said in Arabic with a perfect Baghdad accent. The beer was delivered.

"Yes," I said, "and I assume you are, too, from your accent." I watched him take a sip of his pilsner.

"Unfortunately, no longer," he said. "I'm nearly a German now. I've been here more than twenty years. I came here to study in the late sixties and decided to stay. There are a lot of Iraqis here, you know, but I'm really too busy to keep up with them. I'm just here to meet some businessmen, as a representative for my company. I decided to come down and relax with a drink. It's my wife's night out with her girlfriends." He winked and tipped his glass toward me in a toast. "What about you?"

Of course, the first thing I thought was that the bosses in Baghdad were testing me. It was the perfect approach. I had a million dollars in the bank and a wad of cash in my pocket. What better time to approach me than when I was alone, far from my family, having a drink at the end of a trying day? My first reaction was to turn the man away. Then again, I decided, no risk, no gain. I decided to play along.

"I teach at the university in Baghdad," I said. "I'm just here to buy a few things for the labs." I sampled my scotch.

"Sounds interesting," he said earnestly. Then, out of the blue, he asked, "Did you eat? We could get a bite nearby. Then later, if you'd like, I could show you around." He flashed a genuine smile, but now I was certain he'd been assigned to plumb my political leanings.

"Sure," I said, "but only if we split the tab."

"Great," he answered. We settled the bill, got in his Mercedes, and drove to an unremarkable German restaurant. "The food is good here," he said as we took our seats. And it was, the schnitzel being particularly tender. At first we just talked about our families and life in Iraq and West Germany. Nothing serious. He gave me his card. His name was Omar. He was an engineer turned executive, married to a German woman. For some reason, they hadn't been able to have children. The tests were inconclusive, but he'd stopped worrying about it, he said.

Then talk turned to matters closer at hand. Omar's interest in trading with Iraq had waned, he said, when he found out how crooked the embassy was. I went on alert.

"You can't do anything legal, as far as the Iraqi contracts go," he groused. "You either have to arrange for higher prices and give a cut to Abdul-Muttalib or somebody else in the ruling clique, or you don't get any of their business." He turned up his nose in disgust.

"My company is doing okay without that kind of hassle," Omar said. "We don't need it. Anyway, a whole bunch of people are going to end up in jail here once the war clouds clear. When the West no longer needs Iraq to carry the fight against Iran, the hammer is going to fall. Just wait. Germans are going to be arrested, too, but being an Iraqi expatriate, I'd make a good target once the scandal finally breaks."

It was a strange disclosure, I thought, from a man who'd just met me. Incredibly unguarded. But maybe I'd just spent too much time soaked in the intrigues of Baghdad. He was free, he reminded me, a German citizen, inoculated from Saddam's reprisals. Or maybe he was a spy sent to draw me out. If so, he was a very good actor. His loathing for Abdul-Muttalib and the embassy seemed genuine.

The next day, during a lunch break, I called the main number for Omar's office from my hotel. A German woman with broken English answered and repeated the name and address of the company for me. I wrote it down and checked it against his card. They were the same, and not far from my hotel.

I took a cab to the building where his company occupied a couple of floors. In the lobby I called his direct number and said I was just walking by. Would he like to meet for lunch, or perhaps a drink later? He sounded delighted. If I could just wait a minute he'd be down and we could get something to eat.

I felt confident now that this was not a setup. In all my time in Baghdad, I'd never met a man of this caliber working for the Mukhabarat or any other security agency. Even the security officials around Kamel, the second most powerful man in Iraq, were thugs, murderers, rapists, and con men.

Over the following days, I met with Omar several times. By the weekend, I felt comfortable enough with my new confidant to broach the subject.

"Is it possible," I asked carefully, "to arrange foreign travel documents for people inside Iraq? I have friends who'd like to get out— just so they could live somewhere more peaceful, you know? They've got the money."

He nodded slowly, encouragingly. I went on.

"They might like to live someplace remote, maybe as far away as

Brazil, Panama, or the Cayman Islands. Are there any law firms here you know of, or maybe in London, who could arrange for second passports to someplace remote like that?"

Actually, I'd seen ads for such law firms in the *International Herald Tribune,* but I'd been afraid to call them cold. I asked him if he knew of anybody who'd had any experience with the firms.

"Yes," he said, lowering his voice. "I know of a couple of cases where people managed to get a friend or somebody in trouble out of Iraq using these passports. But to use these passports to leave Iraq you need them stamped, and for that you need somebody on the inside. The stamps can be faked, but it's a hassle, and dangerous. If your friends think the risk is worth it, however, then an arrangement can be made."

We looked at each other. He understood the risk I was taking just talking about it. I decided to trust him. I glanced around the restaurant, then took the plunge. "I'd like to know which of the law firms is the most reliable, especially the experience of somebody who's actually used one."

He nodded. "I'll have to get back to you. I didn't bother to get details at the time from the people I talked to. But I'll get in touch with them and let you know." With that, we quickly paid up and left, going our separate ways.

Back at the embassy, Abdul-Muttalib eyed me strangely all through an afternoon meeting. Afterward, he approached me privately.

"Where do you know Omar from?" he asked.

"Omar?" I asked, stalling. He waited for my answer.

"Oh, him," I said. "Yes. He's just someone I met at the hotel. He was kind enough to invite me to dinner and take me around. Why, is there a problem with him?"

Abdul-Muttalib stared at me. "I was just curious. The Iraqi community here, you know, has all sorts of allegiances. It could be trouble if you . . . unknowingly associated with people with the wrong political orientations. I'm sure you know what I mean."

I listened, hopefully without giving anything away, trying not to panic at the idea that I'd been under surveillance.

"I don't need to remind you that you are on a sensitive mission," he lectured now. "And we're responsible for your safety. So we'd appreciate it if you would make our job easier and avoid possible sources of trouble." He then walked away.

My heart pounded. I was under surveillance. Or was Omar a plant? Whichever, the fantasy of getting my family out of Iraq, tantalizingly close only minutes before, evaporated.

But I had to stay calm. I walked to the bathroom, turned on the tap, and lifted cold water to my face. In the mirror, my face looked as if it had aged ten years. Fighting off a surge of melancholy, I turned back to the business at hand.

Which was Heinz Number Two. I tramped down the hall to my office. When I entered the room, he rose and extended a firm handshake, nearly clicking his heels. This Heinz, at least, looked like a German businessman, in a nicely tailored suit, starched white shirt, and tightly knotted tie.

He was an engineer with a computer factory in Taiwan. In the late 1980s, even desktops with higher processing speeds (back then it was the 386) were on the restricted list of exports from Western Europe and the United States. But companies like Hewlett-Packard were able to sell us 386s from their Singapore subsidiary. Heinz Two promised he could do the same from Taiwan. But we needed something more powerful for designing the bomb, a VAX, a very fast, compact mainframe computer. After some discussion we ordered a dozen desktops from Heinz with the best processors, memories, and storage capacities he could get, and decided to shop for the VAX in London.

There were two more black marketeers lined up. I decided to go for a touchdown with Heinz Number Three, zeroing in on the possibility of buying uranium. My first reason was simple: Kamel didn't have much faith in Jaffar. The centrifuge group was just getting started with uranium enrichment. Even if we could get only low-grade uranium abroad, it would reduce the challenge of amassing bomb-grade stocks. My other reasoning was bureaucratic. I could pass the uranium issue to Kamel's people this way, and if they failed to buy any, it was their fault, not mine.

"Is it possible to get us uranium metal?" I asked the German. "Any degree of enrichment would be useful, but just uranium metal would be fine, too."

He blanched. No question, this was nuclear bomb territory, even though uranium metal is also employed to make armor-piercing shells and we were manufacturing it at AE for use against the Iranians. Later, the United States would use it against our own tanks and troops with devastating effect. But uranium metal with any degree of enrichment was on the proscribed list, because it could be used to make reactor fuel and produce plutonium outside IAEA controls. To Heinz Number Three, as well as another man we talked to, any attempt to buy enriched uranium metal would set off bells all across Germany. It was just too obvious. The controls on uranium were much tighter than on other components of the bomb-making process.

I knew a dead end when I saw one, so I left Abdul-Muttalib to deal with it.

The fact was, despite media reports leaving the impression that the world was awash in black-market bomb-grade uranium or plutonium, it was simply not true. At the same time, con men were always showing up on our doorstep peddling fakes. It got to be such a nuisance that AE chairman al-Ghafour finally forbade us to follow up on feelers. In his opinion, chasing down the flimflams was a waste of time, and possibly exposed us to a sting by the Israelis or some other foreign intelligence agency. But the offers kept coming.

One day he gave me an offer of plutonium to follow up, probably just to make his point. In 1986, we received a letter from a man claiming to be a professor of physics at the University of Geneva, in Switzerland. He said that if we accepted his offer of plutonium in principle, we should take out an ad in the personals column of the Sunday Times of London on a specified date, wishing so-and-so a happy birthday. To many at AE, it was like coming upon a cold beer in the desert. Here we'd been laboring with Jaffar for years to produce bomb-grade uranium and along comes a man with plutonium to sell. He promised to make arrangements to deliver a sample once we published our acceptance.

Al-Ghafour's secretary dropped the letter on my desk with a note attached that the chairman wanted an answer in a few days. At first, I was in a daze. The more I thought about it, however, the more ridiculous it seemed. Our response would be advertising our intentions to somebody we didn't know, most likely the CIA or Israelis. I wrote a note to al-Ghafour recommending we ignore the letter and took it to him personally. He merely laughed and tossed it aside.

"We get letters like that all the time," he said. "I just wanted to see how you'd react." Blushing, I backed out of his office.

But not everybody had the same response. The Defense Ministry and the slugs at Mukhabarat were easy marks for this kind of thing. Both went along with any off-the-wall offer for classified bomb designs or other nuclear materials. Mukhabarat even went the extra step of chasing down leads in the United States and Europe. They always came back empty-handed or with boxes of phony documents. But they managed to spend a lot of money on their junkets.

Unfortunately, as AE's liaison to Mukhabarat on such matters, it fell to me to show them how they'd been scammed. And it was a daunting task.

Mukhabarat's technical intelligence–gathering branch was run by a spindly, dark-skinned Egyptian with well-coifed, receding gray hair, Dr. Mohammed al-Masri. Al-Masri was the epitome of the urbane, quiet-spoken spooks who haunt the world's intelligence services. As head of Mukhabarat's Technical Affairs branch, al-Masri was not only responsible for directing intelligence-gathering operations, but also for developing bugs, wiretaps, and possibly even the poisons and other drugs required for Mukhabarat's "wet work." Meeting him to discuss the latest nuclear secrets his agents had allegedly stolen from the United States or elsewhere had become a weekly affair.

Just negotiating the gauntlet of checkpoints required to get into his building in a fashionable part of Baghdad was a pain in the neck. Al-Masri's courteous manners and apologetic smile helped lighten the burden, but there was no doubt he was running a dubious operation, and badly. Not a single foreign document acquired by his outfit was legitimate or even marginally useful. Most of their finds were crude fakes ginned up by enterprising hustlers who copied old U.S. bomb designs from books in public libraries, slapped Los Alamos letterheads at the top, and sold them to credulous Mukhabarat agents for immense amounts of money. At AE we hardly gave them a glance. Over time, accordingly, my meetings with al-Masri grew less cordial, as he realized to his dismay that he couldn't charm or browbeat me into accepting such junk. Without AE backing, of course, his intelligence coups were falling on deaf ears at the palace, threatening not only his credibility but his budget, too. His people responded with childish efforts to intimidate me during my visits.

"Your people took away my briefcase," I told al-Masri as I walked into one of our last meetings. "I cannot continue our meeting without the documents. So if you don't mind, I'd like to have my briefcase back." He picked up the phone and barked into it with a melodramatic flourish. A few minutes later, one of his oafish lieutenants walked into the room with my briefcase and handed it over.

"I thought you'd need more time to break the combination and photograph the contents," I jibed.

"No sir," he answered stiffly. "We needed only two minutes to solve the lock. The photocopying took five minutes, with four men and two machines." He checked his watch. "We had your briefcase just under eight minutes altogether." Al-Masri smirked at this silly performance, then returned my jibe when he dismissed the man.

"You have not touched your tea, Dr. Hamza," he said as we took our seats. I glanced at the cup. The infamous Mukhabarat tea was rumored to be laced with poison, so I never, ever drank it.

"Well," I parried, "with the evaluation I'm about to give your intelligence reports, I thought it better to be cautious about what I swallowed here." Al-Masri chuckled. "Dr. Hamza, please. You can have *my* tea if it makes you feel safer. Or I can taste yours if you're comfortable with that."

I smiled tightly. "No thank you."

I snapped open my briefcase, pulling out a sheaf of the latest fabrications his agents had gathered. I dropped them on the table. They were all junk, I told him, mostly crude photocopies of openly available information with phony "secret" stamps at the top.

"We're spending an awful lot of time checking these things, at God knows what cost," I said. "You haven't sent us one authentic report in all my time here. Now, the chairman has sent me to tell you we have better things to do with our time and we're not going to accept your reports anymore."

I sat back. Now it was my turn to smirk.

Al-Masri was nonplussed. Accustomed to flattery and deference, he clearly found it a shock to be told, in effect, that his operation was a fraud. As he searched for a response, I stood up and left with the situation unresolved. Only when I got to my car did I wipe off my sweating hands.

The Defense Ministry, likewise, was always a sucker for hustlers.

Word was that they'd paid out a lot of up-front money for sand over the years. In a case I personally witnessed, they offered a European arms merchant up-front money on just the promise of a uranium sample. When he coyly turned it down, a junior officer stepped forward and slipped fifty thousand dollars into his briefcase. The "uranium" the man sent back, of course, turned out to be no such thing, but the Defense Ministry never saw its fifty thousand again. On another occasion, a con man took a huge deposit and just disappeared.

At first I was perplexed at this kind of profligacy. Only after I moved into the palace did it all begin to make sense.

The key to the mystery was in the accounting for discretionary funds. When I arrived at the palace, I was given about a hundred and sixty thousand dollars to spend any way I wanted, the only requirement being I fill out forms reporting expenditures. Well, I thought, who was going to report how much money they'd actually paid for an item? Certainly not Mukhabarat operatives. The system encouraged them to buy a phony document for a couple of thousand dollars, report it as a ten-thousand-dollar expense to their boss, who in turn reported it as a hundred thousand. And so on. The system also explained why so many Mukhabarat foreign station heads were defecting when they were ordered home. They were afraid they'd been discovered.

My German trip was generally fruitful, not counting our long shot at acquiring uranium. And, of course, my failure to find a rat line to escape. A few days after my encounter with Abdul-Muttalib, I saw Omar sitting in the hotel lobby. When he smiled and began to walk my way, I nervously waved him off. He went away, and I never saw him again.

I cannot remember ever feeling so despondent, or fearful, in my nearly twenty years inside Saddam's rotten regime. Was it mere coincidence that Abdul-Muttalib had spotted me with Omar? Or was I constantly being watched? Was Omar really working for them? I couldn't be sure. I was only sure of one thing now: I could not be certain of anything. I was wandering in a wilderness of mirrors without the slightest idea of how to escape. As the elevator lifted me to my hotel room, I nearly shook with loneliness and fear.

• • •

Our contacts obtained a Japanese streak camera through a front company in Singapore, and a German flash X ray was eventually delivered to the embassy. Our agents also got several types of explosive lenses. They weren't powerful enough for my bomb tests, but they were good enough to get the explosives group started on replicating the technology with the help of information they'd gotten at a conference in Portland, Oregon. Both Degussa and Leybold, meanwhile, combined to offer to build us a foundry for a hundred and twenty million dollars. It would be the Islamic world's most sophisticated, capable of making every bomb part except for the explosives.

The German foundry offer also had a bonus: It itemized its components and equipment, with uses, specs, and prices. The Germans had no idea how they'd helped us. AE officials had determined that if we let the Germans alone build the entire foundry, we could end up with another Osirak, with a single supplier knowing too much and potentially helping the Israelis destroy it. So we split the list into several sections and obtained most of the parts from a variety of vendors.

In all this, of course, we were just taking advantage of the West's "don't ask, just sell" attitude toward Iraq. While I was obtaining important bomb components in Germany, a state-owned firm in Austria was selling us large pole magnets for calutrons, or accelerators, used to enrich uranium. Nobody asked what they would be used for. Half of the magnets made their way to Iraq by truck through Turkey, half by ship through Hamburg.

It was a trip to England, however, which exposed me to another dimension of the trade: Behind the scenes, at least in some cases, Western agents seemed to be helping Iraq get what it needed.

Our key man in London was Anees Wadi, a dark, stocky expatriate who'd been living abroad for years. His firm was called Meed International, set up with Kamel's quiet help. Wadi's British partner was Roy Ricks, a blond, aristocratic-looking Englishman, about thirty-five, whom I immediately suspected of working for British intelligence. There was simply no way Wadi could be shipping such sensitive technology out of Britain without some kind of unofficial blessing.

When I voiced my suspicions, Wadi listened intently, nodding and seeming to agree without explicitly offering confirmation. But why would he be concerned? Ricks, after all, was giving him cover to make millions. (As it turned out, Ricks later went into business with a former head of GCHQ, Britain's electronic snooping agency.)

When I first arrived at Wadi's plush new headquarters adjacent to the fashionable Selfridge's shopping center, he gave me a tour, keening all the while about the expensive china his wife had bought for the office. "Eight thousand dollars for coffee cups!" he moaned. But Wadi had a much grander acquisition in the works: a British high-end machine-tool maker, Matrix Churchill. The idea was to use Matrix Churchill, which had an Ohio subsidiary, as a front to acquire particularly sensitive items, not just for the nuclear program but for Iraq's arms programs in general. It would also serve as an overseas perch for Safa al-Haboby, the powerful head of the Al-Nassr arms complex, whom Kamel had taken me to meet on our memorable late-night jaunt from Baghdad. Another one of Wadi's fronts, the Technology Development Group (TDG), was handling the deal. When I met with Wadi and Ricks, we decided that we'd add another layer of subterfuge to my purchases by having Meed International designate other front companies in Europe as end users of exports.

Kamel's orders were to trust Wadi completely, although I quickly found grounds for second thoughts. My shopping list included mainframe computers and advanced mechanical design programs for the bomb, among other things. At our first meeting, Wadi had arranged for a long line of purchasing agents to meet with me, but whenever I tried to discuss prices he'd interrupt and say, "Leave that to me."

"Look, Anees," I finally said, "if I don't start getting numbers from your people, I'll have to stop working through you and start making calls on my own. I just can't keep working in the dark. Cost is a major factor in what computer system we buy."

Wadi snorted, but he didn't want to antagonize me unnecessarily. He made a few calls, and I finally started getting prices by fax. Then I understood why Wadi wanted me to leave the negotiations to him: The offers were three or four times over what we'd paid for similar equipment at AE. After seeing a modest computer offered at three million dollars, I blew up, left the office, and called the salesman myself from a public booth.

"What is this?" I demanded. "Is this your final price or are you expecting a counteroffer?"

"Whatever do you mean?" he said in British high dudgeon.

"What I mean is this is a rip-off," I said. "If you want to do business with us you have to come down to a real-world price."

"You know I can't do that," he countered. "Not with the cut I've got to give to Wadi."

I sighed. "But his cut shouldn't be more than the standard ten or fifteen percent. These prices are at least three times normal," I said.

At that he broke out laughing. "Mr. Hamza, you obviously don't have any idea of the cut your countryman gets. You better take a look at the other offers to understand who you're dealing with. I've been working with Wadi for more than a year, and his cut is never less than fifty percent."

I grunted.

"I'm telling you this," he continued, "so that you'll understand that I am on the level. I don't want to lose your business. And you'll be playing fair with me if you do not mention this to Wadi. Because I'd like to keep your business."

I was fuming as I went back to Wadi's office. Every business needs to make a profit, but this was too much. Plus, if I accepted Wadi's way of doing things, then I'd be his partner in crime. If the thing blew up, my neck would be on the block.

Wadi's response was as cool as a Pimm's Cup in August.

"Think about it," he said. "We started this outfit to help Iraq against the Iranians. We supply all kinds of stuff to Iraq. And the British, the Americans, and just about everybody has been looking the other way. But how long do you think this will last once the war is over? Or suppose tomorrow they change the rules and we're raided by British intelligence? What do you think will happen to me and my family? Do you think Saddam will get me an expensive lawyer?"

I had no response.

"And let me ask you this," Wadi went on. "What have you got to lose? Why are you so riled up?" I still said nothing. He turned impatient.

"Let me tell you something that *will* get you riled up," he said, wagging a finger. "You know your friend Abdul-Muttalib and the black marketeers he brought to see you in Germany? They'll probably charge at least five or six times the real value of the things you want. As for the really sensitive items, you can count on ten times the base price. And by the way, how much do you think Iraq is paying smugglers for all those military spare parts they buy on the black market?

"You should think about yourself," he declared. "Eventually, you know, some investigative reporter is going to blow our cover, and we'll all be exposed. Then what? You'll be a prisoner in Iraq, but at least I'll be able to slip off to some backwater in South America." I considered that. "We both face a very insecure and dangerous future, my friend. Both of us. So don't go complaining about how much extra I charge for my services."

It was a persuasive speech. What Wadi left unsaid, however, was that not all the overcharges were earmarked for his family's safety; some of it went into Kamel's private accounts. I thanked him for his explanation and left. But when I got back to my hotel, something prompted me to stop at the desk and inquire about my current bill. The concierge told me it had been paid. "Meed International has instructed us not to accept any money from you whatsoever," he announced happily.

Walking away, I shook my head. Wadi and Abdul-Muttalib controlled my travel expenses. If I protested about the bill, I'd lose the money, which amounted to several thousand dollars. Even more clever, Wadi sent over a copy of the bill for me to submit when I got home. Defeated, I decided to use the extra money to buy a few things for my wife and kids.

They had me. I was in.

Dafir al-Azawi, head of the explosives group at Al-Qaqaa, was so excited about the availability of American bomb detonators and triggers that he thought he'd try to buy some directly. U.S. Customs, however, quickly got wind of the deal and infiltrated an undercover agent into the operation. Eventually, in what turned out to be the most widely reported bust of our black market operations, two Iraqis and a British woman were arrested at Heathrow in March 1990 with a shipment of forty U.S. capacitors bound for Iraq.

The sting was hatched, according to news reports, after two Egyptians and three Americans were arrested smuggling missile-guidance components through Washington, D.C. In return for lighter sentences, the Americans gave up the names of several Iraqi front companies, including Matrix Churchill, which eventually, in another highly publicized case, was exposed as a conduit for the infamous Gerald Bull's super gun, an artillery piece capable of hurling nuclear, chemical, or biological shells all the way to Israel. Bull was eventually assassinated in Belgium, almost certainly by Israeli agents.

After the Heathrow arrests, though, Saddam had gone on TV and turned the affair into a propaganda extravaganza.

"This is one of our own capacitors, which they did not capture," he said, waving it in his hand. He bragged that our engineers had produced it within five days of the Heathrow bust, and invited the United States and Britain to buy one of ours, made in Iraq. The truth was, we *had* made our own capacitors, but it took us a lot longer than five days. The story behind that operation was even more interesting, and began behind the Iron Curtain in the sunset days of the Soviet empire.

In mid-1988, we had asked the International Atomic Energy Agency in Vienna for information on how to do research in the sophisticated field of plasma physics. The IAEA proposed that we buy a very fast electric-discharge machine called a plasma focus device. Triggering a nuclear reaction by exciting gas with a fast electric discharge, of course, was exactly what we needed for the bomb. So we accepted IAEA's proposal, which steered us to the Poles, who offered to supply us with a plasma focus device and train our people on the miniaturized version we really wanted.

I flew into Warsaw in May 1989, just as the Solidarity movement, led by the charismatic Lech Walesa, was sweeping into power. Everywhere I went, people were jubilant. Freedom was in the air. For the first time in over forty years, people could speak or read what they wanted. The theaters were showing documentaries about abuses under the communists. At the same time, the country was so run-down, food and clothing so scarce, the currency so worthless, that people were nearly crushed by the challenge of rebuilding what a half century of Soviet occupation had destroyed.

The evidence of ruin was everywhere, no more so than in the oppressively bleak countryside around the nuclear research center at

Swierk, fifteen miles south of Warsaw. The fields were fallow, the forests decimated. Only the relatively rich could afford decent food. Just for a scrawny chicken dinner, I had to drive across the river in Warsaw, where I found one minimally acceptable restaurant. Even in the depths of the Iran-Iraq war, average Baghdadis never suffered like this.

I wasn't at Swierk long before some of their best nuclear scientists began approaching me about job possibilities in Iraq, saying they were willing to work for as little as a thousand dollars a month. Since their average pay in Poland was about thirty dollars a month, a thousand must have looked like a fortune. Nevertheless, their fast-electronics technology was top notch—and something Iraq didn't have. Eventually we took some of the Polish scientists up on their offer.

Meanwhile, we got our people trained at Swierk, and together with our laser group, AE embarked immediately on a program to manufacture nuclear detonators. By the time of the busts at Heathrow in March 1990, we were already making our own detonator capacitors, which were as fast as those made in the United States, though not as long-lasting. Not that we cared. Who needed a long-lasting capacitor for a nuclear bomb? It only had to work well once.

By November I was back in Iraq supervising the construction of the plasma focus device when the chairman sent for me.

"We need your help again," al-Ghafour said. "The bomb program is going pretty well under the regimen you devised. Saeed is doing as much as he can, but without some outside technology we'll still be stuck at the most critical stage, producing bomb-grade uranium."

He sighed deeply.

"Jaffar can't seem to surmount the technical problems relating to the ion source," he said, getting up and walking around his desk to me. "I looked over your original plan to resolve this problem, which was to buy a nuclear accelerator from the United States. From Wisconsin, right? That would have solved the problem. But now, with all the fuss about our nuclear program in the news, we can't go back to the U.S. Plus, with the Iranian war over, all the doors in the West are closing to us."

Saddam had learned one thing from the calamitous war with Iran, al-Ghafour's remark reminded me: He needed outside help. And he could usually get it. Despite their ritual declarations of official loathing for Saddam, the West had energetically helped him beat the Iranians. The United States had supplied satellite photos of Iranian forces, attacked Iranian gunboats in the Persian Gulf, and, for a decade, looked the other way while its critical technology flowed to Baghdad. The same went for Britain, France, Germany, and Italy. Some of their technology, along with the help of German scientists, had gone into the chemical weapons program, which proved to be the decisive factor against Iran. Then, after Iraq hit Iranian forces with a barrage of nerve gas in April 1988, Teheran ran up the white flag. Now Saddam, assessing the last hurdles in the nuclear program, decided he could get a bomb ready faster with the help of his few remaining friends.

"So here's what I want you to do," al-Ghafour said. "I want you to go to Russia to buy an accelerator. We'll have the backing of the IAEA again, since they're encouraging nuclear accelerators for the Third World. In fact, they've already accepted our plan to buy one and will even pay part of the cost."

I raised my eyebrows at that. Obviously, Kamel had been busy while I was away. But al-Ghafour had another mission for me.

"On your way back, I want you to look for a solution to the problem of the nuclear trigger. Go see Gy Csikai in Hungary. He's helped us in the past with our neutron generator. See if you can persuade him to help us make a small neutron generator; it would be a good nuclear trigger for the bomb."

I was off once again.

The day I left for Russia was my eldest son's eighteenth birthday. Firas had become a handsome, wiry lad with a quick wit and lively brown eyes. He'd made me a proud papa by excelling at his schoolwork and generally being just a good, upstanding boy. So were Sami and Zayd, my other two sons, who were following in his footsteps. I was overjoyed. But Firas's birthday was cause for melancholy, too, although we all put on our happy faces for a small family party the night before: He was now eligible for the draft.

Although I had a lot of pull with the military, I couldn't be confident they wouldn't just snatch Firas. It would be just like some resentful or suspicious bureaucrat to make him a uniformed hostage to my progress on the bomb. The war with Iran had ended in a bloody draw twenty months earlier, but Saddam was already gearing up for a new fight, this time with Kuwait. What made a new war likely so soon was that Saddam was forty billion dollars in debt to Kuwait and the other Gulf oil potentates for doing their dirty work against Iran. But instead of gratitude, the sheiks wanted repayment, which was driving Saddam up—and against—the wall. The Kuwaitis especially seemed to be taking advantage of Iraq's exhaustion by siphoning off oil from the Rumaila field straddling our frontier. Enraged, and desperate, Saddam was bound to act sooner or later.

Meanwhile, I'd gotten a whiff of freedom in West Germany. As I packed for Russia, I pondered, once again, the possibilities of escape. The Soviet empire was falling apart, pieces flying off like old tires. Eastern Europe was gone, the Ukraine or Georgia was next. With the economy in free fall, Kamel thought we might take advantage of the Russian fire sale and bribe our way into the nuclear club. But as my Iraqi Air jetliner lifted off the runway, I had shopping ideas of my own.

Leningrad (now renamed St. Petersburg) epitomized the collapse. Riding through the snow-packed streets, I saw scenes out of *Dr. Zhivago,* with downcast people in rags warming their hands around barrel fires amid the city's elegant Georgian buildings. Mikhail Gorbachev was being lionized in the West for ending the cold war and permitting legal dissent, but now I could see why his own country hated him. The country was a wreck and chaotic. Indeed, the middle-aged, female KGB agent who was our minder met us with a smile that was more apologetic than welcoming. She delivered us to a hotel that served lunch but no dinner, and advised us to try to buy groceries on the street to take to our rooms.

"Is there a market where we can buy food?" I asked. I hadn't seen any on the way in from the airport, certainly not anything resembling a Western-style supermarket.

She fidgeted, embarrassed. "Actually, you know, there's a problem with finding food. I'll take you to a 'people's market' if you don't mind, and you can go in there and buy anything you want."

We piled back into her old van. A few minutes later, she pulled up at a run-down bungalow and handed us each a few hundred rubles, converted from IAEA-supplied dollars at the official exchange rate—twenty times less than what they would get on the street.

An unhealthy smell assaulted us at the door. Inside the dim room, a few old women in rags were offering badly spoiled meat and shriveled apples from a dirty cloth on the floor. There was no bread. We closed our noses and bought a couple of pounds of apples each and left. Poland, nothing to brag about by Western standards, seemed like paradise in comparison.

The next day the KGB lady drove us to a suburb that was once a small town known as Gatchina. Long ago, however, it had been eclipsed by the sprawl of the Leningrad Nuclear Physics Institute. Some six hundred scientists, more than half of them holding the equivalent of a Western Ph.D., plus another thousand engineers worked there, making it equivalent (in size, at least) to America's Argonne National Laboratory. The director's office, however, was proof that the institute, too, was in dire straits. The crinkled faces of the senior scientists had a look of tired desperation. Their shirts and suits were frayed and spotted. The torn and broken office furniture had seen its best days a generation ago.

During our tour of the factory it was immediately clear from the rusted pieces of metal lying around that nothing had been manufactured here for a long time, and nothing was in the works. The last reactor was made in 1959 and the accelerator they were using was almost as old, with a low precision rate typical of Soviet manufactures. The directors' desperation was manifest in their eagerness to sell us a new nuclear accelerator—no questions asked. In addition, I thought, here was one of the largest repositories of nuclear technology in the USSR, if not the world, and the people here were good enough to solve any nuclear problem we had. One of my orders was to scout for talent we could take back to Baghdad.

Another revelation came at mid-morning, when our guide took us to the cafeteria for a snack. We sat down at one of the bare tables in the small, dingy room. I looked around. We were the only people there. Soon, a small plate with a hard lump of cake was delivered, along with a brown drink that tasted like foul sweetened water.

"Are we dining alone?" I asked.

"Yes," our guide said uncomfortably.

"I was hoping I could talk with your scientists over a meal."

"You wouldn't want to eat the food we eat," she said. "We'll end our talks in time for you to get something decent back at the hotel."

After last night's apples, I looked forward to something edible. As I toyed with my piece of cake, I thought back to a lunch I'd had at Argonne National Lab in 1975, when I was looking into buying an NEC accelerator. The cafeteria was spacious, bright, and clean, with several service areas. The food was good and the staff was obviously happy. Over lunch we'd continued our discussion, which gave me insights into the particular accelerator we were considering. In stark contrast, here I sat with a chunk of cooked dough and an undrinkable soda, alone with a single, sullen guide.

Al-Ghafour had warned me. In fact, he was counting on desperate Soviet scientists to fall like ripe fruit into our hands. The trick was not to go directly to the bomb designers and manufacturing scientists, he said. That would be a dead giveaway, tripping Soviet alarms and slamming the door on our recruitment attempts. Instead, I should look for scientists in support areas like enrichment, and try to recruit them directly. Enrichment was our bottleneck, anyway, since Jaffar had failed. With the equipment we got in Germany, we were confident we had a working bomb design. But as it turned out, finding scientists to work for us was the least of our problems: The Russians were *insisting* on renting us a large number, at a premium price, as part of an accelerator deal.

"If you don't help us with some of the scientists who are in serious financial difficulties," said their chief negotiator, "then we'll probably lose them permanently. They'll leave the country or retire and never come back. Either way it will be a great loss to us."

Later, however, I started getting direct, private pleas from scientists to take them with me, especially the older ones.

"You will be able to accommodate more of us in other capacities than working with this particular accelerator, won't you?" a distinguished-looking man with a gray beard asked me one day. "You see, we have some of the best nuclear physicists in the country. We are working now for twenty or thirty dollars a month." I thought it interesting that he computed in dollars rather than rubles. He looked around to see if any KGB people were watching, then lowered his voice. "How much can you pay us?"

"It depends," I said, "but no less than fifteen hundred dollars a month, plus living expenses. For top scientists, it could go as high as four thousand a month, plus expenses."

Hearing that, the group around him chattered like hungry men passing on rumors of a banquet. "Fifteen hundred!" they whispered. "No, four thousand!" Their eyes glinted like broken mirrors.

By the end of the week we got the institute's price for the accelerator: twenty million, less a million the IAEA would pay. Plus wages and expenses for their scientists—still to be determined.

I left Leningrad for Moscow, my pockets filled with scraps of paper scribbled with the names and addresses of scientists who wanted to come to Iraq in any capacity, whether we concluded the accelerator deal or not. No doubt some would have volunteered bomb-grade uranium or even a warhead to us, but the nuclear weapons were one of the few things still under control in the crumbling Soviet Union. For now.

The Iraqi embassy in Moscow virtually rolled out the red carpet, with an honorary dinner at one of the restaurants for Moscow's new rich and a night out on the town with the ambassador and Munaf al-Ali, the cultural attaché. A fun-loving, U.S.-trained physicist, al-Ali had close connections to Saddam as a member of the ruling Tikriti clans, and had once been an assistant director of the Nuclear Research Center at Atomic Energy. He didn't like the rough-and-tumble, high-security atmosphere of AE, however, so he'd arranged for a soft landing in the diplomatic corps. He really knew his way around Moscow.

Our KGB guide in Leningrad had warned us that there was no way we could get hotel accommodations in the capital without reservations, but al-Ali solved the problem simply by handing a jar of Nescafe instant coffee to the hotel clerk in exchange for a double bedroom. That night, with a hundred-ruble tip to a doorman, he arranged for a front-row table at the nightclub of the International Hotel. As we went in, I looked down the street and saw a line around the block at the newly opened McDonald's.

We gathered at our table. The ambassador was a slim, dark-faced, retired army officer, who seemed to be fawning over our friend al-Ali.

"You know," al-Ali was saying, "we are very well positioned to benefit from the disintegration of the system here."

The ambassador quickly agreed, and told a story.

"Back in the 1980s, Tariq Aziz and the minister of defense, Adnan Khairallah, used to come here all the time with bags full of jewelry and cash. They also had numbered bank accounts to disburse cash. Anyway, that's how we got our weapons and supplies out of here during the war with Iran. Those Russian bureaucrats would not lift a finger without some lubrication. And these same people, especially the technocrats, will be running Russia no matter what the color of the regime is. Right now they'd sell their mothers for a dollar."

We all chuckled and sipped our drinks. Then I brought up the desperation I'd seen on the faces of the nuclear scientists in Leningrad. They nodded somberly. The KGB, they said, was growing weaker by the day, and at some point soon they could lose control of nuclear weapons.

"We probably can't buy a missile-mounted nuclear device yet," al-Ali said, "but the KGB is definitely worried about the safety of components and nuclear materials. If the scientists you saw are in such dire straits, imagine how bad the situation is for low-level people like guards at the bomb factories and missile bases."

The ambassador, his face somber, agreed.

"When this system breaks up, which won't be long now, there won't be any shortage of sellers. The shortage will be of reliable buyers, people with money. And in that area, we're at the top of the list."

I considered what he said. It was true, but what the ambassador failed to fully realize was that for Saddam, the future was now. We already had superior machine shops, along with the German engineers. We had workable designs. We had a small accelerator, whose magnets were already being manufactured to high precision by Jaffar's group, and a bigger one on order from the Russians. For the finishing touches, all we needed was the top Soviet talent to iron out nagging problems. Within a few months, we could have a bomb—perhaps many—in our hands.

The thought chilled me as I walked the streets the next morning, taking in a few sights before leaving the Russian capital. Each step was bringing us closer to the real thing, leaving the theoretical for the practical. Someday soon it wouldn't be an abstract engineering problem at all, but a bright flash in the Iraqi desert.

My pockets were bulging with rubles. I fantasized grabbing a stranger by the lapels and just offering him handfuls, all I had, for refuge, asylum, any escape from Iraq. After a block or so I was jolted out of my dreams by a man offering me a quality Zenith camera for thirty dollars. I examined it and pulled a wad of rubles from my pocket.

"Rubles?" he sputtered. "What can I do with that shit paper? I take dollars, only dollars." Because the camera was so good, virtually a Russian Nikon, I paid him thirty dollars from my wallet and walked on. He scurried away.

Ironically enough, we left Moscow on a flight with hundreds of Jews emigrating to Israel. In fact, the flight had been delayed while Soviet security debated letting us on. Our passports, of course, gave them pause, given Iraq's state of war with Israel. Apparently they thought we might hijack the plane. We finally persuaded them we were just nonpolitical technocrats, traveling on IAEA-issued plane tickets, with no political ax to grind. Little did they know we were building a bomb that might be dropped someday on Israel.

Our destination was Debrecen, a small town a couple hours' drive from Budapest. Hungary, oddly enough, had been the cradle of modern nuclear physics, spawning men like Edward Teller and Eugene Wigner, pioneers in the hydrogen bomb, as well as other major figures in the U.S. nuclear weapons program.

The Center for Nuclear Research at Debrecen was run by the highly regarded Hungarian Academy of Sciences. Despite all the lean years of Soviet dominance, it continued to develop great talent. Though quite modest, and constrained by a small nuclear accelerator, the center also managed to produce an enormous number of high-quality research papers.

The man we came to see was Dr. Gy Csikai, the world authority on neutron generators, having written the main reference on the subject, a two-volume study issued by the well-regarded reference-book publishing arm of the Chemical Rubber Company (CRC), a leading American firm. Csikai had also supervised the Ph.D. research of a longtime Iraqi Baathist, Shakir al-Juboori. I'd brought Juboori along on this leg of the trip because he'd kept in close touch with Csikai, whose willingness to work with us would be critical to the fast success of our program.

Csikai was not a stranger to Baghdad. We'd frequently asked the

IAEA to send him to help us with an old French neutron generator we had. His visits to AE's physics department were always cause for festive dinners and gifts and excursions to historic sights like Babylon. We treated him like royalty, with a car and a driver, and he always expressed his sincere appreciation. But Csikai was the kind of scientist that no amount of oil money had been able to produce in the Arab world, a man dedicated to his discipline, blessed with a rigorous intellect, and undistracted by political intrigue.

We were sure he would never agree to work on a bomb, not if we asked him outright. So we had to devise a plausible cover, one he could accept.

We came up with a pretty solid idea. Miniature neutron generators are used not only to initiate chain reactions in a bomb, but also to trigger neutron bursts in exploratory oil drilling that can help engineers find hidden pools of petroleum. It was natural for Iraq to want to develop such tools and to recruit the best scientist in the world for the job. A neutron generator appropriate for an oil tube would still be too large for a bomb, but persuading Dr. Csikai to make one would be a crucial step forward in the miniaturization of our device.

He agreed to work on the project. As soon as I got back, Kamel asked me how much Csikai knew.

"I don't know," I said. "But he could surely guess."

A cloud passed over Kamel's face.

"But here's the thing," I quickly added. "Telling him would not only be pointless, it would be counterproductive. He does not want to know. Trust me on that. If push comes to shove with the IAEA, this way he can honestly claim that he did not know, that we never told him a thing."

Kamel leaned back, smiled slyly, and nodded. He liked the way I'd learned how to play his game.

The Poles were the same, I added. Our policy was, If they don't ask, we don't tell. And they're not asking. The same with the Russians, who were also coming aboard after some last-minute haggling. And now Csikai. The money was just too good.

So now we had all the pieces in place to make it work, I assured Kamel. The bomb was in sight.

The only problem was Saddam.

On August 2, he invaded Kuwait. And everything came to a halt.

CHAPTER TWELVE

THE WINDS OF WAR

I KNEW SADDAM would never get away with it, but in retrospect, his decision to invade Kuwait had a cranky kind of logic.

Like most dictators, Saddam was bewildered by America. He didn't speak English, he had never visited the United States. He had traveled little, outside of his few years of exile as a young man in Cairo and then, much later, state visits to Moscow and Paris. He lived in a cocoon of yes-men, thugs, palace servants, and a harem. What Saddam knew of America came mostly from his spies and diplomats who tailored their reports to his prejudices.

But as Saddam contemplated what to do about Kuwait in the summer of 1990, nothing confused him more than Washington's hydra-headed policies toward Iraq. Through most of the 1980s the United States helped Saddam against Iran. Then he found out that Reagan operatives were secretly selling missiles to the ayatollah. Likewise, at the end of the war, Washington's attitude toward him had turned chilly, but what was he to think when a delegation of U.S. senators, led by Robert Dole, the Republican leader in the Senate, came all the way to Iraq in the spring of 1990 to express their wishes for closer relations? At the same time, other, Democratic-led congressional committees were digging up embarrassing details of dual-use exports to Iraq. And now the CIA was trying to undermine him from Kuwait.

Washington's relations with Iraq were a bag of contradictions. The leaders of Western European democracies might be equipped to decode the cacophony, but a dictator like Saddam was at a loss.

And he had a deep crisis on his hands. Unbearable financial pressure had been building on Saddam since the end of the war with Iran. Only a blast of chemical weapons had saved his armies from being ground down by another season of human-wave attacks by the fanatical Iranian Shiites. After eight years of war, Iraq was broke.

And isolated. The Persian Gulf sheiks, especially in Kuwait, had been glad to loan Saddam forty billion dollars to exterminate the Shiite germs, but now they not only wanted their money back, they were pumping oil far beyond their OPEC quotas, forcing down the price and making Iraq's recovery all the more difficult. Kuwait was the worst offender.

He had to do something about Kuwait, but the recent visits of General Norman Schwarzkopf and other U.S. officials there troubled him. Schwarzkopf, chief of the U.S. Central Command, had labeled Iraq the main threat to peace in the region—not Iran, not the Russians. What was going on? Saddam wondered. He called in U.S. ambassador April Glaspie and asked her for the American position on his festering dispute with Kuwait.

"The United States has no opinion on Arab conflicts," Glaspie said, according to a transcript released later. Saddam, brushing aside common sense and failing to get clarification from his diplomats in Washington, seized on Glaspie's remarks as a green light to invade. Within days, several Iraqi divisions were rolling across the desert into Kuwait, which Saddam quickly declared a "nineteenth province" of Iraq. Then President George Bush surprised him by declaring that the occupation of Kuwait "would not stand." The U.S. Congress narrowly backed him up.

The looming conflict was horrifying to me as well as other Iraqis who'd come to love America during our student days. I still had my Peter, Paul and Mary albums and had delighted in introducing my children to "Puff the Magic Dragon." Memories of Budweiser and cheeseburgers, dates in my Olds Cutlass, and all-night poker games in Florida filled me with nostalgia. Those of us who had studied in America thought of it as our best years. The country's generosity was bottomless—just the computer time alone for my Ph.D. research probably cost forty thousand dollars.

And now we were going to be at war.

•   •   •

236

The scientists stood in the chill of a desert dawn, watching a plume of dust trailing from a speeding caravan of Mercedes on the horizon, two months after the invasion of Kuwait.

At the wheel of one of the cars was Hussein Kamel, chief of military industries. As usual, Kamel was pushing the Mercedes to its limits, sending the speedometer well past a hundred. In recent months, in fact, he had become increasingly reckless behind the wheel. If pedestrians got in the way, he ran them over. Given a choice of killing someone or chancing an ambush by slowing down, Kamel easily pressed the pedal. His trailing entourage took names and paid off the survivors later. To me, it was a metaphor for the whole regime.

Across the border in Saudi Arabia, American and Allied troops, warplanes, tanks, and artillery were pouring in for the "mother of all battles"—and possibly more, Saddam feared. The Allies might well come all the way to Baghdad to take him out.

Which is what brought Kamel racing at dawn to the secret facility I'd built at Al-Atheer, sixty miles southwest of Baghdad. Saddam wanted to know how close we were to completing the equalizer. In August he'd ordered a crash program to produce enough fuel for at least one nuclear device, a warhead that he could mount on a missile and hurl at the Israelis if the Allies invaded. It was his doomsday weapon. If his own demise were imminent, he planned to take everybody down with him—no threats, no demonstration flash in the desert for diplomatic leverage. The crash program meant Saddam would use the bomb, once. And then we'd all go down with him when the Israeli missiles came whistling back.

Once again, I scrambled for an escape. There was no way I was going to be vaporized with my family in the ashes of Baghdad because of Saddam Hussein's megalomania.

Since August, the Russian reactor at al-Tuwaitha had been running around the clock to produce polonium for the bomb trigger. The overtime was causing the entire plant to pulse with radiation, the cooling water growing especially hot. Workers began to fall ill with radiation sickness. They were sent home so as not to demoralize others. Meanwhile, uranium fuel salvaged from the French Osirak reactor, destroyed by the Israelis in 1983, was being prepared for the process that would turn it into metal for the bomb core. Under Kamel's unrelenting pressure, the design of the device had been partially tested and theoretically modeled, but we still weren't sure it would work. Now he wanted to see how close we were to putting the whole thing together. The Allied invasion was not far off. The regime was running out of time.

And experts. Saddam had badly miscalculated how the West would react to a move that gave him control of 60 percent of the world's oil reserves. Now he faced not only a concerted military invasion but the desertion of his erstwhile friends. A global economic embargo was slapped on Iraq. Foreign experts hired for weapons development were leaving. The Poles, the Germans, the Russians, the Hungarian Dr. Csikai, who'd helped us plan the miniaturization of the neutron generator, were going or gone. The bomb project at Al-Atheer was still a well-kept secret, but only because Saddam had snuffed out a spy.

That episode began when Farzad Bazoft, an Iranian-born journalist with close ties to British intelligence, arrived in Baghdad on assignment for the *Observer*, a London newspaper, in September 1989. Tipped by a British nurse working in a Baghdad hospital, Bazoft traveled to Musseib, close by Al-Atheer, to gather soil samples that could be tested for traces of biological or chemical weapons. Unbeknownst to him, he was under surveillance by Iraqi agents. When word rattled up the chain of command that Bazoft was digging in the sand near Al-Atheer, alarms went off. The soil samples would divulge traces of polonium and uranium, which had but one purpose: a nuclear bomb. Bazoft was arrested on September 13, but rumors were put out that he'd stumbled on a clandestine chemical and biological program, which were picked up and published abroad. The real secret of the bomb went to his grave with him on March 15, when Bazoft was executed as a British spy.

Saddam's invasion of Kuwait, in any event, had killed any chance of building a bomb very soon. Everything was falling apart. The German weekly *Der Spiegel*, no doubt aided by government sources, had already unmasked the German scientists who provided us with centrifuge technology. The bomb program was springing leaks. Iraq was a sinking ship.

But Kamel wasn't about to give up. As he sped across the desert,

Al-Atheer was locked down in an extreme security emergency. No one was permitted to leave. Outgoing calls were blocked. The regime's kingpins were operating at a high level of paranoia now. Or reality, considering the constant rumors of coups and assassination attempts.

Kamel's flash inspection caught me by surprise. I was in Baghdad, tinkering with the design for the trigger. From those at Al-Atheer, however, I was able to piece together an accurate account of what happened.

Waiting for Kamel was the ineffable Jaffar Dhia Jaffar, the willowy bon vivant who'd not only survived the failure of his uranium enrichment schemes but flourished. A few months ago, he'd not only been made deputy chief of military industries but he was awarded a cabinet seat, minister without portfolio. Also waiting for Kamel was Khalid Saeed, the gregarious runt who, on his willingness to carry out Baath Party directives, had risen from a lowly research assistant to director general of Atomic Energy.

Kamel's Mercedes skidded to a stop at the entrance to Al-Atheer's office. Out he stepped, followed by General Amir al-Saadi, his chief weapons adviser. Next came Issam Abdullah, the smirking chief of palace security. Another Mercedes emptied of Kamel's supernumeraries. Armed security agents sped through the gates and took up positions around the grounds.

Kamel was in no mood for pleasantries.

"Where is it?" he demanded.

The bomb was in the bunker. Jaffar led Kamel's entourage into the partially submerged facility, the size of a small aircraft hangar. Technicians in blue coveralls and hard hats, radiation badges pinned to their chests, stood back against the walls. In the middle of the room, under bright spotlights, sat the hulking, blimp-shaped, stainless-steel device, minus, of course, its uranium core. The unarmed, ton-and-a-half bomb was fully four feet in diameter, bigger than a refrigerator, huge by current standards.

Kamel stared at the device with a growing disgust.

"What is this?" he demanded. It looked as big as a boxcar.

Jaffar struggled to reply, suddenly plagued by his long-dormant stutter. "I-i-it's an ac-ac-actual device," he stammered, "wi-wi-wi-without th-th-th-the uranium fuel."

Kamel fumed. "But we can't load this monster on a missile!"

Nobody could remember seeing Kamel explode like that before. The stress of the looming war had taken its toll.

Jaffar struggled to explain. "But th-th-this is not a bomb, sir. It's a d-d-d-device for testing our design. We c-c-cannot provide you a working b-b-bomb imme-me-mediately."

Kamel's eyes flashed. He wagged a finger at the quivering scientist. "If you'd delivered the uranium as you promised, Jaffar, then testing would be feasible. But you didn't. So now all we have is enough uranium for one bomb, and we want it mounted on a missile and ready to go, soon."

Jaffar was stunned. He looked at General al-Saadi, who wore a cool, thin smile on his lips. He'd always thought the nuclear project was a waste of money.

"Al-Saadi has prepared a missile for this weapon," Kamel continued, "and we want you to reduce it to a size we can mount on the missile—before hostilities break out."

Jaffar did a quick calculation. Even if it worked, sending a nuclear missile whirling at Israel not only gave Iraq no military advantage, but the retaliation it guaranteed sealed his own fate. It was Saddam's to-hell-with-everybody strategy.

In any event, for now the question was moot. The behemoth was the best we'd been able to come up with, but was too big and unstable to ride on a missile. The hitch had always been the explosives people at Al-Qaqaa. It had taken them ages to test the lenses, and what they finally produced just wasn't good enough for a smaller device. To compensate, we'd employed an advanced bomb design called levitation, in which a gap was left between the bomb core and the explosives to produce a bigger bang. The result was a device too big for a missile, but one that could be dropped from a plane. Kamel's rage no doubt stemmed from the expectation that any of our planes would be shot down by Israel's formidable air defenses. He was enraged.

Kuwait, meanwhile, was being sacked. Saddam had appointed Ali Hassan al-Majid—Ali the Chemist of Halabjah nerve-gas infamy—as governor of the conquered territory. Ali's deputy was a former assistant of mine, Saleh Hamid, who had negotiated some of the deals with the German firms Degussa and Leybold. Hamid, who'd gotten his Ph.D. in nuclear engineering from the University of Michigan, persuaded Jaffar that Kuwait was rich in technology and equipment that could be useful to the bomb program. Soon, he was made chief of the Kuwaiti Science Research Center, which was commandeered by the Iraqis.

Hamid began by stripping Kuwait University and the Science Research Center of any equipment deemed useful to Iraq, including an IBM mainframe computer. His ignorant soldiers, however, simply chopped the computer cable from the walls, with no consideration of how the machine might have to be reconnected in Iraq. No matter: In the end, it was simply pushed off the back of a truck at Atomic Energy. It broke into pieces.

Hamid was also in charge of issuing checkpoint passes for trucks running loot back to Iraq. Some were sent to Atomic Energy, but others, laden with luxury goods, were diverted to his house and the homes of others useful to his career. In such a way did Jaffar and al-Ghafour come into possession of private yachts. (Jaffar kept his in his driveway; al-Ghafour moored his on his ranch.)

Another service Hamid provided was to round up Kuwait's key officials and ship them back to Iraq as hostages.

Saddam, of course, was the pirate in chief. His Special Security Organization broke down the doors of Kuwait banks, blew the safes, and seized all the cash and gold reserves on hand. Naturally, the SSO officers in charge skimmed off some for themselves. Special teams organized by Saddam's eldest son, Uday, were doing the same.

The plunder piled up in Baghdad. Interestingly, it turned into a public relations problem for the regime. Under the Koran, it was immoral for Muslims to steal from each other. Thus, pious students at the University of Baghdad began to refuse to unload trucks bulging with classroom furniture and equipment stolen from Kuwait. The same went for stolen goods in the central market; Muslims started turning away.

I, personally, saw an opportunity in the chaos and made a bargain with the devil. One SSO officer, eager to unload some of his ill-gotten dollars, offered them to me at a cut rate. Anxious to accumulate hard currency for my family's escape, I bought some of his through an intermediary. My hands shook in the transaction. If word got out that I was accumulating dollars, Kamel's henchmen would quickly be at my door asking why.

More than cold desert winds chilled Baghdad in December 1990. Nearly a half million Allied troops, including Syrian and Egyptian soldiers, were poised in Saudi Arabia to invade Kuwait. A naval armada, including American, British, and French aircraft carriers, was taking positions in the Persian Gulf and Red Sea. Washington was continuing to talk with Iraq, but Saddam was diplomatically isolated; only the Russians were working for a settlement short of Saddam's complete capitulation. The West demanded Iraq's complete, immediate, unconditional retreat from Kuwait. The deadline was set: January 16.

For a man in a crucible, Saddam seemed awfully calm. He'd even taken yet another wife, his third.

I'd watched Nidal al-Hamdani with curiosity as she rose swiftly through the ranks of the Science Research Council. Blond-haired and light-skinned, with a quick wit and fondness for Western clothes that flattered her curvaceous figure, Hamdani was made chief of the Solar Energy Center despite having only a master's degree amid a sea of Ph.D.s. With palace officials bowing and scraping every time she entered a room, moreover, I figured she had to have some kind of connection.

I should have known immediately, but the mystery was soon cleared up. One day in the shadow of crisis with Kuwait, it was announced that Hamdani was Saddam's new wife. Frankly, I had to give my grudging respect to a man who had so much energy he could manage a dictatorship, three wives, countless mistresses, and a household full of troublesome children, all the while steering his country toward a showdown with a superpower.

As for the bomb, once again Jaffar inadvertently came to the rescue. His chemists reported that the crude separation technique they were using on the French fuel would produce only about twenty-two pounds of uranium metal, little more than half of what was required.

The apocalypse was postponed. And I, suddenly, had a way to tiptoe away from the program. Saddam had already started complaining about Iraq's dependence on foreign-trained scientists. "I have met many of them," he declared on TV, "and the first thing they all ask for is a car. Then they start demanding this and that. . . ." With typical hyperbole, he announced the "thousand Ph.D. program" to educate our own scientists at home. The fact was, however, he was broke from the Iran-Iraq war and couldn't afford foreign-trained experts, even if we'd been able to persuade any to come back.

For me, it was an opportunity to take over the AE portion of the training program, which would allow me to retreat from active management of the bomb program. I also turned down a scheme floated by Kamel and al-Ghafour to launch a new, clandestine company in Jordan to make neutron generators outside the embargo clamped on Iraq. My excuse was that I couldn't leave my family, having already spent so much time abroad. They gave me a reprieve. Now I would be based at Baghdad University and the University of Mustansiriya, training a new generation of scientists, where I could begin laying down yet another plan for escape.

As the Allied air war loomed, Saddam ordered evidence of the bomb effort hidden. The palace staff was already relocated. Lights were out at the adjacent Al-Hayat building, where I and other senior advisers had apartments. Key officials were scattered around the city, squirreled inside innocuous-sounding ministries.

At first I was surprised at how calmly Saddam had accepted the demise of his crash program to make the bomb. After a while, I figured out that Kamel must have played the critical role. Only thirty-one years old, with an estimated five billion dollars deposited in foreign banks, Kamel had a lot to live for and a realistic expectation that he could escape sometime and make a deal with the West. But not Saddam, who had nothing to bargain away but his life. Then I learned of Saddam's new diabolical plans.

The problem of using weapons of mass destruction is that they can always be returned in spades by a more powerful enemy. The American secretary of state, James Baker, had sternly warned Saddam that his horrifying threat to "burn half of Israel" would be returned with a "full and complete retaliation." But what, Saddam wondered, if chemical or biological weapons could be used on the Allies without them knowing it? Thus was born the idea of another doomsday defense, this one with chemical and biological stocks.

As the January deadline approached, Saddam had become more of a realist about Kuwait. He knew the Allies could take it back.

The helter-skelter looting was rank evidence that Iraq expected to be evicted. What Saddam still worried about, however, was the capture of Baghdad and his personal vulnerability. For him, there was no escape. Where could he go?

Accordingly, he ordered General al-Saadi to organize a two-pronged defense. The first was to load chemical and biological warheads onto Iraqi missiles, in the event Allied troops stormed through the gates of Baghdad. But the second, and ultimately more relevant prong was to bury thousands of chemical and biological weapons in southern Iraq, at Basra, Nasiriyah, Simawa, Diwaniyah, and Hilla, the likely routes of the Allied invasion. His thinking was that the Allies, following U.S. tactical doctrine, would blow up the bunkers as they advanced, releasing plumes of invisible gas into the prevailing winds and ultimately onto themselves. Any depots the Allies missed could be blown up by retreating Republican Guard units. The invaders literally wouldn't know what hit them, until it was too late—maybe weeks or months after the conflict ended. The pattern of contamination would be so disparate, the symptoms so amorphous, the sources of illness couldn't be easily confirmed.

Iraq would be hell to the invaders, win or lose, Saddam gambled. A corollary benefit was that the chemical shower would decimate the despised Shia in the south, whom he concluded were of little concern to the Allies, given their potential role as troops for Iran. In any event, if chemical residues were eventually detected, the Americans would have only themselves to blame. And the West would tie itself in knots over an appropriate retaliation. Washington, Saddam reasoned, had no stomach for carrying out retaliation in kind.

On the night of January 16, 1991, Iraq's top nuclear officials met for a candle-lit dinner at Le Soufotel, a French restaurant in downtown Baghdad. The dinner was to celebrate my new good fortune at being assigned away from AE.

The gathering was official self-delusion at its worst. The Allied air campaign was scheduled to kick off in four hours, yet many Iraqi officials were still in denial, despite weeks of repeated warnings from Washington.

"It's all a bluff," a colleague uttered, drawing agreeable guffaws around the table. "These guys have no stomach for a land war.

They'll surrender to our forces and we'll have them paraded by the thousands in the streets of Baghdad."

I kept my silence. It was pointless to dissent. In a few hours the truth would be known.

Even the semiliterate Kamel could read the handwriting on the wall. He'd ordered Al-Qaqaa dismantled and its equipment scattered to secret locations around the country.

Al-Atheer was likewise evacuated, the bomb design and assembly groups transferred to a technical training institute in Baghdad. The documents Wadi had sent me from London were packed up by the SSO and carted to my new training center. Employees of the uranium-casting group took their own documents home.

Al-Ghafour, on the other hand, seemed to be sleepwalking through the crisis. He'd taken no steps to evacuate AE's equipment and materials. He had people showing up for work as usual.

The dinner ended sometime before midnight. I drove home through the deserted streets, hoping that America's precision-guided bombs and missiles would work as advertised and keep civilian casualties to a minimum. At home, I fell into a deep, troubled sleep.

At two A.M., Souham shook me awake.

"Get up!" she shouted. "Get up! The bombing has started!"

Before I could even sit up, the house shook with a tremendous explosion. But it wasn't a bomb. A SAM missile battery next to our house had fired off a rocket. Then another house-rattling roar as another rocket was launched. I heard muffled bombing at a distance, and the clackety-clack of antiaircraft guns nearby. We ran downstairs.

Right on schedule, the war had begun. We gathered the kids and huddled in a corner with our arms around each other. I swore at Saddam for moving his missile batteries into residential neighborhoods.

Ba-room! Another huge explosion. Souham and the younger children whimpered. I crept over to a window and cautiously peeked out. A house two doors down was a smoking wreck. An Allied missile aimed at the SAM battery had missed.

I was fortunate, though, not to be at AE. One of the Allies' first bombs had hit the headquarters building, which held the plasma focus equipment we'd gotten from Poland. The Poles—now free of the Soviets—must have alerted the Americans to it. Also hit was the AE library, scattering millions of documents to the wind.

The Russian reactor was also targeted. Somebody must have closely studied its layout, because the reactor was destroyed, though not the fuel in the core. (Later, Saddam would claim to U.N. inspectors that it was destroyed.) The next day, stupidly, tragically, senior scientists and engineers were called in to salvage the computers and electronic equipment, and found themselves wading through radioactive water. Many of them, including Basil al-Qaisy, one of the best electrical engineers in Iraq, would eventually come down with cancers.

It was only a matter of time, I knew, before Allied pilots honed in again on the SAM battery next to my house. We had to get out. My hometown of Diwaniyah, I decided, was the best place to go. There wasn't much there for the Allies to shoot at. I called a friend, who invited us to his ranch outside the city.

In the morning, Souham and I gathered up the children and a few bags, but at the last minute Firas refused to go.

"Someone needs to stay here and keep an eye on the house, Papa," he argued. True enough, looting was inevitable. But I suspected the real reason was that he wanted to stay with his friends, a typical teenage obsession. Almost nineteen, Firas had become difficult to manage, like most boys his age. We argued about it for a few minutes, and my temper flared. But he dug in his heels. Frustrated, impatient, my good sense deserted me. In exasperation, I gave in. I told him he could stay.

We drove off to Diwaniyah, my wife sniffling intermittently about Firas. Along the way, we saw few of the Allied warplanes streaming high over Iraq, but we occasionally heard and saw their handiwork. Smoke rose from military and industrial installations ringing the city. The road was clogged with cars and military trucks and not a few obvious deserters.

The ranch was about twenty miles beyond Diwaniyah, just outside the small town of Daghara, which was filled with military vehicles and officers. We pulled into the ranch after a three-hour drive, exhausted but relieved to be out of harm's way. Our hosts generously welcomed us with hugs and heaping plates of food.

"Why are there so many high-ranking government people in

town?" I asked my friend. Before he could answer Souham came over, tears in her eyes.

"You've got to go back and get Firas," she said. I agreed.

Three hours later I was back in Baghdad, screeching to a halt outside our home. The windows of neighboring houses were smashed, but miraculously, ours looked untouched. I hurried inside and gasped when I saw Firas on the couch. His hands, head, and face were wrapped in bandages.

"Hi, Papa," he said weakly. I rushed to his side.

"I had an accident," he said. He told me he'd been crossing a high bridge in Baghdad in a friend's car when it shook violently beneath them. A missile had been launched from underneath the bridge. They careened into a barrier and didn't stop until the front wheels were hanging in the air ten stories over the concrete below. Firas and his friend, despite their bloody bruises, crawled out the car windows to safety.

Now I was desperate to get him out of Baghdad. Luckily, I'd stored extra gas in the garage. I emptied the last cans into my Passat. We left that night as air raids continued in the city. With the sky lighting up like fireworks, we headed south.

Hours later, I was back in Diwaniyah. It was dark. As we were pulling out of town a guard pulled us over and asked where we were going.

"Daghara," I said.

He shook his head. "Not good, sir. The highway is full of deserters. They'll kill you and take the car." I could tell it wasn't a bluff. My God, I thought: If our soldiers are deserting now, what will happen when the real ground attack starts? Our army will melt like butter.

We pulled off the street and slept in the car. At first light, we left Diwaniyah, wary of the soldiers wandering the highway. Finally, we pulled into the ranch. Souham ran from the house and threw her arms around her son.

"I thought you were dead," she cried, half-angry.

Finally, I had a chance to sleep. The next day, refreshed, I decided to scout the nearby town. I was still curious about the presence of so many high officials there.

It didn't take long to unravel the mystery. Daghara was a major chemical weapons depot, I found out, with maybe as many as a half dozen large bunkers.

We had to get out, *now.*

I sped back to the ranch and told everybody what I'd learned. There wasn't a moment to waste, I said, explaining what I knew of Saddam's strategy with chemical weapons. From the air, the bunkers were designed to look like regular ammunition depots. Saddam hoped the Allies could be lured into hitting them, now or during the invasion.

By nightfall we were all gone, heading back to Baghdad.

Over the ensuing weeks, we sought refuge several times at the Amiria shelter, about a mile from the house. But it was always filled, forcing us to trek back home through the booms and blasts of the attacks and antiaircraft guns. Sadly, our little Pekinese, Lucy, ran away.

The shelter had television sets, drinking fountains, its own electric generator, and looked sturdy enough to withstand a hit from conventional weapons. But I stopped trying to get in one night after noticing some long black limousines slithering in and out of an underground gate in the back. I asked around and was told that it was a command center. After considering it more closely, I decided it was probably Saddam's own operational base.

Saddam never slept in the same place. Several times during the bombing, I spotted him in my own neighborhood, once driving an ordinary car and wearing an Arab headdress covering most of his face. At first I thought I was mistaken, but my neighbor confirmed it later.

Saddam had appeared at his own door, he said, with dark pouches under his eyes. A pair of bodyguards stood at his sides.

"Can we be your guests for the night?" Saddam asked. It was a polite request, not an order, but my friend was alarmed by Saddam's murderous eyes. He quickly stepped aside and invited Saddam and his escorts in.

As Saddam took a seat on the couch, his bodyguards locked the door, signaling who was in charge of his house. Saddam wearily asked for tea.

"Of course, Mr. President," my friend said, starting for the kitchen. A bodyguard raised a hand. "Just show me where it is," he said. "I'll take care of the rest."

A few minutes later the tea was delivered: one cup for Saddam, one for the host. Everyone smiled as the man picked up his cup. It was the last thing he remembered. In the morning he awoke with a terrible headache, sat up feeling abnormally groggy, and looked around. He was in the children's room. He staggered out, noticing the key stuck in the outside lock. In the living room, on the coffee table, was a wad of money. He picked it up and counted five hundred dinars—about fifty dollars. There was no sign of Saddam.

The president went on television frequently during the air raids to taunt the Allies. All the TV channels would be cleared if he had something to say on the evening news. Most of the occasions were devoted to making fun of the bombing of Iraq.

"They tell us the Americans have stealth planes you cannot see," he said, chuckling one night. "But that's a lie. Our shepherds see them all the time!"

When the bombing grew even heavier, a new joke made the rounds in Baghdad.

"What happened to Saddam's shepherds?" people cracked when a warplane shrieked over Baghdad. "Did they go blind?"

In the early hours of February 13, the Amiria shelter was hit with a new kind of bomb, one that penetrated several feet of reinforced concrete before exploding and incinerating about four hundred people inside. Rescue workers discovered many had survived the initial explosion, but died trying to get out through the locked doors.

I was told that Saddam had slipped out only an hour before. Several military-only shelters were similarly destroyed in the hunt for Saddam or his top commanders. In one case, a demolition officer said he found a score of officers' corpses plastered to the shelter walls. The adverse publicity over Amiria put a crimp on the Allies hitting civilian targets, at least in Baghdad.

At dawn on February 24, following a ferocious artillery barrage, the ground war finally kicked off. U.S. and British armored divisions crashed across the border, led by swarming Apache antitank helicopters. American bulldozers rolled over Iraq's defensive trenches, burying thousands of soldiers alive. The survivors began surrendering by the hundreds, then thousands. The deserter-execution squads were surrendering, too.

Some officials, meanwhile, used the chaos as cover for an escape. One of the most significant was Ibrahim Bawi, whom Jaffar had press-ganged into Atomic Energy when he returned from Britain in 1990 with a Ph.D. in electrical engineering. Bawi hated every minute of his duty on the magnetic enrichment program. To pacify him, Jaffar gave him a government car. When Desert Storm began, he drove it to Turkey, and eventually made contact with the CIA. He was the first defector from the Iraqi nuclear weapons program.

My old colleague al-Shahristani, meanwhile, now a bearded Shi-ite zealot after years in the hands of Saddam's sadists, managed to bribe his way out of Abu Ghraib prison and fled over the mountains to Iran. Eventually, he got to Canada, then later joined the Iraqi opposition in London.

I deeply envied both, who had nothing to lose but their own lives. Al-Shahristani left with little more than the tattered shirt on his scarred back. Bawi did manage to drive his family out with him, but that was all. He was so young and low on the AE totem pole he owned nothing of value, and nobody missed him for weeks.

The defections filled me with remorse. Saddam's tactic of fatten-ing high officials with cash, cars, and houses had worked. I was too old, too comfortable, too scared to risk my wife and children and leave everything behind. And I had too high a profile just to slip away and not be missed. So I sat, and grieved. Then I resumed plan-ning. My time would come.

The war was over in four days, capped by the infamous U.S. air attack on the so-called Highway of Death out of Kuwait, which incinerated thousands of Iraqis fleeing in their booty-filled vehicles. The world was horrified by pictures of the carnage, but unknown to outside observers, many ordinary Iraqis were not that upset. Pious Muslims believed the thieves got what they deserved.

Meanwhile, a dark, viscous, foul-smelling cloud had blanketed Baghdad, pollution from the Kuwaiti oil wells Saddam had set afire. My house, given a coat of white paint only the year before, turned gray. Food was contaminated, too. Word spread that fish in the markets was inedible because of fallout from burning chem-ical weapons depots. Hospitals in southern Iraq were crammed with soldiers and civilians complaining of lung and intestinal problems.

Inevitably, defeat is midwife to plots. One story that is widely believed among Iraqis—and not dismissed by knowledgeable CIA officials—swirls around one Salah Omar al-Ali, a suave former Iraqi ambassador to the United Nations. Salah had staged a noisy defection to the United States during the Iran-Iraq war, then gone underground. After Saddam invaded Kuwait, Ali surfaced as a leading member of the Iraqi opposition abroad. Then, when President Bush declared a cease-fire, al-Ali is said to have floated a plan to eliminate Saddam, which eventually found receptive American ears.

It had irresistible simplicity: At its nub was the question of whether Saddam would be permitted to deploy his helicopters, a key issue in the cease-fire talks between Iraq and General Norman Schwarzkopf, Desert Storm's commander in chief. Saddam, facing an imminent Shiite uprising, and capitulating to Allied demands to ground what was left of his air force, was desperate to keep the choppers aloft to quell a Shiite rebellion that had ignited in the south. Iraq's official plea, of course, was that the choppers were needed for humanitarian relief and the routine transport of high-level government officials.

Ali allegedly let it be known that if the flights were permitted, a plot could be hatched for one of Saddam's personal pilots to assassinate the dictator. The idea was greeted enthusiastically, not only because it promised to rid the world of Saddam, but it would replace him with another member of his inner circle—not a Shiite who might be a stalking horse for Iran. The West would have a unified Iraq, minus Saddam. Accordingly, Iraq's request to use their helicopters was accepted.

According to this story, however, the rumored plot was a sting. What is clear is that the regime promptly put the gunships to work repressing the Shiite rebellion.

The Shiite uprising was probably doomed, notwithstanding al-Ali's cunning. Nevertheless, when George Bush called for a revolt, the Shia rose up. And were chopped down.

There were a thousand tragedies in this episode, but one that took place in Diwaniyah was typical. Soldiers returned, hungry and destitute, to their homes and government authorities indifferent to their plight. People were sick of Saddam and anybody associated with him. Many soldiers traded their rifles for a meal. Rebellion was in the air.

Some of Saddam's local officials, such as the district governor and the head of Diwaniyah University, ran away. Others sat on the fence as the crowds of leaderless Shiites and soldiers swelled. My brother's father-in-law, an elderly, semiliterate zealot by the name of Sayed Mohsen, was enticed into leading the revolt. Entirely unequipped for such a responsibility, he stood by helplessly as the rebellion descended into endless squabbles and looting. The only useful act the rebels carried out before the curtain came down was to free Kuwaiti women and children secreted in a building that was misleadingly identified as a hospital for victims of AIDS.

Nonetheless, within weeks after the war ended, fifteen of Iraq's eighteen provinces were under the control of Shiite or Kurdish rebels. But Saddam's Republican Guards retook the rebel towns one by one. U.S. troops not only failed to aid the rebels, they helped the Republican Guards gain access to local munitions and weapons depots. Then, as they stood by, the rebels were encircled. U.S. troops also held a rebel leader who had approached the American lines for help, the son of the Shiite Imam al-Khoi. After that, the imam knew the insurrection was doomed. He agreed later to appear on TV with Saddam.

The Shiites were even more viciously betrayed in An Najaf, their principal holy city in Iraq. A helicopter with Iranian insignia landed, disgorging a gaggle of purported mullahs speaking fluent Farsi. They announced that they had come from Iran to support the rebellion.

"Where are your leaders?" they asked. When some came forward, the mullahs announced they needed help back in Iran with logistics. The rebel leaders stepped aboard and the chopper lifted off.

It landed in Baghdad. The rebels promptly disappeared into Saddam's dungeons. Similar operations took place in Shiite towns across southern Iraq, and the rebellion was soon crushed. Luckily, my brother's father-in-law and his family were able to flee to Saudi Arabia. Later, Saddam demolished their houses and gave away their property.

Fifty thousand Iraqis died in the abortive revolt. Six months after a half million Allied troops had been mobilized against him, they were leaving, and Saddam was still in power.

CHAPTER THIRTEEN

AFTERMATH

Eventually, the food and medicine ran out—except for the officials who looted Kuwait. They had plenty.

A year after defeat in Desert Storm, most Iraqis were doing very poorly. Even I, supporting the family on a professor's salary, plus consulting fees at Atomic Energy and speculative profits from the stock market, was growing wheat to make bread, albeit on a ranch I'd bought on a branch of the Tigris north of Baghdad.

Only the thieves were doing very well, led by Saddam's volatile oldest son, Uday. Like his father, Uday had a mean streak and an explosive temper. Like his father, he favored black leather jackets and had a gangster's instinct for exploiting other people's problems. Since most people had a problem getting food, Uday's immediate target was imports.

The shortages guaranteed corruption. Under Uday's direction, merchants began importing molding meat, eggs, and milk and repackaging them as fresh. Baklava was fried in automobile grease instead of oil. Tea was made from sawdust and coloring material. A new type of shortening distributed by the government stuck to the throat and made people sick. The inspectors, of course, were paid to look the other way.

Likewise, expired medicines were repackaged and sold as new. Since the price of most drugs was beyond the reach of ordinary Iraqis, however, it hardly mattered. Meanwhile, anesthesia was in such short supply that limbs were being reset and appendixes removed without it. Surgery, in any event, was a gamble: The operating rooms in government hospitals were so contaminated that infection was nearly guaranteed. Only the very rich had access to competent medical care. At the same time, the hospitals were filling with people exhibiting the same ailments that soaring numbers of Gulf War veterans in the West were complaining of. There was no doubt in my mind: Saddam had stricken his own people with biological or chemical weapons.

The cost of the war came home one day when a friend described the starvation death of his neighbor, a young war widow. One of her babies was found dead next to her corpse, but the other was still suckling at her breast. Since I used to live in the neighborhood, the tragedy was particularly sad. But what also made my friend and me angry was that the woman was a devout Muslim who lived not far from the neighborhood mosque where Friday prayers were held. Instead of the mullah looking to the needs of his flock, he wasted his time on fiery speeches about the evil Americans and kept donations for the poor to himself.

In contrast, Iraq's Christians, some 850,000 strong before the war, seemed to me to take better care of their people. The priests, mostly Chaldean Catholics, personally knew the needy among their flock and turned their churches into distribution centers for food and medicine. To my amazement, a Christian friend told me proudly that his own brother had cut him out of the food line because he was considered too well off.

Unlike the mullahs, who seemed indifferent to the poor in whose names they collected donations, Christian priests eschewed lavish lifestyles. You never saw them driving around in shiny luxury cars, as you commonly did the mullahs. To be fair, rich Muslims who donated alms for the poor never seemed to complain about the mullahs squandering their money. It was just the timeless way of doing things in Iraq, where Saddam weeded out any clerics who showed a less than slavish enthusiasm for his own Friday sermons. In religion, as with everything else in Iraq, loyalty flowed up, not down where it was needed.

Crime, meanwhile, mushroomed in the wake of the war. Army deserters and defeated Shia rebels alike wandered the towns and cities, breaking into houses for food and cash. It was not unusual for an overnight bus to arrive someplace with its passengers stripped of everything they owned, including their clothes. Women were often abducted from the buses or their homes. Murders of whole families were common in Baghdad's neighborhoods, too, leading me to suspect that government death squads were carrying out political hits under the cover of the economic chaos. There was no shortage of executioners and assassins. The long war with Iran had created a surplus of hit men. A generation of interrogators had been trained to torture people without regard to due process. Now they were let loose on the population, gunmen for hire.

Complaining to the police was useless. Even honest cops said they were incapable of protecting anyone because they didn't have the money to keep squad cars on the street. They advised people to make "citizen's arrests," then demanded pay for the paperwork. No such deprivations were visited upon the internal security organs protecting Saddam, his family, and cronies, who continued to live in luxury. Only ordinary Iraqis had to fend for themselves.

With conditions deteriorating, I put down money on a second ranch, this one near Taji, thirty miles north of Baghdad. The purchase served two objectives, the first to make ourselves more self-sufficient, the second to lull the regime into thinking that I was staying. With defections common, the security organs had formed close links with land-registration and sales offices. If someone sold off a house or large parcel of land, the agents quickly took note; names went on the watch lists at border controls. Before the embargo grounded Iraqi Air flights abroad, the agents dragged a friend of mine off a plane leaving Baghdad. It turned out to be a case of mistaken identity, but the lesson was not lost on me. The border controls kept a list of any official who'd sold a house.

The new ranch was suitable for an even more important purpose: It was located off a seldom-traveled road ten miles west of the highway from Baghdad to Mosul, the main route for my planned escape to the north.

Soon after I arrived, however, I found I wasn't the only person looking for a discreet hideaway. The ranch next to mine, it turned out, housed a secret training camp for Palestinian commandos.

I learned about the camp entirely by accident. The ranch, about eight miles north of the village, had a reputation for growing high-quality vegetables in a maze of greenhouses. I decided to stop by one day to investigate. With Iraq's food shortages, truck farming was a lucrative line of business, and I was looking for any means possible to fatten my nest egg for an escape.

The wiry young man who came out of the main house greeted me warily until I told him I was his neighbor.

"Oh, you must be Dr. Hamza," he said with a smile, offering a handshake. "I am Abu-Khalid."

I took his hand, surprised. How did he know my name?

He chuckled. "Everybody around here is investigated before they can buy land," he said.

He didn't look to me like the usual Mukhabarat agent. Even after all the years in Saddam's Iraq, I was caught off-guard. "I didn't realize I was in some kind of special security zone," I joked.

He laughed and waved it off. "I'll explain it to you some other time," he said. "Meanwhile, take all the vegetables you want." His cockiness was unnerving.

A few days later, the young man dropped by my place for a visit. I made tea and put out a few snacks. Clearly, he knew who I was, if not all the details. At one point he addressed me as "general," but I brushed it aside. We talked farming. I told him I was considering going into the vegetable business. Then, as casually as possible, I asked, "Who owns your ranch?"

He hesitated.

"I guess it's all right to tell a man like you," he finally said. "It belongs to President Arafat." Yasser Arafat, chief of the Palestinian Liberation Organization, the PLO.

"It's about six hundred acres, all in all," he continued. "President Saddam gave it as a gift to our president. He has other ranches in Iraq, as you probably know." I did. There were about a half dozen, I recalled. "This one supplies our people with vegetables but, as you saw, we're building more things, including some chicken sheds. By the time we're finished we should be completely self-sufficient."

He smiled in evident pride. I managed to mumble "That's fantastic," but having a PLO operation next to my ranch, needless to say, gave me pause. It could only draw more of Saddam's security people. On the other hand, it certainly made the neighborhood safe, no small benefit in postwar Iraq. "Abu-Khalid," certainly a *nom de guerre*, hired himself out to organize security for other ranches, and, unlike other parts of the country where break-ins were rampant, the area around Taji never had a problem with thieves.

Over time, as I got to know Abu-Khalid, I learned that the ranch was a major sanctuary for PLO guerrillas. In exchange for providing a safe haven for the PLO, Saddam got the use of its veteran fighters for anything he wanted. But it was also a training base, he indicated, where Iraqi operators passed along their expertise in unconventional warfare to PLO recruits.

What I found provocative was Abu-Khalid's description of some of the training missions, which, he confided over time, took the budding commandos to Kuwait and Saudi Arabia.

"We enter Kuwait clandestinely by night," Abu-Khalid told me one day with enthusiasm, describing how they neutralize border controls. "Mostly we stay away from populated areas." Kuwait was the main training ground, he added. "Only rarely do we go to Saudi."

Each trainee carried a device they were required to plant at their targets, including "major water reservoirs and food storage areas," he said. "On some missions we even wear gas masks and special protective suits." He was coy about divulging further details, beyond saying they were required to bring back a photo of the device on the target taken with "a special camera." But he clearly meant to imply that they were training to plant chemical or biological weapons abroad.

Over the months, I was led to believe there were many groups like this. A constant stream of recruits passed through the nearby ranch en route to tactical training camps elsewhere, he said. There they fired weapons and ate only what they could forage or capture, sometimes the raw meat of rabbits or rodents. It was classic commando training, I knew, but for what?

Hitting Israel, I assumed, or perhaps U.S.-occupied Kuwait. Saddam had the weapons, the PLO had the means, and using Palestinians to plant the devices abroad gave Saddam some measure of deniability, even if his support for the PLO was open and of long standing. Virtually every Middle Eastern guerrilla group had at least toyed with the idea of using chemical and biological weapons, I knew, but only Iraq and a few other rogue states actually possessed them. The arrangement also fit with Saddam's way of doing things. He had permitted an Iranian opposition group, the Mujahideen Khalq, to operate from Iraqi soil, but he also drafted them into action against their own people during the Iran-Iraq war. According to a friend, they'd been forced to fire some of the chemical weapons on the Iranian Revolutionary Guards.

But the truth of Abu-Khalid's disclosures was hard to measure. After Desert Storm, Iraqis were constantly slipping back and forth across the Saudi border to visit refugee and POW camps, so developing targets there could not be ruled out. Hitting Kuwait, or attacking U.S. units there with biological or chemical weapons, would also be a means of avenging a loss that stuck in Saddam's craw. Israel was always a target, but its border controls were tough.

But PLO recruits weren't Bedouins at home in the desert. They were city boys from the slums of Gaza. To carry out training missions as Abu-Khalid described them, they'd have to jump off from camps in the south and not from anywhere near my ranch, which would require them to navigate the trackless sands. Yet, as with most things in Saddam's Iraq, almost anything was possible.

I decided to sell the ranch, for the simple reason that if Abu-Khalid was right and his secret were leaked, everybody in the area would be suspect. And in that case, Saddam's men would not waste time sorting out the innocent from the guilty. We'd all be hung by our thumbs until somebody confessed.

Over the years I remained curious about Abu-Khalid's tale. I never came across an independent corroboration, but one thing stuck in my mind. On a cold day in January 1994, when I stopped by his ranch for the last time, he greeted me with the embrace of a fellow revolutionary after a long separation.

"I just came back from a trip," he said with a wink. "It was fun."

Oddly enough, for all of President Bush's dire alarms about Iraq's nuclear program, only three of our seven major nuclear sites had been destroyed in Desert Storm. My weapons-development site at Al-Atheer survived essentially intact, with only the explosives bunker damaged when a pilot evidently unloaded a bomb returning from another target. The bunker, built with several feet of reinforced concrete and set on sophisticated shock absorbers, merely tipped over when it was hit. It was so sturdy that, after the war, the

International Atomic Energy Agency couldn't even blow it up. They finally filled it with eighty truckloads of cement.

Baghdad was swarming with inspectors from the United Nations Special Commission on Iraq, known as UNSCOM, who were charged with making sure Iraq destroyed its strategic arms, from missiles to remnants of its chemical and biological programs. The IAEA was responsible for nuclear weapons. From the beginning, of course, the inspections were an elaborate cat-and-mouse game, the kind at which Saddam excelled. He declared that Atomic Energy was being split into several groups to rebuild the country's infrastructure, such as power plants and electrical grids. In reality, AE's Group Number Four was transferred to the Technical Training Institute adjacent to the Saddam Bridge, where it continued to work on the design and components of a nuclear bomb. Likewise, al-Azawi's explosives group, which Iraq had declared destroyed during Allied raids on Al-Qaqaa, was hidden in a Baghdad military barracks and continued its experiments.

AE's Computer Center, likewise, was retooled and parts of it hidden in downtown Baghdad. Although some AE programmers had fled to the Gulf states before the war, the best ones who stayed were relocated to a new company called Babylon Software. Ostensibly, its job was to support various government agencies in the rebuilding effort, but the programmers soon found that their major contracts were with the Mukhabarat and classified. Their headquarters was tightly guarded.

I knew many of the programmers, having launched the Computer Center and hired many of its people over the years, so I started poking around. They told me they'd initially been recruited to work on computer viruses and virus-protection programs, and had been provided with an extensive array of imported software. Some programmers, I was told, were sent to Amman, Jordan, so they could order more equipment through Jordanian front companies.

Next they were put to work as hackers, with the explanation that they needed to become familiar with techniques to protect Iraq's computers. After a while, however, the better ones were segregated into a highly compartmented unit and tasked with breaking into foreign networks. In some cases, their mission was to download sensitive information; in others, to infect the foreign computers with viruses that would destroy their files. Gradually, I was told, the hackers accumulated enough experience to break into computers with moderately difficult protective systems. Bonuses were awarded for hacking into more sophisticated systems. Eastern European and Russian computer technicians were also brought to Babylon, I was told. Whatever the case, Babylon Software became Iraq's largest employer of programmers, even though it produced no visible software products, its only work was classified, and its only customer was the Mukhabarat.

Iraq had long been expert at deception, of course, so foiling UNSCOM or IAEA inspectors was nothing new. Talib Jindeel, an old hand in AE's physics department, for example, made a before-and-after videotape of nuclear equipment allegedly being destroyed. To the inspectors, that meant Iraq could no longer enrich uranium. They were wrong.

Jindeel's schoolboy trick pointed up a weakness in UNSCOM's approach, which concentrated on the capture of equipment and documents. Finding and facilitating the defection of scientists was beyond its mandate. That was a double loss for the West, because Saddam kept his captive weapons makers at work. In the meantime, superficial, incomplete, and even phony documents were served up to mislead the eager inspectors.

In September 1991, for example, a joint team of inspectors from UNSCOM and the IAEA, led by David Kay, barged into my old office in the high-rise across from the Al-Rashid Hotel. Ibrahim Saeed, my former boss, was in the process of clearing the building of sensitive documents and materials. Kay saw a big metal box in plain sight and pounced on it. Inside were hundreds of files about the bomb program, including a full list of employees with their pay and employment grades—a virtual Rosetta stone for the program.

Kay thumbed through a few documents and immediately understood their significance. His team latched on to them like a rugby scrum and made for the exit. The Iraqis, belatedly figuring out what was going on, cut them off in the parking lot and blocked the exits. Thus began a tense, three-day confrontation that riveted the world's attention on Baghdad and Saddam's effort to hide the weapons programs. Under a brutal, searing sun, neither side would give in.

I didn't understand, at first, what Saddam thought he could accomplish by such tactics. Under U.N. resolutions he could comply with the inspections, get the embargo lifted, and conspire to fight another day. If he dug in his heels, he risked another round of bombing. In fact, David Kay was making that perfectly clear in an adroit stream of interviews with the international press corps in the parking lot outside my old building. Saddam risked retaliation if he didn't cooperate. He had put himself in the headlines once again, just as the world had forgotten about him.

On the other hand, the United States had made it clear that sanctions would stay in place as long as Saddam did, no matter what happened with UNSCOM. So he had little to lose. He decided on a tactic of not complying but appearing to comply. (Later that would change.) For months he'd allowed U.N. teams to go through various stages of weapons "discovery" and then slammed the door, provoking a stalemate. That was what was happening in the parking lot. Finally, however, a compromise was reached that allowed Iraq to inventory the documents Kay had before they were taken away.

Now another deception plan kicked into gear. Saddam sent a team headed by my former assistant in the AE theory group, Mohammed Habib, through the rear door of the building. As documents were being inventoried by Iraqi officials, they were slipped to Habib's experts, who stealthily erased critical data, removed important papers, and doctored others with half truths to mislead the inspectors. Only then were they handed back.

Kay's people left with a box full of tainted documents. For years afterward UNSCOM, as well as Washington, believed that my facility at Al-Atheer was no more than a material sciences lab, where bomb designs were merely explored and no more. The extent of the nuclear program, as well as its ongoing work, remained hidden.

In contrast, one incident underscored the value of defectors in penetrating Saddam's smokescreen. For months the IAEA had accepted Iraq's explanation that its huge magnets had been used for maintenance at power stations. Finally, however, information supplied months earlier by AE defector Ibrahim Bawi made its way to the IAEA. Photos of the Tarmiya magnetic enrichment plant, analyzed by experts at the Oak Ridge laboratory in Tennessee, were recognized for what they were: proof that Iraq had a uranium enrichment program. And incredibly, Iraqi intelligence had failed to clean out Bawi's office. IAEA inspectors went there and harvested everything he had left.

Events like that had consequences for Iraqi officials, of course. Saeed paid for Kay's discovery of the nuclear documents in my old office with a demotion of two grades in pay—a slap on the wrist that could only be explained by some hidden financial arrangement between him and Saddam. The demotion was rescinded later, with the official explanation that Saeed had given the Baath Party years of loyal service. Those farther down the chain of command, however, did not fare so well. Imad Khadouri and the AE documents group he headed were all jailed in harsh conditions for a month, then permanently demoted in pay. Upon release they were warned that if they screwed up again, the penalty would be far more severe.

AE's engineers, meanwhile, were being touted as national heroes for getting the electrical system back on its feet in only three months. The same went for telephones, oil refineries, new factories for chemicals, and even bridges: Much was working again, and AE was doing it all. A new, can-do spirit swept the beleaguered country, whose people were badly in need of a morale boost.

Naturally, Saddam joined in and drafted AE's engineers to build him a string of new, lavish palaces.

Meanwhile, like Gulf War veterans in America and elsewhere, the number of Iraqis falling ill with a mysterious soup of ailments—from skin rashes to headaches; neurological, intestinal, and lung problems; unbearable fatigue; birth deformities; and cancers, especially in the liver—continued to mount. The symptoms were showing up predominantly in the south and southwest, in the Shiite territories where chemical and biological weapons were cached in advance of Desert Storm and where, in some cases, the Allies blew them up, scattering their deadly spores to the wind.

Dr. Adnan Ayoubi, a friend and a neighbor of mine, was chief of surgery at the Jumhouria Hospital in Baghdad, Iraq's largest government hospital. A British-trained ethnic Kurd, Ayoubi was regarded as one of Iraq's best surgeons. He told me that, in the past, he usually saw twenty bowel cancers a year. Now he was seeing twice that number in a month. His colleagues were reporting spikes in other cancer rates. The pediatric wards, meanwhile, were becoming a nightmare, as a growing number of mothers just walked out after giving birth to deformed babies. Most of them were Shiites from the contaminated zones.

Gulf War Syndrome was well known to everybody in Iraq, but Saddam remained silent. In this he had a secret ally—the U.S. Pentagon, which continued to deny that there was proof of a war-based disease despite growing evidence to the contrary. But evidence soon leaked of Allied forces blowing up chemical dumps during the war, and of the U.S. government's efforts to suppress repeated reports of contamination by units during the conflict.

The conspiracy of silence has remained to this day. Saddam has no interest in confessing his use of chemical and biological weapons, nor does Washington, which would be confronted by an outraged people to do something about it—and Saddam—if the deliberate contamination became known. Both sides have suppressed the real causes of Gulf War Syndrome because it has been convenient for both. Saddam blames the sickness on malnutrition and drug shortages caused by the embargo, and Washington blames it on . . . nothing.

After the war, officials like me were prohibited from visiting Baghdad hotels or other public places frequented by UNSCOM inspectors. The regime figured, rightly, that we'd be tempted to contact a foreigner and run.

My friend Ahmed Numan had a chilling experience with one of the inspectors. U.S.-educated and fluent in English, Ahmed was assigned to the Iraqi team that dealt with UNSCOM. His attitude was friendly but careful, especially with the Americans, who often quizzed him on why he didn't return to the United States. One day one of them pressed a scrap of paper into his hand with his name and telephone number on it. Numan tucked it discreetly into his pocket and went home. At midnight, a security officer knocked on his door.

"Where is the paper?" he asked. Numan didn't even consider bluffing. He turned around, walked back into his house, retrieved the scrap of paper, and handed it over to the security man. It was a warning, he knew. A lot of questions and trouble would follow.

Many others had run. Jaffar's cook had disappeared with his

family on the eve of Desert Storm, reportedly surfacing in the United States. The cook's daughter had worked on Jaffar's personal staff, so there were suspicions that she had traded stolen nuclear documents for green cards for the whole family. We never knew.

Husham al-Shawi, a former chairman of AE and Iraq's ambassador to Canada, defected to England, together with the Iraqi ambassador to Spain. Then the ambassador to the United Nations, Mohammed al-Mashatt, defected to Canada (after the United States turned him down). The whirl of defections tempted me to discard a cover story I was carefully developing to explain an extended absence from Baghdad and just make a break for it, too. But then news would come of something like the fate of Muayed Naji, an engineer in our centrifuge uranium enrichment program, and I'd quickly reconsider.

Naji and his wife managed to get to Jordan with fake documents and plead for asylum at the U.S. embassy. After interviewing him, the CIA clumsily told him they would consider his petition, and they asked him to return later. He used the time to contact people for a job in Libya. Of course, Iraqi agents were all over Jordan like flies. A two-man hit team from Naji's own neighborhood in Baghdad approached him on an Amman street, hailed him with a friendly greeting, then shot him on the spot.

"Why?" he said, falling to his knees in front of his wife. "Why?" He bled to death on the street.

His assassins were arrested, then handed over to Iraq after solemn but empty pledges from Baghdad that they would never come back.

Jordan had long been servile to Saddam's needs, but the Naji incident prompted Iraq foreign minister Tariq Aziz to negotiate a secret arrangement with Jordan to return defectors to Iraq. The arrangement came to light when a secretary to Iraq's vice president, Izzat al-Douri, fled to Amman and contacted the Iraqi opposition there. When Baghdad charged that the secretary had taken cash from the vice president's safe, he was arrested by Jordanian authorities, returned to Iraq, and shot, reportedly by al-Douri himself. Now even the door to Jordan was locked.

If I needed confirmation that getting my whole family out without careful preparation was impossible, there was the case of Adil

Fayad, Jaffar's energetic mechanical engineer–turned–purchasing chief. Fayad handled several billion dollars yearly in foreign acquisitions for AE. As such, he had to know he was closely watched, yet he continued his homosexual forays despite having a wife and children. Security didn't mind, because Fayad's indiscretions just gave them another handle on him in a pinch. What they did take note of, however, was his contacts with foreign military contractors, especially those with intelligence connections. And Fayad must have done something wrong, for one day he turned up dead in a ditch at his ranch.

Fayad's longtime farmhand was arrested and charged with the murder, but it was an obvious frame-up. That night, about half a dozen distraught AE colleagues came to my house. None of them believed Fayad had been shot by his trusted helper. They wrung their hands and grieved in fear. Fayad's murder was the first in our own circle to be carried out by the regime, and they didn't know what to do.

I did. I was leaving, but on my own schedule, with my own carefully laid plans. In late 1992, I made my move.

The Baghdad stock market was an insider's game, a stacked deck for people with connections. Millions could be made by speculators who knew what the government was up to. And I did.

A friend from my student days in Florida, Talib Abbas, who'd become a stockbroker after retiring as vice president of Basra University, encouraged me to get in on the game. Buying stocks was like shooting fish in a barrel, he said. But we both knew it wouldn't last long. Eventually Saddam and his cronies would get involved and rig it for themselves. First, though, they had to fatten the Iraqis for the slaughter. It was only a matter of time.

As with any inside dealing, the key to making a bundle was advance word of a new stock, or initial public offering (IPO). With windfall profits from the sale of my Taji ranch, I was able to buy stock in several companies before they went public, in most cases earning profits of 2,000 percent or more in just a few months. In one transaction alone, I made the equivalent of a couple hundred thousand dollars on stocks of a new import firm owned by the chief of internal security, Saadon Shakir. I concentrated on food and auto part imports because, unlike Iraqis who believed Saddam would negotiate an end to the embargo, I knew he'd never give up his weapons. The economic embargo, likewise, would not be lifted soon.

People started to think of me as a financial whiz, which gave me another opening. I began to cut other officials in on my deals. My reputation grew as someone who would never think of leaving, which was exactly my idea. If the security people sniffed at my heels, moreover, the high officials I was helping could also turn them off.

Now I was ready to launch the next stage of my plan. My son Firas, now twenty-two, had already been discreetly scouting for someone who could smuggle me to the no-fly zone in the north. News trickling in from the region indicated that Iraqi opposition groups were well established and supported by the CIA. One of them, the Iraqi National Congress, was headed by my former schoolmate at MIT, Dr. Ahmad al-Chalabi. I was confident that if I could reach al-Chalabi he'd put me together with Americans, who I figured would gladly get all of us out in exchange for the information I had. All I needed was a persuasive cover story to explain my disappearance from Baghdad for a lengthy period of time.

I decided I'd make noisy plans to build a date syrup factory in my hometown of Diwaniyah. While date syrup is as popular with Iraqis as Vermont maple sugar is with Americans, shortages were common. Building a plant there would make sense.

But I needed more than plans. My story would have to hold up if government agents started sniffing around. So I went down to Diwaniyah and bought an option on an industrial site on the outskirts of town. Back in Baghdad, I showed pictures of it to all my friends and asked their opinion. Everybody, of course, loves to kibitz. Next, I got estimates for the plant and equipment, and showed those around. Finally, I applied for a sabbatical from my teaching duties and consulting at AE. Since I was making my bosses so much money, they granted it without a hitch. Greed was the new byword. The new attitude toward me, in fact, was amazing. I was the man with the golden touch. Every official I visited received me like royalty, even al-Ghafour.

Hussein Kamel, hypervigilant in the past, was no longer a threat either, thank God. In 1992, the removal of a brain tumor had left huge gaps in his memory. Two years after, he didn't even recognize the new chairman of Atomic Energy, a man he knew quite well. But I decided to steer clear of his office, on the odd chance that he'd spot me, not remember my face, and order up an investigation.

The next step was to disentangle myself from longtime friends and colleagues who might make inquiries in my absence and inadvertently stir up trouble. I began to act like a grouch and pick fights. I stopped calling people, and withdrew from dinners and other social events. One day I gave a longtime friend, a high Baath Party official, such a hard time that he said he'd never speak to me again. After a week or so of no calls, I knew he meant it.

Friends, indeed, began falling away. Looking back, it sickens me to think how badly I acted toward even my closest friends, people whom, in some cases, I'd known all my life. The targets of my obnoxious behavior included my brothers, who had no inkling of my plans to leave and were mystified by my change in behavior.

As was my wife, whom I excluded from my plans for the longest time out of fear that she would tell her sisters. They in turn would tell their husbands, who might tell others. It was just too dangerous. Only Firas, my eldest son, knew everything from the start.

Finally, however, it came time to tell her. I sat down with her and explained what was going on, reminding her in no uncertain terms of the consequences of letting out what I was about to tell her: death, or worse. She sat silently as I explained my recent behavior with our friends and told her what I had planned. Her eyes grew misty. She thought I'd stopped loving her, she said, or that maybe I'd become one of the regime's cold brutes, like so many others. Tears ran down her cheeks.

"No, my sweetheart," I murmured, putting an arm around her. "Never. That will never happen. I'm doing this so we'll have a chance at a better life. I have a good plan. And I'll be coming back to get you and the boys. I promise."

She sniffled on my chest, and I smoothed her silky black hair. We sat holding each other wordlessly for a long while. I said nothing of my plans to contact the CIA or my determination to reach America. And after all these years, she knew better than to ask any questions. Knowledge like that was too dangerous. Saddam's interrogators could wring it out of her in a minute.

The room darkened in the Baghdad twilight.

"But how will I manage without you?" she asked, prompting another flood of tears.

"Now, now," I whispered. "I've thought of that." I hugged her again, hoping I sounded more confident than I really was. We'd been together twenty-three years. Never had she really been alone to fend for herself. Even when I went abroad for months at a time, she had the protection of the regime and a steady flow of money. Now it would be different. If I disappeared without a trace, she could hardly ask them for help.

My mind flashed back to Diwaniyah and the shy Muslim girl who had shown up at my father's house so many years ago, captivating me with her beauty and laughter. Back then, especially after years of dating in America, I couldn't imagine myself in an arranged marriage. But it had worked—a mystery.

I took Souham's face in my hands. "Firas is a man now," I said. "He'll take care of you while I'm gone. And you've always gotten on well when I've been out of the country."

Privately, however, I worried. Firas had begun smoking heavily with the stress of recent months, pacing the floor, peering out the window for surveillance. If something went wrong, I guessed that he'd be the first to be picked up and questioned, and he'd eventually spill the whole story. He was only human, and a boy at that. I made no mention of that as I handed over to Souham the document that gave her power of attorney for our affairs.

That night, Souham screamed in her sleep.

It was too late to turn back. Firas had a friend who had a friend in the army. The officer was a Kurd, who was very privately opposed to the regime. "Adnan" had gotten others out before.

Firas began bringing him by, and a subtle, tingling dance began. We each knew the risks of misplaced trust. We each knew how efficiently Saddam's police had turned friends against friends, neighbors against neighbors, children against parents. Iraq had become a Soviet-style state without the hammer and sickle. Trust was a luxury we couldn't afford.

Adnan and I ate, we drank, we had coffee, watched television, played cards. For weeks neither of us dared broach the subject, which floated above us like a bomb. Finally, Adnan asked why a high official like me, with so many privileges and so much money, seemed so unhappy?

I took a deep breath, then I poured out my laments about Saddam, who had done so many good things for Iraq in his early years, despite his undeniably violent record. But long ago he had crossed a line, I said. He'd dragged us into two wars, gassed his own people, made Iraq an international pariah, and turned the country into a kleptocracy for his friends. The hospitals were filled, children were starving.

Adnan looked into my eyes.

"Okay, my friend," he said. "When do you want to leave?"

———

CHAPTER FOURTEEN

THE FUGITIVE

"Hello, Dr. Hamza, this is the CIA, in Washington, D.C."

The voice sounded as if it were coming through electrical coils. In fact it was originating in a cubicle at CIA headquarters in Langley, Virginia, ten thousand miles away. From there it bounced off a satellite and down to the Netherlands, where it was pinged off another satellite to Ahmad al-Chalabi's headquarters in the no-fly zone of the Kurdish north. I'd finally escaped.

It was the moment I'd been anticipating for so many years. Al-Chalabi, my corpulent patron, many years past his svelte days when we'd been schoolmates at MIT, sat across the upstairs desk from me, listening hopefully. He was chief of the Iraqi National Congress, an umbrella organization that joined together all exile opposition groups in the north.

The transmission from Washington was clear enough. And it was completely secure, al-Chalabi assured me. I'd used it to call home and let Souham know I'd arrived in the north safely, albeit using code words we'd agreed on before. Our boy Firas had gotten back all right as well with the half-dinar note, she said. Suddenly, everything seemed great.

The CIA man called himself Bob.

"Tell us about yourself, Dr. Hamza," he said evenly, as if it were a job interview. That was the first of my surprises, since I thought al-Chalabi had told them everything before. Surely they'd checked me out during the many hours after his call alerting them to my arrival. Al-Chalabi and I had sat at the table for hours waiting for the call-back, picking at our food and exhausting every topic, from our student days at MIT to gossip about Saddam and the situation in the north.

What were they waiting for? My school records were public. Plus, many other defectors had come before me.

But Bob wanted the basics. I took a breath and told him about my master's degree at MIT, my Ph.D. in nuclear physics from Florida State University, and my years teaching at both FSU and tiny Fort Valley State College in Georgia. He merely murmured assent, with a hint of boredom, but I plowed onward.

I recounted how I'd returned to Iraq in 1970 and headed up AE's physics department. I'd become an adviser to AE's chairman and then later, head of nuclear weaponization. . . .

"Right," Bob said.

"I started the Al-Atheer nuclear weapons site . . ."

"Nuclear weapons at Al-Atheer?" he asked, sounding incredulous.

"Yes," I said, puzzled. I glanced at al-Chalabi and continued. I'd represented Iraq at the International Atomic Energy Agency, I said, and at United Nations conferences.

"Earlier, I'd started the uranium enrichment by diffusion," I said. "I worked with Jaffar Dhia Jaffar on the establishment of the enrichment program. . . ."

"Right," he said again, sounding amused. I told him about Saddam's order for the "crash program" to build a bomb before the war. . . .

Now I heard the unmistakable sounds of a snicker. What was going on? Did he think I was making this up? Before I had a chance to ask, he interrupted.

"Dr. Hamza," he said lightly, "I have a nuclear expert with me here. He's on the other line. He knows everything about atomic weapons. He's going to ask you some questions, and if you'll cooperate with him completely we'd be grateful."

I was still rattled by the strange experience of the past few minutes, but not so much that I'd lost my wits. Al-Chalabi had emphatically warned me that the CIA would try to wring everything it could from me for nothing. If pushed, they might offer me money, but that wasn't what I'd risked my life for. I had plenty of money. Al-Chalabi strongly advised me to hold out for resettlement before I handed over the family jewels.

"On what terms?" I answered. "I can't give you any serious information until I get a commitment from you for asylum in America for me and my family."

Bob sighed, and then his voice turned steely. "I am afraid that is going to be very difficult," he said. "Answer his questions first, so we can confirm who you really are."

Now I dug in my own heels. I'd dealt with tougher guys than this bureaucrat in Washington.

"If you don't know who I really am, after three years of UNSCOM and IAEA inspections, then you don't know much about the Iraqi nuclear program," I said. Then I took a deep breath and calmed down. I ticked off the names of previous defectors who knew me. I repeated the dates of my attendance at MIT and Florida State. Surely those were in their files, or they could easily confirm them.

Then a different, thinner voice came on the line.

"Dr. Hamza, I am a nuclear scientist. I know all there is to know about atomic bombs. You tell me, in as much detail as you can, about the program, and we'll straighten this out."

I sighed. I considered hanging up right there. But then I remembered all the years I'd spent preparing for this. I thought of Souham and the boys, depending on me to get them out. My mind flashed on Saddam's secret police, and the long trip from Baghdad over the mountains.

But I also remembered the story al-Chalabi had told me about my old friend Mouafaq, a researcher in AE's biology department who'd come out two years before. A pleasant, low-key fellow, he'd palmed himself off to the CIA as a Ph.D. scientist and high-level AE official. Without checking him out, the CIA had flown him to Turkey, offered him resettlement in the United States, and taken over the entire floor of a posh hotel for a week's debriefing. Mouafaq gave plenty to the CIA, from AE's organization to the names of key personnel. But when they learned he'd puffed up his credentials, al-Chalabi said, they dropped him like a rock. When he woke up in the morning, the agents were gone.

A cautionary tale, al-Chalabi put it.

Now I was paying for Mouafaq's nervous foolishness, and perhaps al-Chalabi's as well, for backing up Mouafaq's bona fides without more care. Now the CIA was responding by not budging an inch with me. But I couldn't turn over everything I knew without at least the possibility of getting my family into the States. I understood why the CIA might feel burned because of Mouafaq, but that was their mistake, not mine. I wasn't a low-level official. I had designed Saddam's bomb. That should be easy enough for them to confirm. I also knew about the chemical and biological programs.

"I will answer you in a limited way," I told the CIA man. "But until I get an acceptable deal I just won't answer all the questions you have about the nuclear program. I will, however, give you enough to establish my identity, and then we can take it from there."

The CIA scientist answered with a moment's silence. Then he said, "Well, okay, we'll do that, Dr. Hamza, but first tell me about . . ."

I shook my head. The man was unspooling a complicated question about uranium enrichment. I let the phone dangle in my hand for a few seconds, then I came back on the line.

"Look, sir. Please try to understand. I am not going to talk to you until you offer me and my family some sort of sanctuary. That's the deal. That's the whole reason I've risked my life to get here."

The line went silent again.

"I could have left on my own years ago if I was willing to leave my family behind," I continued. "So, now, you've got to at least promise that you'll give this your very serious consideration, or I just won't talk. I'm sorry."

The scientist muffled the phone. I could hear him talking to someone else, then "Bob" came on the line again.

"What seems to be the problem?"

"What seems to be the problem?" I repeated. "The problem is that your other guy wants to keep asking me questions about the program."

"And why don't you tell him?"

I was ready to scream. "Because I told you. I will not answer questions about the bomb program until you *promise* that you will at least seriously consider taking me and my family in. And you must take some steps to show your good faith."

There was a big sigh on the other end of the line.

"Well, that's very difficult to arrange," he said, brushing off any possibility. Suddenly I remembered their mocking chuckles when I

274

told them about Al-Atheer and the bomb. They were treating me like a fool. I was tired. I lost my temper.

"You gave sanctuary without hesitating to twenty thousand Cubans," I said. "A lot of them are jailbirds. Why can't you do the same for me and my family? I'm a hell of a lot more educated than they are. And I'm not going to be causing you problems."

The CIA man sounded like he was stifling a yawn.

"That's different," he said. "We can't do the same thing for you."

I was speechless. What kind of intelligence agency was this? I didn't know what else to say.

"Well," I finally said, "good-bye then." I handed al-Chalabi the phone. Walking out of the room, I heard him say something like, "Well, he seemed to know what he was talking about."

Downstairs, I smoldered. Sure, my pride was bruised; I'd been dismissed like a nobody. But there was more at stake than my ego, or even my uncertain future. The CIA's chortling response to my answers told me they had no idea how far we'd gotten with the bomb. They didn't seem to know who I was. They had no idea that our scientists were still working on bomb design and explosive lenses in new, hidden locations in and around Baghdad. It sounded to me as if they'd been lulled by Saddam's phony documents, or blinded by his concealment schemes, or numbed by a stream of low-level defectors. I'd learn later that Iraqis had been turning up every week at U.S. embassies all over the Middle East claiming to be Saddam's bombmakers, clutching childish diagrams. But that was no excuse: The CIA was the leading superpower's principal espionage agency, with thirty thousand employees and a six-billion-dollar budget. Supposedly, Iraq was an important target. Separating fact from fiction was its job. And I'd just been turned away. It blew my mind.

Another problem with his demand for instant information was that it jeopardized my family. If the CIA passed my information to the IAEA and the IAEA acted on details I provided, Iraq would quickly trace the source. Since I was the only senior figure missing, they would know it was me. I had to secure my family first, but Bob refused to listen.

When al-Chalabi came back downstairs, I chuckled ruefully, remembering a spy thriller in which a CIA director played by Henry

Fonda knows everything about a Russian defector, Yul Brynner, within minutes after he turns up. The CIA even has videotapes of him in its archive. What a joke. On me.

"Don't give up so easily," al-Chalabi said, plopping into his chair. "These guys are usually suspicious."

I sighed. "Yeah, but this one's supposed to be an Iraq specialist in the CIA. I explained the danger my family is in, but he doesn't seem to care. He should give me some slack, but he's totally indifferent. Besides, all they can think about is Saddam's weapons and equipment. There's no attempt to try to find out who the scientists are and what they think. They can take away all of Saddam's equipment, but he knows how to replace it. Even with the embargo he can buy it through his network. To find out how he does it they have to talk to people like me."

Al-Chalabi shrugged. He looked very tired. Outside the window the sky was smudged with gray. The sun would be up in an hour.

I couldn't stop talking. "Both of these guys are supposed to be experts on Iraq, but aside from Jaffar, I have the feeling they didn't recognize any of the names I mentioned," I complained. "How can they disarm Iraq that way? Who are they talking to?"

Al-Chalabi was silent. Little did I know that he had fallen out of favor with the CIA, not because of the fiasco with Mouafaq but for an earlier episode when he tried to stampede the United States into a military intervention in northern Iraq. The White House consensus was that al-Chalabi was "poison," but I didn't know it then. To me, he was still a generous patron. He was trying to help me get out.

"Look," he finally said, "you can bring your family here. I'll have my chief of security arrange for somebody to bring them out along the same route you came. If the Americans don't give you sanctuary, I can arrange for you to settle somewhere in Europe, most likely Holland. I can get you through Syria to Lebanon and you can fly from there. Meanwhile, I can give you a salary, about seven hundred dollars a month, and you can stay here. You can live well here on that, and you'd have a house and guards and a car. Until we solve this problem, you can work with me."

I nodded. It was a generous offer. Even two hundred dollars a month would be more than sufficient to live on there. But it was a dangerous neighborhood. Al-Chalabi's house had already been fire-bombed once by Saddam's agents. Few things were secret for long here, and I had little doubt my identity would soon seep out.

Nor did I like the idea of going to Holland. I'd never spent any time there. I was sure it was a nice place for its own people, but I didn't know its language or culture. In general, moreover, Europeans hated the Iraqi refugees who were washing up at their borders. Living on the dole as foreigners didn't appeal to me. And what would I do for work?

No, I thought, I risked all this to go to the United States, a heterogeneous society where my sons could get a new start, a place where we could eventually become citizens. Refugee status here or in Europe looked like a dead end.

Al-Chalabi urged me not to give up on the CIA, but I had slim hopes they would reconsider. The way I saw it, they'd dismissed me out of hand. On a practical level, however, I couldn't just sit around and mope. That just wasn't my nature. So I tepidly accepted al-Chalabi's offer, met with his chief of security to go over a plan to get my family out of Baghdad, and moved into a house he provided—after dismissing the guards, who I knew would just draw more attention. At the same time, I decided to explore every possible alternative.

The other exile opposition group operating in the north was the Iraqi National Accord, headed by Dr. Ayad Allawi, one of Saddam's former physicians. Allawi was smart enough to get out of Baghdad in the early 1970s, as Saddam was consolidating his grip on the regime. But Iraqi agents caught up with him in London. Two gunmen entered his house. His wife woke up and started screaming. They killed her but only wounded Allawi, who was able to escape. By 1994, he was one of the oldest hands in the Iraqi opposition abroad.

Unlike al-Chalabi's headquarters, the INA offices were low-key and spare, with only a few exiles permitted to hang out and gossip. Samir, an untalkative Kurd, ran a tight ship, restricting access to a locked room with a radio transmitter and a satellite phone linking the office to London.

A few days after my dispiriting encounter with the CIA, Samir came looking for me and handed me an envelope. It was a fax from Allawi, congratulating me for my successful escape and welcoming me to the growing ranks of Iraqis fighting to bring democracy to our country. He offered his services in any way he could be of assistance, particularly in getting resettled safely abroad. Relative to that, he had a list of questions.

I read down the list. The questions were all about the nuclear program.

"Dr. Allawi would like to talk to you," Samir said. We drove to INA headquarters, a large house on a treeless ridge overlooking the Kurdish valley. A forest of antennae sprouted from the roof. In the communications room, Samir punched in the numbers for London. After a few words with somebody there, he handed me the phone.

It was Allawi. "How are you, Dr. Hamza?" he said slowly and respectfully. His baritone was measured and reassuring. We exchanged a few pleasantries, then he said, "Dr. Hamza, we have a secure, encoded communication system here through the satellite phone. Nobody can listen in on us. You can talk openly and freely on this system. Do you feel we can discuss things now?"

"Yes," I said. "Your secretary here, Samir, gave me a list of questions. But I should tell you I can't answer those questions without some understanding of what's going on."

"Well, if you must know," Allawi said soothingly, "Dr. al-Chalabi reported you to both intelligence agencies, the one in Washington and the one here in London. I am of the mind of giving you a choice, and this is the purpose of my call. The British here have agreed to provide you safe haven and a salary of three thousand pounds a month"—about five thousand dollars. "If you say yes, we will make all the necessary arrangements and I can get you out of the north right away."

Now we're getting somewhere, I thought. No hassles or headaches. No haggling, no questioning my bona fides. These guys knew who I was and how to do things. My spirits soared.

"Very good," I said. "But what about my family? Without a safe haven for them, it's pointless for me to come. As soon as Saddam finds out I'm there he'll slaughter my family. You, of all people, should know that."

"Yes," Allawi murmured. "Yes, of course I understand."

"I can have my family up here in a few days," I added.

"I understand," Allawi said again. "But, unfortunately, I have no authorization to offer you anything for your family. If you come to London, we can work on it. But I can't promise anything."

I sighed. The roller coaster was racing downhill again. The phone suddenly felt slippery in my hand.

"I know that may not be satisfactory," Allawi added apologetically.

"Well, Dr. Allawi," I finally managed. "I thank you very much. You've been very kind. I appreciate your unconditional offer. Please thank your British friends for me.

"But I just can't do it. Without my family, my escape is meaningless. I can't go public against Saddam, I can't join any meaningful effort in exposing his lies and schemes. I can't leave my family to face a horrible fate if I do anything rash."

Allawi again murmured understanding.

"So I think for the time being, I'll stick with al-Chalabi," I said, "and see what happens. Any information I gave you right now would affect the IAEA inspections and Saddam would trace it right to me, since I'm the only figure in the nuclear program who's not under his thumb these days. He'll ask where I am. My family would be doomed."

"I understand," Allawi said. "I'm sorry we can't do more for you right now."

"I am, too," I answered wearily. "But I appreciate your offer. It's certainly more than the Americans offered, which was nothing."

We exchanged amiable farewells, and that was that. I hung up.

Now what?

No America, no U.K. No going back. Where else could I go? Iraqis didn't have many options. Only four countries allowed us in once the embargo was slapped on Iraq after the invasion of Kuwait: Turkey, Jordan, Sudan, and Libya. Turkey limited visits to only two weeks, and visas were hard to come by. Jordan was unacceptable, because I might be recognized and Saddam's assassins were crawling all over the place. Sudan, another Islamic dictatorship with close links to Saddam, was too far away even if I wanted to go there.

That left Libya, another rogue nation with a megalomaniac at the top. Many professional Iraqis had landed there, not because they wanted to trade one house of horrors for another, but merely because they could get in. Muammar Khadafy, vying with Saddam for leadership of the Arab world, welcomed Iraqis. For his part, Saddam was more forgiving of Iraqis who settled there, because at least they weren't likely to be talking to Americans, who had no diplomatic relations or embassy there. For me, however, Libya could only be a temporary solution, because Khadafy would inevitably pressure me to help him build his own nuclear bomb.

I reached into my pocket and pulled out a piece of paper. I'd saved it for just this worst-case scenario. It was a letter from a former AE colleague offering me a teaching job at a small university near Tripoli.

The only route to Libya was overland through Turkey, and then by ship from the Mediterranean port of Izmir. But since my old passport had expired, I first needed papers. To see what the possibilities of buying a new passport were, I decided to take a bus to Dohuk, the dusty smuggling capital of the north, four hours up the winding mountain road toward Turkey. The brother of Adnan, the Kurd who'd taken me out of Baghdad, worked for one of the Kurdish faction's security services there, and if anybody could fix me up, he could.

The legend of Kurdish smuggling came alive on the hairpin turns through the mountains, as black market gasoline tankers came careening down the rock-strewn highway past our column of overloaded buses and trucks chugging up the road. Everything was for sale here, but one of the region's biggest exports was hashish, sold in one-kilo bricks that earned immense profits for the Kurds as well as their overseers in Iraq, Iran, and Turkey. The pious Muslims Saddam Hussein and the ayatollahs of Iran allowed the Kurds to export drugs while applying the death penalty for their use at home. The unspoken rationale, of course, was that keeping their own societies clean while addicting the West was a sound, anti-imperialist strategy. But the money cut closer to the truth. Saddam's son Uday had a piece of the action.

Two Kurdish factions vied for dominance of the region, Massoud Barzani's Peoples Democratic Party of Kurdistan (PDK), and the Peoples Democratic Union (PUK), led by Jalal Talabani. Ideologically, there was little daylight between them; clan always trumped politics among the Kurds. Barazani held sway over the region around Dohuk, but Talabani's people were always challenging his rule, making the region a powder keg that Saddam was always ready to ignite. Al-Chalabi was constantly trying to broker a peace between the two, but by his own dolorous account he'd failed, giving me just one more reason to get out of the area as fast as I could.

Dohuk's hotels were full of Iraqis and their families waiting to be smuggled into Turkey by the Kurds, but it was a very dangerous gambit. The Turkish army was fighting its own Kurdish insurgency and hypervigilant. Once caught, the refugees were stripped of their belongings and trucked back to Iraq, where they were jailed, tortured, and often even murdered. After hearing a few graphic stories, I decided to buy a passport.

Adnan's brother took me to a "tourist agency" that was run by a genial, compact Kurd in his mid-forties. He had an Iraqi passport for me, stamped and ready to go, in my own name. Before I left, however, I asked about foreign passports, whereupon he opened a drawer and nonchalantly tossed a stack on the table. He pointed to a blue one. It was American.

"That one's about your age and appearance," he said. "It's two thousand dollars." I picked it up and opened it. The picture of a smiling brown-haired man, age fifty-two, looked up from the page.

"I separated out the passports that might fit you," the proprietor said, fingering the stack. "You speak good English, so you could use almost any of these. I wouldn't recommend a Swedish one, however. The Turks are getting suspicious and have Swedish translators these days. If they start asking questions, you could end up in jail and deported to Iraq."

I studied the U.S. passport, which, like the others, had been stolen from a tourist in Turkey. This one had an Anglo name that would immediately cause me problems, even after my own picture was glued into the space. But there were other reasons I didn't like the idea. U.S. law permanently barred anyone from entering who'd been caught using a false passport. More important, I just couldn't steal another man's identity. I had lived cleanly all my life, except for working on Saddam's bomb. I wasn't about to start my new life as a common criminal. I handed back the passport, paid him for the Iraqi one, and left.

Back at my hotel, I found al-Chalabi's man waiting for me.

"Where have you been?" he said urgently. "We've been looking all over for you. Dr. al-Chalabi wants to see you right away." He ushered me into an SUV and we raced down the highway toward Salahiddin. Four hair-raising hours later, dirty, sweating, and tired, I walked into al-Chalabi's office. He looked very nervous.

The CIA had called again, he said. They wanted to talk to me. We had to go right to his house and call back.

"You can't have things up front," al-Chalabi lectured me as we drove to his home. "You have to cooperate with them. Tell them what you know, then they will see what they can do."

I looked out the window at the valley below, wondering whatever happened to "Don't tell them anything until you get a guarantee."

"Dr. al-Chalabi, look," I said, "I'd start talking if there was a deal in the air. But your friend at the CIA was very clear: There is no deal. He said, 'Tell us what you know, and if you don't, good-bye.' There's nothing to negotiate. He's dead set on getting everything for free."

At that, al-Chalabi had a hard look in his eyes. Whoever had worked him over in my absence had done a good job. Now he was on their side, totally unsympathetic to my needs or point of view. Apparently, he'd decided he needed them more than me. Now I was entirely alone in this godforsaken place, with no allies and no place to go.

Upstairs on the satellite phone, it didn't take long for the CIA man to take me into the same cul-de-sac. Again he wanted everything for nothing. Again I said no.

"We cannot take you to the States, no," he said. "Nor your family. That is impossible. But we can offer you money. Plenty of money." He sounded like a mortgage salesman.

I was incredulous. No wonder top Iraqi officials ended up somewhere else. The former AE chairman, al-Shawi, had gone to England, finally settling in Saudi Arabia. Our ambassador to Spain had gone to the U.K. Wafiq al-Samarrai, the chief of Iraqi Military Intelligence, a confidant of Saddam's, also defected to England.

I had to give the CIA man one thing, though. He played a losing hand for all it was worth.

"Why don't you cooperate with us?" he said. "We're the good guys."

The good guys! Like in the movies. I couldn't believe it.

"Just tell us what you know," he said. "If you'll fax us the descriptions and diagrams of the bomb design, we'll put in a good word for you with al-Chalabi."

A good word with al-Chalabi—now that was surreal. I laid the phone on the desk and walked away, not even bothering to eavesdrop as al-Chalabi picked it up and started talking to him. Downstairs, frustrated, I remembered a security lecture a Mukhabarat officer gave us on the eve of a foreign trip many years ago. It came back to me with a stunning clarity.

"A foreign intelligence operative has one mission," the security man, a tall blond Iraqi, said. "It's to get everything out of you with the minimum cost in the shortest time. The only way to foil him is not to play the game. He'll always have a leg up on you, for the simple reason that he's trained and has all his agency's resources at his disposal. Don't try to feed him false or misleading information. The more you talk, the more he'll have on you. Even wrong data helps him. Don't delude yourself that you can outsmart him. He will win every time, because you're playing on his turf. Do not try to outsmart him, simply drop him. That's his nightmare, because then he's utterly failed at his job. He'll panic. He's had a contact and then lost him. Later, you can report the incident to us, and we can start playing our own game on him."

Those were prescient words, I thought. I was more certain than ever now that I'd done the right thing. They were fools.

And unpredictable. As al-Chalabi chattered along upstairs, I knew I had to break for the border. The situation around his place was too fluid, with Kurdish rivalries a tinderbox ready to blow and Saddam perhaps ready to pounce. With my value so low to the CIA, maybe al-Chalabi would sell me to somebody else. Or maybe he'd lock me up until I agreed to talk to the CIA on their terms.

I really didn't know. All I knew was that disaster was lurking, and I had to slip away. When al-Chalabi came downstairs, I sidestepped any more talk with a protest of extreme fatigue, and went back to my house.

By nightfall I was gone.

The route across southern Turkey is a two-lane, rock-strewn, pot-holed highway jammed with overloaded, exhaust-spewing trucks and buses with people hanging out the windows and sitting on the roofs. Every few minutes a driver played a game of highway chicken, pulling out to pass and bearing down on the oncoming traffic until the other guy got out of the way. Wrecks littered the barren fields at the sides of the highway. Treeless tan hills curtained the horizons.

Officially, Turkey is part of the Western alliance, a member of NATO, and host to American air bases and supersecret radar sites eavesdropping on Russia. But that's where any integration with Europe ends. Culturally and linguistically, Turkey is Middle Eastern, descended from the caliphs. Despite its secular government, its habits are thoroughly Islamic, anchored in the rhythms of the muezzin's calls to prayer and the cutthroat customs of Arabic rule. I was headed for Diyarbakir, where I hoped to hop a flight to Istanbul to visit the Libyan embassy. At the wheel of my taxi was an excitable Turk who plied the border trade. The fare was immense, by his standards—maybe a hundred dollars for the hundred-mile trip—but it included a certain risk. Young, trigger-happy Turkish soldiers were searching for Kurdish rebels at checkpoints along the highway.

Within a few hours we passed a bus full of Iraqis headed south under guard.

"They made big mistake going with smugglers," my driver said. The checkpoints were forbidding, requiring us to get out of the taxi. Nervous soldiers searched our bags and thoroughly examined my papers. The troops were serious about choking off the Kurdish insurrection, unlike Iraqi soldiers, who were almost all available at a price.

My visa, obtained by putting eight hundred dollars into the hands of a border official at the crossover point at Zakho, was good for only two weeks. I had decided to accelerate the process after visiting my old AE friend Mouafaq, who had been discarded by the CIA for imaginatively rewriting his résumé. When I rang his doorbell in the dark, after fleeing al-Chalabi's compound, he squinted out the door in puzzlement until he recognized my face, then brightened like a lightbulb and insisted I stay for dinner. Over plates of lamb and rice, he told me that he'd heard about my arrival in the north; he'd been building drones for al-Chalabi to fly over Iraqi troops, taking pictures and dropping propaganda leaflets. And then he whispered a warning.

"You are in danger," he said. "Al-Chalabi's house was bombed before because Saddam's agents infiltrated his headquarters. They don't know who you are yet, but they will, even if you're using another name. They'll find out who you are."

I stopped chewing for a second, but I was hardly surprised. Saddam was a master spy.

"Do you have a passport?" Mouafaq asked me.

"I just got one," I answered, tapping my shirt pocket.

"That's all you need," he said. "I know the officer in charge of the border checkpoint and I can get you through to Turkey."

Mouafaq's wife then walked into the room. She was a pretty, lithe young woman, much younger than her squat, middle-aged husband. Her eyes were red, and I could see that she'd been crying.

After a brief introduction, she got morose again.

"We were all right in Baghdad," she said. "We had a furnished house and were getting by okay. Then Mouafaq got it into his head to join the fight against Saddam. He talked about nothing else. He said we'd be taken good care of by the Americans. The Americans were encouraging everyone to rise up." She sniffled into a handkerchief and dabbed her eyes.

"Now look," she said. "After a few months up here people just forget about you. He has no job except the airplanes he does for al-Chalabi. The Americans won't talk to him anymore. He won't even go back to Turkey to try to get us visas to go someplace else."

Mouafaq fidgeted. His wife sat down next to me.

"Maybe he can go with you and find a way to get out of this place," she said. "There's no future here. Saddam's agents are everywhere and for sure one day it will be Mouafaq's turn to get hit." She began crying again. "Then where will I go with the children?" She put her face in her hands and sobbed.

It was a sad story, all too common. No question, the Americans had raised everyone's hopes and then squashed them. Fifty thousand Shiites were dead because they had risen up at the call of President Bush, only to be slaughtered while U.S. troops stood by. Ever since, U.S. officials from Bill Clinton on down had ritually called for the overthrow of Saddam. But at the end of the day, we were all alone. In Iraq, Uncle Sam was an empty suit.

Mouafaq left with me in the morning.

• • •

At Diyarbakir we picked up a flight to Istanbul without a hitch. An hour later, I was nudging through the exotic city's clotted traffic. Mouafaq had gone off on his own to get a visa. Libya was out for him, because he didn't have a job lined up or a permit to seek work.

Outside the Libyan embassy, a dark-skinned man in a fez sitting in a metal chair asked me what I wanted.

"Is there a Libyan ship that goes directly from Turkey to Libya?" I asked.

"You just missed it," he said, smiling through broken teeth. "It goes once a month. The last one went three days ago."

My chin hit my chest. It was already mid-September. The teaching contract in my jacket pocket stipulated that I had to be there two weeks ago. I broke out in a sweat. Inside the embassy, however, an official told me not to worry.

"You can go anytime," he said. "They always need university teachers." He handed back my passport. "Good luck."

Izmir is a Turkey's Riviera, a sparkling modern port city of four million people, new hotels, and casinos on the Aegean Sea. Five thousand years ago, Homer lived here researching *The Odyssey,* his epic tale of "a man of twists and turns, driven time and again off course . . . fighting to save his life and bring his comrades home." It seemed an appropriate place for me to wash up.

The sight of it was heaven. I looked across the white-capped, azure waves and felt better just taking in lungfuls of clean, salty air. I'd made it safely out of Baghdad, out of Iraq, out of the dirt of Kurdistan, the traps of the CIA and al-Chalabi, and now, across the badlands and roadblocks of Turkey. Things had to get better.

And better fast. Time was running out on my fourteen-day visa, but the ship to Libya wouldn't be in for another three weeks. I had to find a place to hole up. Luckily, the police were less inclined to round up Iraqis in Izmir than they were in Istanbul, where the authorities aggressively hunted them down. The simple reason was that most Iraqis came to Izmir to get out, and the police weren't going to stand in our way, especially if we looked prosperous. Nevertheless, I had to keep my head down. Having gotten this far, I didn't want to tempt fate. The last time I saw Mouafaq, he was banging on embassy doors in Istanbul, desperately seeking a visa. By now he was probably on a deportee bus south, or dead.

I found a mid-range hotel in Izmir that, in Turkey's depressed economy, cost the equivalent of fifteen dollars a day. A very good dinner cost three bucks. Drinks were mostly free at the foreigners-only casinos, where I could play the roulette wheel all night with only five dollars' worth of chips.

My story was that I was an Iraqi businessman in the import-export trade. Nobody thought twice about it, including the proprietor of my hotel, who turned out to be an Iraqi Kurd who didn't speak English. With American and European tourists flooding the hotel, he latched on to me like a charm, and I was only too glad to help, even manning the desk and chatting up the guests. After three weeks, however, my visa had long expired. By law, he was required to fill out a daily police log on foreigners at the hotel. But in an unspoken favor, he forgot to enter my name. Even when the local chief of the secret police dropped by for a chat, he never said a word.

Finally, the day of my ship's scheduled arrival came—and went. The ship had become hostage to a fight between Istanbul and Khadafy, who owed money to Turkish construction companies working in Libya. After the Turks threatened to seize the ship if it came in to Izmir, Khadafy kept it at sea.

I waited, making myself look busy with business deals, and taking turns at the hotel reception desk. The local police chief and I became pals. Finally, in late October, the ship docked. Its name was *Tulaitula* (Drawing Nigh). On November 1, 1994, we sailed.

That evening, as the ship steamed up a crimson path toward the setting sun, I leaned over a deck railing, enjoying the soft sea breeze. Along the blue Turkish shore, lights twinkled on. For just a moment, I felt at peace. Iraq and all its tawdry conspiracies seemed far away.

The *Tulaitula*'s glory days as a Spanish cruise ship were well behind her. All but one of its restaurants and bars was closed. Dinner was spaghetti with ground meat and boiled vegetables. No salad or fresh fruits. The only beverage was a foul-tasting soda. It reminded me of Leningrad in the last days of the Soviet Union.

I was already upset from our passports being confiscated for the duration of the voyage. If it were misplaced or lost, I could never replace it. I'd have to visit the Iraqi embassy in Tripoli, which would telex Baghdad, and the answer would come back that I was traveling on a forged document. I'd be hustled to an airplane and disappear back into the maws of Saddam. I cursed myself for not buying a duplicate, but it was too late to worry. I could only pray it wouldn't be misplaced or lost.

I'd already had another shock. As I was boarding the ship, I turned around in the loading area and found myself face-to-face with someone else from Atomic Energy, a woman named Leila.

We both started, but I quickly pretended not to care and proceeded to check in as if nothing happened. When I got out of her sight, however, I leaned against a bulkhead and breathed deeply. What was she doing here? How did she get out of Iraq? I'm sure she was wondering the same.

There were a number of Iraqis going to Libya for work, I noticed. Later, I found a way to strike up a conversation with an older Iraqi woman whom Leila seemed friendly with, but she said they'd just met. Then, as if on cue, Leila walked in with a man she introduced as her fiancé, a pleasant Tunisian we'll call Ihsan, and they sat with us. In time we all began to let down our guards.

Leila and Ihsan told me they first met in the 1980s, when they were students in biology at Baghdad University. Ihsan then left for France to get his Ph.D., but they kept up through letters and a few trips he made to Iraq to see her. Their fondness for each other grew. Finally, they decided to get married and live in Tunisia, where Ihsan was building a food refrigeration business. First, of course, Leila had to get out of Iraq.

She had left Baghdad the same way I did, she said, but not being able to get a Turkish visa in the no-fly zone, she'd hooked up with a Kurdish smuggler. Once over the border, he stole her passport— just as I'd been warned—then sold it back to her at an exorbitant price that left her penniless. Fortunately, she had an uncle in the States who wired her enough money to get on the ship. Ihsan flew over to fetch Leila and take her back to get married.

They smiled broadly at the happy ending. I was happy for her, too. As a single, thirty-year-old professional woman in Iraq, Leila faced bleak prospects. So many Iraqi men were poor and incapable of providing a home, they had given up on marriage. Some women married anyone who asked. To me, it was just another one of Saddam's cruel legacies.

That night the Mediterranean winds came up, gently rolling the ship and hurling spindrift onto the deck. I walked for hours, staring out into the darkness, alone with my thoughts. My enthusiasm for Libya had waned. Now it looked like a parachute on a burning plane. Once I landed, I had to work on rewiring my contacts with the Iraqi opposition, even the Americans, elsewhere. Saddam was still hiding and building his weapons. Nothing had changed about that.

At least I had my passport back. Unfortunately, however, there was one more drama before we moved on. Dr. Ihsan foolishly thought he could carry a sealed bottle of whiskey through Libyan Customs, since he was going straight on to Tunisia. But Libya had strict Islamic regulations. When the Customs man opened his bag he was promptly arrested. He faced six months in jail and a fine.

I went with Leila to the Customs office, where she began pleading with a Libyan officer to release him, saying that they were jailing him on their honeymoon. Eventually she broke down and wept, begging for mercy. After several hours, to my total surprise, he relented, saying that because she was an Iraqi they would release her husband and be satisfied with payment of the fine, the equivalent of a hundred dollars.

It was late night by the time we all cleared Customs. The ordeal had lasted eight hours. I could have left them behind, but I pitied poor Leila. I knew what she'd been through in Iraq, and I knew what humble standing a lone female had with officials in Libya, a self-styled Islamic religious state.

It was the right decision. In the end, I was able to grease the paperwork with the men at Customs. Leila's husband, Ihsan, meanwhile, became a close—and eventually valuable—friend.

Libya is a strange place, one of those oil states like Kuwait and the other Gulf sheikdoms where foreigners do all the work: Moroccans clean houses, Sudanese grow vegetables, Egyptians fix cars and drive trucks. Iraqis run the power stations, and American and European technicians keep the equipment and systems humming. All the Libyans do is show up for make-work government jobs, put their sandals up on the desk, and consume. One wonders what they'll do if the oil ever runs out.

Iraqis also teach, among other things, in the sand-blown country. I had an appointment as an associate professor in the physics department at the University of Zawia, a small, palm-potted city on the Mediterranean thirty miles west of Tripoli. As it turned out, however, there were no physics courses being offered. So I was assigned to teach math and computer sciences. The students were so lazy and obnoxious I ended up failing half the class.

But that wasn't serious business. Not long after I arrived, the head of the physics department asked if I'd like to visit the Russian nuclear reactor at Tajoora, ten miles away, which had been shut down for more than a year. The last time it was spooled up the air ventilation didn't work and many workers got sick from high doses of radiation. They hadn't tried to start it again since. Clearly, however, they were sniffing at me with the idea of rejuvenating the program. An overture was also made for me to help them recruit Iraqi chemical weapons specialists.

I had no interest in visiting the reactor, I told the department head. I was out of that business, I just wanted to teach. He kept at me for several weeks, however, insisting that Libya was no longer interested in building a bomb and had dropped the program in 1982. He pressed me to explain my reluctance, but I usually begged off with excuses that I was tired or ill and would take it up with him another day.

But the Libyans clearly knew who I was. I was surrounded by Iraqis who, insecure and eager to please, worked as informants for the Libyans. Every foreigner also had to register with the local security agents and get a picture ID. I'd dodged it for a while, but after getting hassled at a few highway checkpoints I finally went in to register with the security chief of Zawia.

It was an odd experience. My passport was taken away by the clerk, who disappeared for a moment and then came back and ordered me rudely into the chief's office, nearly shouting as he followed me in.

The chief was standing behind his desk with my passport in hand, obviously agitated. He braced me in front of him.

"Look," he said, "any head that rises above the crowd in Libya gets chopped off. You understand? You better watch yourself." He glared at me. "You should behave with more respect. Take this as a warning."

I was bewildered. I didn't know what he was talking about. "Heads"? "Respect"? "A warning"? In all sincerity, I asked, "Sir, what's the problem?"

His lip curled in derision. "You know exactly what the problem is. The problem is you're not cooperating. Everybody here serves the Jamahiria"—the Republic of Libya.

Now it dawned on me: My refusal to visit the reactor, brushing off the feeler about chemical weapons. I'd taken them too lightly. I'd rejected them for fear of becoming enmeshed in the kind of security web I'd had in Iraq. Now I had a security problem because I had refused to be involved.

Catch-22. I decided to be contrite.

"Officer," I began, "we Iraqis are here to serve our Libyan brothers."

He sat back.

"You know," I continued, "I could make more money almost anywhere else. But I chose to come to Libya because it's Iraq's friend. It's the only friend we have. And believe me, we're grateful. If, at any time, you feel I have overstepped your hospitality, please, all you need to do is point a finger and I'll be packed and gone in no time."

The chief raised an eyebrow, and assessed me. He'd probably expected a different response. He stared at me for a long moment.

"Why don't you sit down, Professor," he finally said. He called to his orderly to bring us some tea.

When it came, I took the tiniest sip I could, praying it wasn't laced with an Iraqi-style poison.

"You know, Professor," the chief said, "we live a very uncomfortable life here. Our people are boiling with anger and we always have to be on the lookout for trouble. People are simply unhappy with our system. Things could blow up at any time."

Now I was befuddled. One minute he was denouncing me as disrespectful and the next he was letting down his hair. Why? And why me? Whatever, I decided not to be drawn into a snare.

"Officer," I said carefully, "we are here as mere guests. And guests should not overstep their bounds. But . . . I can talk to you about the international situation. Libya still had many friends in Europe and the Arab world. Iraq has very few. So at least in this respect, your man Khadafy is doing much better than ours."

I put down my cup. The chief was listening closely without revealing himself. I looked at my watch.

"But I really must go now." I stood up. "I have a class in half an hour." The chief came out from behind his desk and walked me back into the front office.

"Give him his passport back," he told the orderly. "And fill out his security pass."

We shook hands cordially at the front door. As I walked away, I didn't know what to make of it all. He seemed appeased by my speech, but no doubt he'd also been used to deliver a message: Somebody in Libya was unhappy with me.

Libya was a carbon copy of Iraq, just not as efficient. Posters and murals of Khadafy in heroic pose were everywhere, just like the ones of Saddam all over Baghdad. Mustachioed soldiers in black berets rushed around self-importantly in their jeeps. The plain-clothes police gathered ostentatiously in the cafes. To be sure, dissidents were taken away at night, tortured, and shot, just like in Iraq, but the Libyans didn't seem to have their hearts in it. Compared with Saddam, Khadafy was material for Gilbert and Sullivan. He had retreated to his desert tent after Ronald Reagan placed a few missiles on his home, and appeared to have lost his enthusiasm for building weapons of mass destruction. In contrast, Saddam seemed to grow stronger with every cruise missile Bill Clinton flung at Iraq.

I was intrigued, meanwhile, by Libya's chemical weapons effort. Oddly enough, it was during a professorial outing, a barbecue at a ranch that was a rare break in our dreary routine, that I got a chance to learn more about it.

One of the guests was an Iraqi named Anas Barbouti, whom I'd known to be well connected with our Mukhabarat as well as with top officials like al-Ghafour, the chairman of Atomic Energy. Now he was a professor married to a prominent Libyan who was head of the government-sponsored women's organization. He'd also worked for Libya's AE and had extensive connections to Khadafy, or so he hinted when we first bumped into each other after my arrival. He even pointed out one of the two men accused by the Americans of blowing up Pan Am 103 over Lockerbie, Scotland, in 1988, whom he said was his neighbor.

Barbouti was probably sending reports about me to Baghdad, but since I was being careful not to do anything suspicious, my worries were tempered. With every passing week, in fact, I'd grown more curious about the lack of any reaction from Baghdad about my disappearance. There were several possibilities: One was that Saddam was acquiescing in my Libyan sojourn, which I thought unlikely. The other was that the intelligence channels were in such disarray from a river of defections that reports on my whereabouts were getting lost. Finally, I remembered how feebleminded Hussein Kamel had become. It was entirely possible that the intelligence reports had landed on his desk and he'd forgotten who I was. Little did I know then that he was planning to defect himself, and might well be sitting on the reports.

Whatever the case, now that Barbouti had warmed up to me, I decided to ask him about the Libyan's pitch to me about recruiting chemical weapons engineers. At first he looked a little nervous, but then he loosened up and told me a startling story.

His cousin Ihsan Barbouti, he said, had been Saddam's agent in chemical weapons deals with the West Germans and others. Then one day in the 1980s he showed up in Libya offering his services to Khadafy, who was ecstatic. Soon Ihsan was allegedly exporting poison-gas components to Libya through his companies in the United States and Europe.

But then Ihsan started playing games, Anas said: Deals for which Khadafy had advanced him money stopped materializing. One day, after Ihsan got an advance of several million dollars, he simply vanished.

Khadafy, of course, couldn't let something like that go unpunished. He dispatched assassins to London, where they supposedly tracked down Ihsan and killed him, Barbouti continued. Pictures of the corpse, the grave, and the tombstone with Ihsan's name on it were shipped home for Khadafy's inspection.

Barbouti smiled. It was all a ruse, he said. Ihsan paid off the hit men and bought a cadaver and phony headstone. Somebody else molders in Ihsan's grave. He was living happily in the United States.

I chuckled at the yarn, but I really didn't know what to make of it. Later, however, I did some checking. It turns out there was an Ihsan Barbouti with connections to both Khadafy's and Saddam's secret weapons networks in the States, according to news reports and congressional investigations, including a deal to supply almond extract to a company in Florida—whose main by-product would have been hydrogen cyanide, a key ingredient in nerve gas. Barbouti also had a half-billion-dollar contract to build airfields in Iraq and admitted to designing Khadafy's notorious German-built chemical weapons plant in Rabta, Libya.

But he was not living happily ever after in the 1990s, as his cousin claimed. After U.S. Customs shut down the Florida plant, Ihsan Barbouti apparently went underground. Past close associates won't say where he is.

A postscript: Ihsan had been exporting highly controlled materials from the United States all through the 1980s, until the Iran-Iraq war ended. Only then did the authorities shut him down. Having been involved in that game for a very long time, he, I had not the slightest doubt, had been operating with the approval of U.S. intelligence. When it came to weapons of mass destruction, the regulations simply weren't that loose.

I figured it would take me at least a couple of months to lull Baghdad into concluding I was staying put and keeping quiet. But it wouldn't hurt to open up another channel of disinformation, I decided.

There was an Iraqi at the university by the name of Rabah whose clumsy ways immediately revealed him as a Mukhabarat informant. I decided to make him my housemate, much to the disgust of my friends.

I gave him the first floor all to himself. I took him to the hospital when he got sick. I stayed by his bedside until he got well. Eventually, he told me all about his work. I was the best friend he had.

My reward was a steady stream of glowing reports to Baghdad, in which Rabah vouched for my innocent activities. I was most assuredly not in touch with the Americans or any Europeans, he told them. He'd made certain of that.

Rabah was grateful to me for making his job so easy.

"Not at all," I said. "Don't thank me at all."

Indeed, all was quiet on the home front. I'd been in Libya five months. On the last day of March, I called Baghdad. Everyone sounded happy that things were going well and that I'd settled down in a safe place. Souham wondered aloud whether I might even persuade the government at some point to let them join me. Nobody had been bothering them, she said. Not even an inquiry. We guessed that since I hadn't caused Saddam any problems, and didn't intend to, the agents had left them alone. We rang off with our usual bittersweet farewells.

Then suddenly, two days later, all hell broke loose: The world's leading newspaper reported me dead.

"Disappearance of an Iraqi Nuclear Expert," the headline said. It was April 2, 1995. The front page of the *Sunday Times* of London was reporting I'd disappeared in Greece after faxing the newspaper some fifty secret documents revealing that Iraq had revived its effort to build a nuclear bomb. The story, by Jon Swain, the paper's veteran foreign correspondent, quoted Souham saying she feared I'd been kidnapped or killed by Saddam's assassins.

Ridiculous, all of it. Other details in the story were equally fantastic.

The *Times* said that I'd fled Iraq *with my wife* on August 18, and been pursued across Turkey by the Mukhabarat. We'd escaped safely to Greece, where I'd made contact with the *Sunday Times* and faxed it a few documents. Sensing Iraqi agents were shadowing me, the story went on, I'd gone out in my slippers to call the paper again from a telephone booth, but I never returned. Souham had discovered the slippers in the booth, called the paper asking for help, then vanished herself.

Both of us were feared dead, the *Times* reported, saying it had a stack of faxes about the bomb program and my handwritten notes explaining what they meant.

Utterly false. I'd never contacted the paper, from Greece or anywhere else. But it correctly reported I'd worked directly for Saddam's son-in-law Hussein Kamel in the presidential palace. It was the first time my name had surfaced in the press. The question was: Why? Who planted the story, and for what reason?

I was caught up in something much bigger than myself.

Before I could begin to investigate, the story circled the globe, reinforced by the authoritative broadcasts of the BBC quoting the *Times*. Newspapers throughout the Middle East put it on page one. Iraq even published a full translation of the *Sunday Times* story, with the added comment that it was all lies.

No one believed it. The Iraqi press, everyone knew, was rigged.

Then the wave crashed on my family. Condolence calls poured in for my wife. When she told them I was alive and well in Libya, people dismissed her out of hand as covering for Saddam: If the *Sunday Times* and BBC said I was dead, then I was dead. Period.

Saddam was probably as alarmed as I was, for different reasons. At least part of the story could be true —that I'd blown the nuclear program to the *Times*. To him that would mean I was also talking to British intelligence, as well as the CIA. Within hours Mukhabarat agents appeared on the road near my house. The Iraqi ambassador called with a feeler that we meet. Suddenly, once more, I was trapped. The rivalry between Khadafy and Saddam that prohibited Iraqi "wet work" on Libyan soil might save my life for a while, but not for long. As soon as Saddam persuaded his Arab "brother" that I was as dangerous to him as I was to Iraq, I'd be run down like a dog.

Desperate, I called Ayad Allawi, the head of the Iraqi National Accord in London, on an open line. I was certain my phone was tapped, but he'd been around a long time and I was confident he would be discreet. With his connections to British intelligence, I hoped he could surreptitiously arrange for a fast visa, this time for the whole family. The *Times* story had changed everything. Now all of us were in immediate, mortal danger.

To my astonishment, Allawi himself expressed surprise that I was alive. I'd suspected *him* as a culprit in planting the story, with the idea of flushing me out. Since our last telephone conversation in the no-fly zone, we'd completely lost contact.

Allawi said he was eager to help, but then he made a grave mistake: Over the open line he gave me explicit instructions to go to Tunis, where he said I'd be met by British intelligence.

I slumped in my chair. Allawi had pronounced my death notice on the tapped line.

My head spun for a few seconds. Finally, I pulled myself together and emphatically rejected his plan.

"That's out of the question," I shouted, primarily for the benefit of the phone tappers, although some of my anger was genuinely for him. "Absolutely not. I have no intention of contacting, or cooperating in any way, with Western intelligence. I would never do that." For the next few minutes I larded my rejection with disgust for the West, especially the Americans, for bombing our country and starving Iraqi children with the embargo.

"I will always be a patriot," I added. "Saddam and I have our differences, but not so much that I would betray Iraq. That filthy *Times* newspaper story was designed for only one purpose: to sow intrigue. I am happy here in Libya and plan to stay here. I hope I can bring my family here as well," I added for good measure. "We talked about that on the telephone just two days ago." For once, I hoped the Mukhabarat was tapping my home phone, too.

Allawi listened to my tirade without interruption, and finally seemed to get the point. If the Libyans, not to mention Saddam, had the slightest idea I was talking to the CIA or British intelligence, they'd take care of me themselves. I'd be walking along the street and a truck would run me over. They could poison my drinks, just like they did it in Iraq.

My conversation with Allawi ended with awkward good-byes. Once again, the Iraqi opposition had not only failed me but put my life at risk.

I sat back on the couch, yearning for a scotch in this godforsaken Muslim country. Instead, I had to settle for a rotten Libyan soda.

A few minutes later, I decided to check in with my family in Baghdad. As the phone rang, I rubbed my face, completely exhausted.

Souham answered and was relieved to hear from me. We talked about everything that happened, as best we could with the code words we'd perfected. The newspaper story was still causing havoc, she told me, with friends and relatives calling in alarm. It put her in a tight spot, because all she could do was keep repeating that I was happily ensconced in Libya. When one of her relatives began arguing about why I'd deserted her to go there, she had to cuss them out and hang up. The pressure on all of them was getting to be intolerable.

As usual, I did my best to buck her up with vague statements that plans were in motion and everything would be fine in the near future. But long ago she'd taken that as a signal to hand the phone to one of the boys.

This time Firas came on the line, sounding nervous. I asked him all the usual questions about himself, but he was strangely unresponsive. To every question, he answered only "Fine." And then he interrupted me.

"Father," he said, "watch out for yourself."

I waited for more, but he only repeated himself.

"Father," he said again sternly, "watch out for yourself." And then he was silent.

Father: He always called me "Papa."

It could only mean one thing: Saddam's hit teams were coming my way.

CHAPTER FIFTEEN

IN FROM THE COLD

WHICH WAY would they be coming?

I held the phone after Firas clicked off, considering the possibilities, telling myself to stay calm, not to get paranoid.

My oldest son was not a frivolous boy. He'd been my closest confidant and helpmate while I developed my cover story. He'd manufactured my escape from Baghdad. He'd skillfully deflected inquiries from nosy relatives and friends concerning my whereabouts. For months, he'd kept the family together at home, especially Souham. If Firas was signaling that Saddam was coming after me, I had to take it seriously.

On the other hand, the *Sunday Times* story had inadvertently set up a standoff between Saddam and myself. It would be watched very closely at the United Nations and in Western capitals. Despite all its fabrications, the newspaper's account of my disappearance had sparked an international inquiry, one that Saddam could ill afford at the time since he was seeking relief from sanctions. No matter how much he wanted my head, no matter how desperate he was to prevent me from taking his secrets to the West, he could not move against me until the spotlight had dimmed.

In my calmer moments, I also thought hard about who would have planted such a patently false story in the *Times*. What was the point? The more I thought about it, the more I concluded it was planted by the CIA, with the help of their British friends in MI-6. Who else could fabricate such a story from whole cloth, including the phony faxes, and peddle it to a veteran correspondent? Who else knew so much about me? Who else had an interest in embarrassing Saddam and flushing me out of hiding with one stone?

It was the CIA that had lost track of me, and now they were using the planted story to find out where I was. But it did have a silver lining: If they wanted to know where I was, it meant they wanted me in from the cold.

Now the pressure was on. There was no way of telling how long the world would remain interested in my fate. I had to move quickly, first to protect myself, then to find safe harbor for Souham and the boys before the U.N. moved on to other issues and left us at the mercy of Saddam.

Fortunately, I had a blueprint to fall back on: the security lessons the Mukhabarat itself had taught me for my clandestine shopping trips abroad. Back then I'd had to worry about the Israelis gunning me down, now it was Saddam's agents I had to think about. From now on, I'd be careful of where I went, where I slept, and what I ate.

I sprang off the couch. I emptied the refrigerator of all my food and bottled water. From now on I wouldn't touch anything at home: It would be too easy for Rabah, the Mukhabarat agent in my own house, to poison me. Next, as I'd done in London, I'd eat randomly in different restaurants. Luckily there were numerous Egyptian-operated eateries that catered to foreign workers where I could blend in. A rabidly anti-Saddam Syrian ran another where I felt safe.

No walking at night. I'd taken to clearing my mind in Libya with long, late-night strolls along the seaside boulevard, but that would have to cease. As far back as my earliest days in Baghdad, one of Saddam's favorite techniques for getting rid of people was running them down with dump trucks. Putting a bomb under a car was another standard trick, so I'd dismissed the idea of buying my own car in Libya. From now on, I'd even be careful about taxis, picking one from the middle of the queue outside hotels and restaurants instead of the first one that drew up.

Saddam himself was a hunted man. I asked myself what he would do. I remembered how he'd moved from house to house during the bombing of Iraq. I'd do the same. With the help of trusted friends, I began moving from house to house every night, interspersed with visits to a government-owned hotel and nights at home. I changed the locks on my bedroom door to make it difficult for Rabah to slip in while I was asleep.

For big, special targets Saddam usually dispatched a team from Iraq, but I wasn't sure how much of a free hand he had in Libya these days. When an anti-Saddam professor was hit by a car in a dark alley one night in 1993, all known Iraqi operatives were fired from their cover jobs and deported. That included Rabah, who'd been dismissed from Tripoli University. But unaccountably, he managed to return the next year with a job offer from the university at Zawia. I kept myself in a high state of alert.

But Saddam never gives up. The Iraqi ambassador to Libya invited me to the embassy for dinner to discuss matters, but that was the last place I was going to eat. An Iraqi opposition activist in Czechoslovakia had been foolish enough to go to our embassy in Prague to renew his passport; he was drugged and shipped back to Baghdad in a container. When the Czech police arrived to inquire, they were told that it was an internal affair on embassy grounds and they had no right to interfere.

After I declined the invitation, the ambassador sent a note saying we could meet in any place of my choosing. When I failed to respond, he resorted to intimidation, placing a couple of agents in the lobby of a hotel where I sometimes stayed, as well as around the university. Rabah also suddenly lost all enthusiasm for going out every night, and became a constant presence at the house. No doubt prompted by the ambassador, he also began pestering me about the London *Times* story. Beyond pointing out that I couldn't have been in Greece and sharing a house with him in Libya at the same time, I refused to discuss it. My story was that I'd legally left Iraq through Jordan, and I was sticking to it.

Shortly after I rebuffed the ambassador, ominous word came of threats to my family in Baghdad. One day Firas was driving to college when a military truck pulled out of a side road and gunned toward him for a head-on collision. Firas swerved, barely managing to get by before the truck sideswiped him. On another occasion he spotted a similar truck waiting for him and changed his route. Even the younger boys were not immune. Zayd, only thirteen, was beaten on the street by a security agent and his son. Threats were made to Sami. Mukhabarat thugs started hanging around outside the house, bothering Souham whenever she stepped out. Her blood pressure soared to over two hundred and, according to Firas, she had turned into a quaking shadow of herself.

At the same time, anti-Saddam Iraqis in Libya were nearly giddy over the developments.

"Look, Hamza," one said, typically, "you have Saddam over a barrel. He's accused of violating the cease-fire agreement. He's kidnapped and killed one of his own scientists, according to the papers. You've caused an international uproar. The U.N. Security Council has passed a resolution and the IAEA is investigating." He laughed. "You're more useful to us dead than alive."

In another time, I might have chuckled along. But right now I valued my life more than his cause. Interestingly, Saddam had not only failed to tell the media that I was safely alive in Libya, but had put out the story that I was involved in the import-export business and simply not available for interviews, which I interpreted as his way of buying time to decide what to do. With the situation unsettled, I decided to give the Iraqi opposition in London another chance to get me and my family into the U.K. I didn't have to worry about phone security now that the cat was out of the bag.

I quickly reached Ayad Allawi, head of the Iraqi National Accord, who seemed pleased to hear from me again. He told me to send him photocopied pages of my passport as soon as I could, then added, "You have to make a copy of all the pages so we can confirm that you haven't been to Greece."

That was odd, I thought. He knew damn well I hadn't been to Greece. He knew I'd exfiltrated Iraq through the no-fly zone. I assumed he was trying to put distance between himself and the London *Times* story, which included details about my house that only he could have known, through a relative of his I'd helped get out of Iraq. Then again, it was hard to be sure. Someone had planted that story to flush me out and put Saddam on the spot. My guess was that a high official at the CIA had panicked when he learned that "Bob" had brushed me off and lost track of me. They'd concocted the phony nuclear documents, perhaps used Allawi's people to impersonate me and Souham on the telephone, and peddled the ruse to the unwitting reporter at the *Times*. Now Allawi was trying to signal he had no connection with it.

Whatever the case, it was far over my head, and not my immediate concern. I photocopied all sixty-four pages of my passport and took them, along with a cover letter asking for a visa, to the DHL office in Tripoli for fast shipment to London. I was surprised that the Libyans would permit a foreign mail carrier to operate in their security-crazed country. As it turned out, they of course had it covered. When I came back two days later to make sure the package had been delivered, the clerk looked at me in total fright. Later I heard from an Iraqi who been in the DHL office right after me that Libyan intelligence agents had rushed in, demanded the package, ripped it open, pored through its contents, then ordered the clerk to reseal it and send it on. Everybody was jumpy.

Meanwhile, I began to get a feeling that the Libyans wouldn't mind if I moved on. The long U.N. embargo on Libya for its terrorist activities had made deep ruts in the economy. Khadafy had raised a white flag. The last thing he wanted was to be linked with Saddam in the assassination of an Iraqi scientist on Libyan soil. The dean of the university at Zawia had even told me point-blank that I should go. With that, I figured the Libyans no longer cared who I talked to on the telephone, as long as I was on my way out.

Now, however, London's Iraqi exiles threw up a new roadblock. Allawi told me, on my next call, that the only way I could get a visa was to talk first to "some people" at the British embassy in Tunisia.

My head spun. Whatever happened to the offer of immediate asylum and a salary when I was in northern Iraq? Allawi mumbled excuses about "difficulties" and "changing conditions" that added up to mush. To me, it sounded like the CIA had gotten the upper hand once again and was calling the shots. What else could explain the changing conditions? I had become a pawn in some fathomless bureaucratic game.

Now the telephone rang, throwing yet another wrench into my plans. It was Firas.

"Papa," he said, "I'm coming to see you."

It wasn't good news.

In retrospect, I shouldn't have been surprised that Saddam would use Firas to lure me home. Intimidation had failed. Now they were sending my son to get me. When I asked him who was paying for the trip, he hesitated, then said it was my "former boss"—Saddam.

"He wants you to come home," Firas said. "He says all will be forgiven."

I sighed. This was one of Saddam's oldest tricks, luring people back with promises of amnesty. I was always amazed when people took the bait. They promptly disappeared into the prisons. I certainly wasn't going to fall for it. On the other hand, the call told me that Firas had fallen under the control of the Mukhabarat, and the only way I could break its grip was to get him alone.

"Of course, Firas," I said with gentle enthusiasm, "I'm always glad to see you. Please come as soon as you can." He would come in a week, he said.

Now I had only a few days to explore every escape hatch before Firas arrived. I had to have a viable alternative or he'd not only lose faith in me, but sink into greater danger if he went back empty-handed. I scoured around for the fastest avenues to political asylum. Neither the British nor the Americans had embassies in Libya; their small "interests sections," tended by other embassies in the absence of diplomatic relations, were tightly watched. Likewise, the embassies in neighboring Tunisia, sympathetic to Saddam, were under surveillance. One Iraqi who'd visited the U.S. embassy a few times to make arrangements for his son to attend an American college was picked up by Tunisian security, interrogated, and beaten. If the Tunisians found out who I was, they might do Saddam a favor and ship me home.

Despite my misgivings, I tried the Turks. The embassy clerk was a squat bureaucrat who spoke brisk, fluent Arabic. I got in line and heard him offering the Iraqis in front of me a one-month tourist visa for summer vacations. My hopes jumped. When my turn came, however, he flipped through my passport and squinted at the page with my previous entry visa stamped at the Kurdish border. Obviously, I was a renegade. The Turks were losing billions of dollars from the U.N. oil embargo on Iraq and wanted to stay in Saddam's good graces.

"I can give you only two days' transit," the clerk said. "You cannot vacation in Turkey." He picked up his rubber stamp, but I took back my passport and left. It was fruitless to argue with a Turk.

The story at the Moroccan embassy was the same, except that

they sat on Iraqi visa applications rather than rejected them outright. It was a four-month minimum wait, I was told. The same for Egypt. I was rejected outright by Malta. Western Europe was entirely closed: Nobody wanted any more Iraqis seeking asylum.

Eastern Europe, however, was a possibility. A friend told me Hungary would allow me in under two conditions: that I have an invitation from a local sponsor and proof of a job to return to in Libya. He said he could arrange the invitation through a contact there for three hundred dollars.

"Let's do it," I said. "I'll pay your friend when I get to Hungary."

The only hurdle now was getting from Libya to Budapest. There were no direct links. The only flights were from Tunisia, which had clamped down on visas for Iraqis. Even transit visas had become very difficult to get.

Then I remembered the friends I had made on the ship from Izmir. I pulled a card from my wallet, picked up the phone, and called in a favor.

"Dr. Ihsan?" I said over the crackling, clicking line. "This is Dr. Hamza, calling from Libya. How are you and Leila doing?" I told him I needed a visa—fast.

As I expected, he had a friend in the foreign ministry.

Firas arrived in mid-July. I was shocked by his appearance. He looked like a bag of skin and bones when he walked into the hotel, chain-smoking like a soldier.

He brightened like a lightbulb when he saw me. I grabbed and squeezed him like a rag doll. He was my oldest, dearest son.

The first thing I wanted to do after I got him settled upstairs was to take him somewhere we could talk. He instantly understood when I put my finger to my lips when we walked into the room, so we merely traded empty pleasantries until we were back out on the street.

We walked for a short while along the seaside promenade. With Firas carrying an offer from Saddam, I calculated we weren't in danger. If anything, the Libyans seemed to be keeping me under a careful watch now to discourage an embarrassing incident.

Firas told me about his mother and her blood pressure problem. They'd found a doctor to treat her privately, fearing what might happen if she was treated by a government physician.

"But she is not looking well, Papa," he said sadly. "She is very worried."

The Mukhabarat had interrogated him almost daily in the past few weeks, he said. "But I gave them nothing," he added with a shy smile.

I put my arm around him. "You are a brave boy," I said, struggling with a towering wave of guilt. What had I put them all through?

I decided to show him around the campus, which would also be a safer place to talk. In the hallway outside my office, I introduced him to some of my female students, who immediately began to flirt, telling him how much they loved Iraqi boys. He blushed and began to banter a little, and finally I could see his spirits start to lift. It was the best medicine I could have offered. When finally I dragged him away, he was laughing and much less a wreck. Finally, we found a shaded spot under the palms and took a seat.

The Mukhabarat agents were planning on sending someone else to talk to me, he said, but he'd persuaded them he was the only person I would trust.

I nodded. Firas toyed with a few stones before continuing.

"The head of Mukhabarat personally told me to tell you," he finally resumed, "that the president will give you anything you want, including a full pardon, if you will come back to Iraq." He looked me hopefully in the face. I smiled noncommittally.

"He says you'll be rewarded with huge riches and can resume a very happy life." He pulled out a piece of paper from his pocket and handed it to me. I opened it and saw the presidential seal at the top.

"They want you to sign this. Then they'll arrange a press conference for you in Tunisia to refute the lies published by the *Sunday Times*. If you sign, they'll fly Mama, Sami, and Zayd over for the ceremony and they'll issue you a legal passport and a work permit to work in Libya legally."

I was scanning the letter. It was written in English, obviously for the benefit of the Western media. An Arabic translation was attached.

"I affirm my loyalty to the heroic leader of Iraq, Saddam Hussein," it read. "The lies concocted by the British and American colonialists and published by the *Sunday Times* of London are meant to maintain sanctions on the heroic Iraqi people. The documents cited by the newspaper are forgeries. I never sent any such documents to the paper, nor did my wife accompany me to Greece, a country I have never set foot in."

The letter went on with stilted praise for Saddam and the regime and my unswerving loyalty to him. There was a line for my signature at the bottom.

It was standard boilerplate, the kind of text we'd seen a score of humiliated Iraqi officials read on TV, with Saddam beaming in the background. Of course I wouldn't sign it. Not only would no one believe it, the videotape of my press conference would demoralize every opponent of Saddam inside and outside Iraq. Then, once the spotlight moved on, he'd have my family picked up and order me to return to Iraq or they'd be executed. The minute I stepped off the plane I'd be taken away, never to be seen again.

That was simply the way things were done. There was the case of Mohammed al-Hakim, the head of the Iraqi Islamic opposition based in Iran. His sons were picked up, and his brother summoned to the dungeon. The first son was executed in front of him, and the brother was sent to al-Hakim with the message that if he didn't surrender the rest would be killed. When he refused, they were murdered one by one. And no one could forget the night of the long knives, when Saddam had his top officials murder each other in the courtyard as he laughed. The lessons were endless.

I looked over at Firas.

"You should sign it, Papa," he said softly. His cheeks were hollow as he nervously smoked.

I nodded noncommittally.

"They'll kill us if you don't," he added.

I put my arm around his shoulder.

"Firas, my son, this is an old trick," I said softly. "You know that, don't you?" He shrugged off my arm, got up, and stared into the distance. A late-afternoon breeze rustled the palms.

"No," he said evenly. "I don't see that."

I studied him. "Let's walk," I said.

Changing his mind was going to take time. The Mukhabarat had thoroughly turned him around. I was disappointed but not surprised. They were very good, and he was still a young man. Right now he was too scared to think straight.

We walked down through the campus and back along the sea-wall. We ambled slowly and talked. An hour passed, then two. I made my case that Saddam was setting a trap, not just for me, but all of us in the family. I reviewed our lives under the regime and how Saddam had proved again and again that he could not be trusted.

I was not getting through. Firas was lighting one cigarette off another, avoiding my gaze, and only half-listening without comment.

Finally I hailed a taxi and we returned to my house. No one was there. I led him upstairs to my room and turned on the radio to muffle our conversation. Music to the glory of Khadafy came on. I turned it up.

"Papa," he finally said, raising his voice, "they made it clear. If you sign the letter, then everything will be fine. And that makes sense to us. If you don't sign, we are dead. Why would they want to cause a stink?"

I was growing alarmed at his stubbornness.

"Firas, listen," I retorted. "Only if I don't sign will he keep us alive. He has to prove that he did not kidnap me. The only witness to that is your mother. He has to keep her alive and happy so she can tell reporters and U.N. investigators that she never went to Greece and that the whole story is a fabrication. Do you understand me?"

He shook his head.

"If I sign, I kill the goose that's laid the golden egg. The goose is the *Times* report claiming I'm dead, plus the documents I've supposedly sent them saying that Saddam is rejuvenating his nuclear bomb program."

He nodded slowly this time.

"What's keeping us alive is the pressure on Saddam to produce me, plus the Security Council's orders to the IAEA to check out the documents. If I sign that paper you've brought me, then the pressure will be off. Saddam will let things cool down, the inspectors will go away, then he'll come after us—all of us. Do you see now?"

He started to listen.

"The next time I die it will be for real, not just a newspaper story. Saddam will do away with all of us then tell the world he has no idea what happened or where we have gone."

I put my hand on Firas's knee and lowered my voice. "Ironically, the only thing that is keeping us alive is the story that I am dead."

Firas shook his head, his face grew red. The pressure was too much. Now he burst into tears, put his head between his hands, and started to cry. I put my hand on his neck, but he shrugged it off.

"I always knew you would do this to us," he sobbed. "I always suspected it, but now I know. You'd let us die rather than be tainted with the Americans by a pledge of loyalty to Saddam. You're only thinking about yourself."

He sniffled. "You've never really loved us!" he shouted through tears.

"Firas, son. . . ."

He was trembling. He stood up, volcanic in his rage.

"If you won't save us, I can't stay under the same roof with you for another minute." He picked up his bag and stomped from the room. Downstairs, I caught up to him at the door. He said he was taking a taxi to a hotel.

I had to let him go.

I called the government hotel, the only one in town that might have a room, and told them to give Firas the suite that I had kept leased. As it turned out, that was the only room available.

It was still only mid-afternoon, so I decided to let Firas cool off for a while. In a couple of hours he'd be hungry, and we could talk again. Meanwhile, I decided to reach out for help. I called a trusted friend who'd been out of Iraq for fifteen years and knew all of Saddam's tricks. Ali—a pseudonym—knew all the stories, with names, places, and dates, of the people Saddam had pardoned and then killed. He knew their friends and relatives, whom Firas could call for corroboration. He was quietly persuasive and not connected to any of the squabbling Iraqi opposition groups. He kept a low profile and spoke discreetly. He had sheltered me for a few nights while I kept on the move.

A few hours later, I found Firas lying on the bed in my hotel room, his eyes worn from crying. I sat down on the edge.

"Listen, Firas," I said softly, "I'll sign the letter."

He looked at me, not believing what he'd heard. I let it sink in.

"I'll sign the letter," I repeated. "But there are two things I want you to do."

Now he was listening. "First, I have a friend who would like to meet you. He's invited us for dinner at his house and I'd like you to come along."

He nodded cautiously.

"The second thing is, you wouldn't want me to sign that letter without guaranteeing the safety of you and the family, would you?"

No.

"So I have the following proposition. . . ."

He looked annoyed. I held up my hand.

"Since they've said that the family can leave if I sign, then I'll offer them this: I'll say I'll sign if they let your mother and brothers leave the country right now. I'll sign if they can leave first."

Firas listened.

"Since you're going back anyway, I'll propose that you stay as a hostage. If I don't sign, they can kill you, or threaten to, figuring that I'd never let that happen. But at least they have a hostage, which is you, while the rest of the family gets out safe."

His eyes narrowed as he considered the idea.

"Do you follow?" I asked. "Would you accept being a hostage for a while? It would take some work to get you out after that, and maybe we'd fail, you know. Maybe I'd have to go back and give myself up if they were serious about killing you. But at least we could save the rest of the family. The way it is now, if I sign that paper, they'll never let your mother and brothers, and you, out. And when the issue dies down they'll make me come back and then kill us all."

Finally, it was sinking in.

"So we'll test them and see if they are lying," I said. "If they refuse my offer, then we'll know they never intended to honor their end in the first place."

Firas sat up, gingerly weighing the proposition. And looking a little sheepish. I had proved I was serious about saving the whole family, not just myself. If it worked, it ensured the safety of his mother and brothers. The rest of the risk would be shared equally by Firas and me.

"I'm sorry, Papa," he said. "I was wrong to accuse you."

I squeezed his shoulder. Saddam, I knew, would never accept the deal. Not a chance. He had all of them hostage now. Why would he give any of them up? But I knew Firas had to see that for himself.

Suddenly he stood up. "I'm going to go see the Iraqi ambassador right now and tell him our offer."

"All right," I said. "But be careful. And don't forget our dinner tonight."

After he left, I lay down on the bed for a nap, knowing what the answer would be.

Hours later, Firas returned, downcast, and slumped into a chair. I knew what had happened. The ambassador had brushed him off, he said, without even bothering to call Baghdad for instructions.

"He said, 'We're not the Mafia, we are the Iraqi government, and your father cannot negotiate with us.' He said you must sign right now, and that those are the orders of the president."

Firas sagged. The reality of who he was dealing with was starting to hit home. Now I really needed my friend Ali to cinch the case.

We arrived for dinner at Ali's house as the sun set. He put out plates of hors d'oeuvres and we chatted lightly for a while. Then, over bowls of lamb stew, we got down to business. Without any melodrama, in a matter-of-fact way, Ali told him one horror story after another—of whole families disappearing into Saddam's prisons after they'd accepted his phony offers of amnesty.

"You have to keep the screws on Saddam," Ali said softly. "You can never let go. You can never trust him. The only thing your father has to save your lives is what he has in his head—the nuclear secrets. Saddam is afraid that your father will jump the fence and go over to the Americans if anything happens to his family. So he has to play it carefully. And so do you."

Firas listened respectfully, but he wasn't quite ready to give up.

"You want more proof that they are lying to you?" I interjected. He looked at me.

"They said in Baghdad that you could pick up a new passport and work permit for your father in Libya, right?"

Ali chuckled.

"Well, tomorrow, why don't you go down to the embassy and pick them up?" I said. "I'll even sign the loyalty letter, and you can take it with you."

Firas hesitated. Now even he was leery about my signing anything in advance.

"No, that's okay," he said. "They told me they would be ready. They didn't say anything about signing anything."

The next day, Firas went down to the embassy again and got an entirely different reception. After inquiring inside, the guard said the ambassador didn't wish to see him. After Firas protested, an Iraqi diplomat came out and told him they didn't know anything about a passport or work permit for me.

"Go away," he said. "Don't come back."

Firas looked crushed when he returned to the hotel.

"I guess you were right, Papa," he said. "They were lying all along." He looked embarrassed.

I let it sink in.

"What are we going to do now?" Firas said.

I leaned forward, put my hands on his shoulders, and locked my eyes on his.

"The same thing we were always going to do," I said. "We're going back to the plan."

The taxi raced along the coastal highway, taking me to Tunisia. This was my last chance. Saddam surely was closing in. There was no heading back. I'd sent Firas home.

What was my plan? A little vague, to tell the truth. I would slip through Tunis, board a plane for Hungary, and start banging on embassy doors in Budapest. If nothing opened for me there, at least I'd be within striking distance of the International Atomic Energy Agency in Vienna, including the head of inspections for Iraq. Maybe I could latch on to a temporary position and then arrange for the safe passage of Souham and the boys from Baghdad under U.N. protection.

It was ambitious, wild, desperate. But it had its advantages: No more middlemen. No more scheming exiles, no more game-playing CIA agents on the telephone. I was going to get inside the U.S. or British embassy and dare them to throw me out—with all of Saddam's secrets.

The timing had to be perfect. I'd concocted a cover story that would hold for only a month, the length of my summer vacation at the university. I'd told friends I was going on vacation at a seaside resort near the Egyptian border—the opposite direction from Tunisia. Then I put a story in the exile rumor mill that Saddam was letting my family come to Libya. Firas would also tell the Mukhabarat that I was seriously weighing their offer to sign. With all that, I thought, I'd be able to buy time.

I was pushing the taxi driver to the max. He gunned along the coastal highway, swerving to avoid potholes, wooden carts, pedestrians, and oncoming trucks. The sun heated the sand-blown road as if it were a frying pan. I looked out the window at the trash-strewn highway and was disgusted: The six-hundred-mile road, a crated ribbon of colonial-era asphalt entirely absent of such amenities as gas stations, restaurants, bathrooms, or even water fountains, was a monument to the empty rhetoric of self-styled Arab revolutionaries. The beaches were filthy, devoid of tourist shops and sailing boats common even to Tunisia and Morocco. Khadafy, awash in oil billions, was running the country down and piling up cash in numbered Swiss bank accounts. The people got nothing but speeches. I hoped I'd never see this part of the world again.

Firas had gone ahead to Tunisia en route to Iraq to stay with Dr. Ihsan and let him know I was coming. When he checked in by phone he confirmed my worst fears. Tunisian television sounded like Baghdad TV, he said, with constant anti-American rants and paeans to Arab "heroism." The security services were ubiquitous and alert for renegade Iraqis.

When I saw the border ahead, my stomach lurched. A mile-long line of vehicles backed up in each direction. People were standing beside their cars, trucks, and buses, fanning themselves for a breeze, rather than bake inside while the engines boiled over. An eerie, resigned quiet filled the air. To our left, the desert stretched to the horizon. To our right, even the turquoise ocean looked like it could boil.

A border guard came walking down the line of vehicles, collecting passports. Once again, I panicked. So often in this part of the world, papers got "lost." But there was no choice. I handed it over.

Six nerve-racking, sweating hours later, we inched across the border. I rushed to a bank in Tunis and got there just as the doors were being locked. Inside, I cashed my Libyan checks, then went down the street to a travel office to buy a ticket to Hungary. To meet my contact as planned, I had to be on the first flight out in the morning.

"I'm sorry, sir, there are no seats left," the travel agent told me after checking his computer.

I slid into a chair, looked at my watch. I was exhausted. The agent could see my distress. "There are always cancellations," he said.

I shook my head in despair.

"If you want to wait . . ."

"I might as well," I said, looking around the clean, well-kept office. Nothing like this existed in Libya, where everything seemed covered with dust. On the table was a pile of local magazines and newspapers. I picked one up and started thumbing through. Two hours went by and I'd read them all, not absorbing a thing, then the phone rang. After a few seconds, the travel agent's eyes lit up. He lifted a thumb.

"You're in luck," he said, hanging up.

Next was a hotel. I figured the Tunisian police, and perhaps even Libyan security, checked the guest register, so I went to the front desk and put on an imperious act about being late for a government appointment, saying I had to register later. The flustered clerk handed over a key. Early the next morning I gave him a fifteen-dollar tip and he didn't even ask my name.

One border down, one to go.

Ihsan picked me up at the hotel and took me to the airport. I had wanted to thank him personally for arranging my visa, as well as for taking care of Firas for a few days.

We shook hands and said a very fond good-bye. It was distressing to leave this extraordinary man. When we first met on the ship, he had just married a college sweetheart he hadn't seen for years, just because she was desperate, stranded, and facing deportation back to Iraq. He'd pulled strings to get a visa for me, no questions asked. He'd taken in my son. All this for people he hardly knew. Perhaps he'd just returned a favor because I'd helped him when he was arrested by Libyan Customs. But I think it was more than that. I think that when the rare opportunity came to show trust and true friendship in this part of the world, we'd both grasped it like gold.

The Tunis Air flight lifted off the runway and banked north over the azure Mediterranean waves. From a few thousand feet, Tunis looked like a beach resort, and to carefree tourists I suppose it was. But as the sandstone mosques fell beyond my window, I felt as if two strong hands were slipping off my ankles. I was leaving behind a fetid world of dictatorship and corruption. For decades, behind the banner of Arab revolutionary nationalism, Saddam and his cronies in Syria, Libya, and Egypt had looted their treasuries and us, hurtling back farther and farther into the past. To millions of people in the "Arab island," democracy is not even a faint hope. I could not leave fast enough.

Ten thousand feet, twenty thousand feet, we soared through a clear blue sky. Europe, finally, lay ahead. Freedom!

Freedom, I decided, was underrated.

My contact was an Iraqi who'd lived in Hungary for several years. He met me at the airport.

"Do you have the three hundred dollars?" he asked before we left the terminal. Business as usual. I handed him the wad as soon as we got into his car.

He was briskly professional. He informed me that he'd arranged to put me up in a private home because the police checked the hotels. That way, if my plans hadn't materialized by the time my thirty-day visa had expired, I could disappear underground. If all else failed, he said, he'd arrange for some Kurdish friends to smuggle me into Holland.

I had turned my nose up at Holland the year before. Maybe not this time.

We drove through the city and over the Danube, past the ancient domes poking into the scudding clouds. The city shone like a jewel on gray velvet. On the edge of Budapest, my contact delivered me to a nice studio apartment in the back of a private home, close to tram service and taxis. For the first time in weeks, I got a good night's sleep.

Early the next day I took a stab at calling Ahmad al-Chalabi, whom I'd last seen in northern Iraq some eleven months earlier and a world away. He'd moved his operation to the comfort of London.

He sounded annoyed when he came on the line.

"Why did you disappear on me?" he said without formalities. "We could have gotten a temporary visa for you to be debriefed by the CIA in Turkey."

I sighed. What the hell did he mean? Had he forgotten that it was he who persuaded me not to talk to the CIA before my family was out? I started to protest, then decided it was hopeless: He had nothing for me. After mumbling a few vagaries, he told me to call back the next day. When I did, he was off on a trip, I was told. He'd left no forwarding number or instructions. So much for that.

The noose was tightening. Now it was on to Plan B, to link up with the U.N. weapons inspectors in Vienna. Little did I know that it would end in a tutorial on the cozy relationship between Saddam and the United Nations.

The first person I called was Maurizio Zifferero, the Italian leader of the IAEA inspection team for Iraq. Few outsiders knew that Zifferero had a long history with us in Iraq, beginning in the late seventies when he represented Italian companies that built our plutonium separation labs. Back then he was a frequent visitor to Baghdad, where he was plied with gifts and provided with escorts for his jewelry-shopping excursions to fancy boutiques along the Tigris. Fair or not, Kamel joked about him as "our man at the IAEA."

Following Desert Storm, Zifferero was appointed to head the IAEA inspections. He played a soft game with Saddam, figuring he'd get better cooperation if he avoided confrontations. Of course, it didn't work.

Despite my misgivings, I decided to call Zifferero at home and try to win him to my side.

"Dr. Hamza," he said, sounding pleasantly surprised, "it's nice to hear from you at last." We exchanged a few pleasantries, during which I parried his lively curiosity about where I was or where I'd been.

"Actually," he said after a while, "your case is assigned to my assistant, Gary Dillon. If you'll give me a few minutes, I'll call him first and let him know you've surfaced." He gave me Dillon's number.

When I reached Dillon, he was on the other line with Zifferero and put me on hold. Several moments later, he came back on the line.

"Dr. Hamza," he asked in his clipped British accent, "where are you?"

I hesitated. Dillon worked for a man too close to Iraq. To stall, I thanked him for visiting my family in Baghdad right after the London *Times* story. "It might have saved their lives, Mr. Dillon. I'll always be grateful."

"You're quite welcome," he said, adding that he looked forward to sitting down with me and getting the real story behind that episode.

"But Dr. Hamza," he said, "please tell us where you are."

I took a deep breath. "I will, but I first need you to provide me with U.N. cover. You, more than anybody, know that I'm in danger and need help."

"Yes," he said evenly.

"Is there any possibility you can put me on one of your teams? That way I'd have U.N. cover and possibly a means to get my family out."

He exhaled. "No, I'm sorry, we can't do that," he said. It was against U.N. rules to make temporary hires of defectors. It would jeopardize their official neutrality. "But I can arrange to get you here to Vienna for a debriefing. Unfortunately, the visa would be good for only a few days. After that you would have to leave." Now it was my turn to sigh. "I can't do that. It'll only endanger my family. You visited them; you know the situation there."

"Yes," he said, then shocked me with his next suggestion.

"Dr. Hamza, we more or less are convinced that this story was planted in the *Times* and that the documents they got were forged.* For us, once we report to the Security Council, the file is closed. Since that's the case, why don't you think about going back to Iraq and making those points with your government? I'm sure you would be well rewarded."

I was stunned. Go back to Iraq? Get my old job back? I could barely gather my wits enough to respond.

"I don't think so," I said, before hanging up.

I sat holding my head with both hands. I couldn't believe IAEA's policy was to advise Saddam's nuclear bombmaker to go back to Iraq—at any time, but especially not when he was right on their doorstep desperately trying to defect.

I picked up the phone and dialed.

"Mr. Zifferero," I said, "I just heard the oddest suggestion from

---

*Two weeks after the story appeared, the IAEA informed the *Times* reporter who wrote it, Jon Swain, that the documents were forgeries. But the newspaper never issued a correction. Swain says now he has "no idea" where they came from.

Gary Dillon, the inspector in charge of my case. He suggested I go back to work for Saddam. Do you agree with that?"

"Why not?" he responded lightly. "It sounds like a very reasonable suggestion to me. You'll make points with your government. They'll be happy, and you'll be back in your home. It's probably the best option you have."

What? I held the phone, unable to speak. The room seemed to spin. Whose side were these guys on?

"In any event, we should talk, " Zifferero said. "Where are you now?"

Not a chance. "Good-bye, Mr. Zifferero," I said, and hung up.

That night I wandered the streets of Budapest trying to clear my mind. I could only guess why Zifferero would want me to go back—as an icebreaker with Saddam? Saddam never gave anyone anything for free. But Gary Dillon? I couldn't figure that at all.

In any event, Plan B was out. And now I was really desperate. If much more time went by, Firas's resolve might crack, and with it, the rest of the family's.

The next day, I pulled myself together, swallowed my pride, and dialed up the Iraqi National Accord, Ayad Allawi's group, in London. I didn't know what to expect . . . except nothing.

To my surprise, a man came on the phone sounding excited to hear my voice.

"Dr. Hamza," he said, "the Americans want to talk to you."
"What?"
"The Americans, they want to talk to you. They've been looking all over for you."

Now I *knew* who had planted that story.

I stood in front of the U.S. embassy, a hulking pile of carved gray stone on a stately park near the Danube, gathering my coat tighter against the early-morning chill.

I noted the date: August 14, 1995, only a few days shy of a year since I'd escaped at dawn from Baghdad. I'd suffered so many setbacks and double-crosses over the months that now, at the moment a door was finally open, I was afraid to walk through it.

My instructions were to go to the gate and ask for "John." That was it, John. Like "Bob," maybe another cynical, insulting CIA man. Somebody wanting something for nothing, to hell with my family's lives.

"No, no," the Iraqi activist had assured me on the phone. "Don't worry, they are very interested. And they're going to help you this time."

I was skeptical. How could it be different from the last time, when "Bob" laughed me off the phone in northern Iraq?

"It's for real," he insisted. "There have been big changes. All you need to tell me is where you are, so we can arrange things."

I took a deep breath. The hell with it, I was out of options.

"I'm in Budapest," I said, giving up.

"Budapest! Fantastic!" the man exclaimed. "We thought you were in Libya. It'll be much easier to get you out from there."

I'd taken a chance, allowed myself a glimmer of hope. And now I stood outside the high, wrought-iron embassy gates. Everything rode on what happened in the next few minutes.

There was a long line of people waiting to get in. I anxiously scanned the avenue, looking for a pair of Iraqi agents who might pull up and shove me into the back of their car. When I first contacted the embassy, they told me to move to another part of Budapest right away because Saddam's agents were all over town. Now I saw a black Mercedes idling across the street. I decided to move.

I walked briskly across the broad avenue, slid through the crowd, and elbowed my way to the front of the line, catching the eye of a stocky Marine guard.

"I have an appointment with John," I shouted. "I am Dr. Hamza."

"John?" he asked. "That's it?"

"They told me just to ask for John."

"And you are?"

"Dr. Hamza," he repeated. "Hamza. Dr. Hamza. From Iraq." I looked around, nervous. I wasn't in yet.

The Marine's eyebrows shot up. "Wait here," he said.

A few minutes later, the Marine returned, followed by a friendly-looking, sandy-haired man in a well-tailored blue suit. They opened the gate.

"Welcome, Dr. Hamza," the man said casually. "Where have you been?"

END GAME

Hɪɢʜ ᴏᴠᴇʀ ᴛʜᴇ Aᴛʟᴀɴᴛɪᴄ, the CIA jet got a flash message from headquarters: Proceed to northern Iraq. Complete the clandestine exfiltration of a woman and her three children from Baghdad.

Finally, the day had come, more than a year after I slipped out of Baghdad, and three months since I'd walked into the American embassy in Budapest. Now, at last, Souham and the boys would be with me.

Far from stopping the roller coaster we'd been on, however, my arrival in the West led to a new series of shocks. The first came with news that my former boss, Saddam's son-in-law Hussein Kamel, had fled Baghdad himself, a few days after I surfaced in Budapest. Kamel, his brother, their wives—Saddam's daughters—and children and an entourage of servants and hangers-on had flown to Jordan and were busy spilling the secrets of Saddam's arms programs to the West, according to the CIA man who took me in.

And that quickly complicated my own situation, he said. "John," as the CIA man called himself, quickly informed me that I had to start talking fast. There wasn't much time, or much of anything, to bargain over, he said. Everybody at CIA headquarters in Washington was focusing on Kamel.

I could only shake my head, once again. "That may be," I finally replied. "But I knew more than what Kamel knew, and what Kamel knew about the bomb he got from me."

I looked around the embassy's high-security meeting room, the so-called bubble that was secured from hostile eavesdropping and wiretaps.

"He is of limited usefulness to you," I said. "Yes, he can give you the big picture, but he has no technical background, he has no understanding whatsoever of what we were doing. He saw the outside of the bomb, but had no idea of what was inside it." I told John how Kamel had assigned me an office to build the bomb on the top floors of one of Baghdad's swaying high-rises. He chuckled.

"Besides," I said. "Kamel has lost most of his memory from brain surgery three years ago."

John's eyes flickered. "What brain surgery?"

"He had a tumor removed," I said. The CIA man sat back, surprised. Either he hadn't been informed, or the CIA itself didn't know. I still had a few cards to play.

"He has huge gaps in his memory," I explained. "Sometimes he doesn't even recognize people he's worked with for years."

John seemed to be assessing me anew.

"I'll admit that Kamel can probably tell you a lot about the system," I continued, "about the major programs and policies. But he doesn't know the details. Actually, what I know will complement what Kamel can tell you. I can shed light on things that Kamel has no idea about."

The CIA man jotted a few notes, then looked up. "We're very eager to hear everything you have to say, Dr. Hamza. We're very happy to have you here."

He seemed to mean it.

"I believe you," I said. "Do you know what happened the first time I talked to you people?" He reacted noncommittally. When I got to the part about how "Bob" and his sidekick had snickered at my news that we'd perfected a bomb design, John was shaking his head.

"So here we are again," I said. "I'm prepared to outline all the subjects I can tell you about, but the details will have to wait until I am on U.S. soil and you've made a firm pledge to get my family out."

John sat back in exasperation. He had his own hardheads back at CIA headquarters to contend with, he indicated. I told him I was sympathetic, but my position was unchanged from the first day I got out of Iraq: resettlement for me and my family in the United States. No more, no less. Then I'd tell him everything.

He said he'd see what he could do.

Meanwhile we reviewed what subjects I could expand upon. At times it seemed no different from northern Iraq, with one difference: John treated me with respect and kindness. As the haggling continued, however, I finally disclosed that I'd prepared a fallback position. I'd visited the British embassy. When I told John a British visa would be ready for me in a week, suddenly all the roadblocks melted: The next morning an embassy car whisked me to the airport.

In mid-October, my oldest son was sitting in a Baghdad coffee shop when a deranged-looking man in rags drew close and started muttering as if he were begging for a few coins.

"Firas?" he whispered when he was close.

He drew back. The man's filthy face, torn pants, and crumbling shoes gave him the appearance of one of the thousands of homeless wandering the Baghdad streets.

The man fixed him with his eyes. "Firas?" he whispered again.

Now my son knew. As prearranged, he got up and walked out onto the sidewalk, the beggar following and jabbering incoherently. They walked around the corner to Firas's car. When it seemed no one was watching, they both got in. The man handed him a crunched-up envelope.

Firas had been waiting for this moment since I'd called him from Washington on an untraceable phone. As usual, we'd talked in our own code.

"I'm in Libya still," I'd said, "but I saw your friends Ahmad and Eqbal the other day and they asked me to say hello." Ahmad and Eqbal were two friends of his who were living in the States. It was our prearranged signal that I'd arrived safely in America. He strained to contain himself with the news.

"That's good, Papa," he'd bubbled. "That's very good."

Now, in the car, Firas raced through my letter, which began with breezy banalities and then stated, "This man is on our side." So Firas could be sure, I then reminisced over our time together in Libya, with details only he and I would know—the places we'd been, the food we'd eaten, the people he'd met with me, the quarrels we'd had. Firas finished the letter, then nodded approval to the man in the car.

"Are you ready to go?" the stranger asked, looking around nervously. Suddenly he noticed Firas staring at his hands. He had no fingernails.

"I'll tell you what happened to them some other time," he said. "Are you ready to go?"

"Yes," Firas said evenly. "We're ready. We can go tonight."

"Good," the man said. "Meet me in Mosul tomorrow at noon." He named the place.

"Are you sure you can make it?" he asked.

"Yes, of course," Firas answered. With that, the man got out and scurried away.

That night neither my wife, Souham, nor Firas slept. They paced in the darkness, watching through the curtains as the ubiquitous security agents patrolled the neighborhood. Saddam's palace was only a few blocks away. The younger boys, Sami and Zayd, slept only fitfully. Tomorrow their whole world would change, one way or another.

They were all excited, but they were also leaving everything behind—friends, relatives, house, land, money, and the personal possessions of a lifetime. Nothing, not even a photo album, not a picture, could be taken. If they were stopped, anything like that would incriminate them.

Finally, just before dawn, a taxi pulled up at the house. Souham and the three boys clambered inside with a few bags and were off. In a few minutes, they were on the outskirts of the city.

As they sped out of town, they turned and looked back at Baghdad, as I had before. Behind them, rising from the ground and towering over the rooftops, were Saddam's two huge, cast-iron forearms, holding crossed swords. The taxi roared on over the hills.

The car was a late-model American sedan, probably looted from Kuwait. But a couple hours north of Baghdad, it began to break down, a casualty of subpar Iraqi gas and oil and the lack of spare parts. The closest repair shop was in Tikrit, Saddam's hometown. The driver was a member of his clan. Luckily, though, he was just an honest, hardworking man. He drove them to Tikrit, picked up another car, and in a short time they were on their way again.

The detour made them late getting to Mosul, but they linked up at the prearranged meeting place with the Kurd who would take them over the mountains. Already, he said, he'd been scouting the region for trouble. Just to be safe, he drove them to a village up the highway, deposited them with relatives, and took a dry run to the north with a few barrels of black market gas and oil. By dawn he was back.

The Toyota Land Cruiser was again loaded with barrels. Sami, seventeen, was stowed in the back with the contraband. Firas, nervously smoking, took the passenger window. Souham sat in the middle, with Zayd on her lap, and told him to scrunch down to look even smaller. They pulled onto the highway as the day broke, heading north.

The first few checkpoints went smoothly. The smuggler had greased the palms of the guards a couple of times already, and now he added fistfuls of dinars to keep them happy. At the next checkpoint, a sentry looked quizzically at Souham and the boys, but the driver explained that he was taking his "aunt and nephews" to a family funeral in the village ahead. The guard checked for suitcases then waved the van forward.

Through the hours, the Toyota crawled up through the hills and around the valley turns, just another vehicle on the endless pulley of black market traffic between Turkey and Iraq. From time to time, Souham and the younger boys dozed. Firas, however, forced himself to stay awake, no doubt helped by the sight of the driver's fingertips, stripped of their nails in one of Saddam's jails, on the steering wheel.

Finally, the border was in sight, marked by a wide swamp. On the far side was the Kurdish zone. Trucks were being loaded and unloaded. The driver started up the Toyota and inched forward into the shallow water. Halfway across, it sank into the muck and stalled. No amount of trying could get it restarted.

The smuggler jumped out of the Toyota and began wading across the water to get help. Souham ordered the boys to get down on the floor. Back down the highway, they knew, the Iraqi army would be launching its morning patrols.

The best thing I learned when I came in from the cold is that "Bob" had left the CIA.

In fact, with every passing hour of my arrival in Germany, where I was first debriefed, the attitude of the CIA grew more trusting, friendly, and respectful. A team had flown in from Washington to hear what I had to say. And from the looks on their faces, they were no longer laughing, they were stunned. Saddam had almost completely fooled the West.

Over the next several weeks, I took them through the two-decade-long bomb program, from its origins around a dining room table in 1972 through Saddam's crash program to put a warhead on a missile on the eve of Desert Storm. And beyond.

Many of my revelations were a surprise, I discovered. Iraq had apparently persuaded U.N. inspectors that:

- Our nuclear effort had never progressed beyond basic research.
- The bomb-design center I'd built at Al-Atheer was merely a materials research facility.
- The equipment to make explosives for the bomb had been destroyed. (I informed them it had been removed a week before the Allied bombing.)

They also had no idea that Iraq had succeeded in engineering the barriers to enrich uranium using diffusion. The Hungarian connection, through which we learned to manufacture nuclear triggers using miniaturized neutron generators, was another surprise. The role of the German firms Degussa and Leybold in supplying Iraq with equipment and components was largely a blank.

Overall, the most valuable information I might have provided was on the central role Atomic Energy played in all of Saddam's programs for weapons of mass destruction. AE's part in developing and hiding biological weapons efforts was almost completely unknown.

I gave them the names and addresses of the key people still working. "Talk to the experts," I urged. "Here's where you can find them." Most, I said, would like to get out.

I had purged myself.

The helicopter landed on a hilltop in Salahiddin, one of a regular shuttle in and out of the Kurdish north. Out popped Rick Francona, a dark-haired, boyish-looking air force intelligence officer assigned to the CIA. Francona, fluent in Arabic, had spent many years in the Middle East, including an assignment as interpreter for General Norman Schwarzkopf at the cease-fire talks with the Iraqis at the end of Desert Storm. Now, he and other CIA agents were assigned to bring my family in.

And they were late.

Souham and the boys had been stranded in the swamp on the border for more than an hour, hiding on the floors of the Land Cruiser as best as they could. The sun was rising over the hills and they were easy pickings for an Iraqi patrol. Another hour passed. Finally, a squad of armed Kurdish rebels showed up on the distant shore, riding a tractor.

In what seemed like endless slow motion, they waded across the muck toward them, coming to the Toyota's rescue. Eventually a thick rope was hitched to the Land Cruiser and the rebels pulled it forward.

"Welcome to America!" the Kurds laughed when they had them on shore.

But the Americans weren't there.

After some animated discussion among the Kurds, the family was piled back into the Toyota and driven an hour north to a safe house operated by one of the rebel groups. They were put inside. The door was locked. Another night of cold, hungry, anxious waiting began.

In recent months the CIA had been struggling to unite the fractious Kurds and plotting with Saddam's top military officers to topple the regime from the inside. Neither effort was showing much promise. The Kurds had too long shown a proclivity to plot against each other in secret league with Saddam. Now the Kurds began arguing over what to do with Souham and the boys, who were not, after all, their responsibility. Night fell.

Finally, the door swung open. In walked Francona and his sidekick, a tall blond CIA man, as if they were dropping in for a beer. Firas jumped up in glee.

"Who are you guys?" he asked.

The CIA man smiled.

"We're not from around here," he cracked.

Their troubles were over, we thought. We were wrong.

The road trip through Turkey and the flight to Germany were

happy, even joyous. Francona and his CIA team couldn't have made it smoother. My family couldn't have felt more secure or welcome.

Then the bureaucrats stepped in.

November turned to December in Germany, then to January. Souham and the boys were cooped up in a CIA safe house waiting for clearance to come into the States. The winter winds and pewter skies dragged down their spirits. While I trudged off for lengthy debriefings for the CIA near Washington, they spent hours idly watching Turkish-language TV, playing cards and video games. Once a week a CIA escort dropped by and took them out to dinner, but more frequent outings were discouraged. Iraqi agents were assumed to be scouring the city for them.

For security reasons, they were not allowed to use the safe house telephone, so Souham and the boys had to arrange to call me from public booths. After a while, the arrangement became too tiresome.

Weeks more passed. The delay was a crushing disappointment. Our nerves stretched to the breaking point when the INS informed us that Firas wouldn't be able to enter the United States with the rest of the family, on the grounds that he was no longer a minor. Later, the FBI would also reject our fingerprint cards four times as technically unacceptable.

Finally, however, the doors creaked open.

February 12, 1996: I waited nervously in the Delta terminal at National Airport, my eyes searching desperately for a familiar face in the long stream of passengers.

Finally, I saw them. Firas, the tallest, then Souham, smiling weakly, and then the two boys, Sami and Zayd. Their eyes locked on mine, mine on theirs.

"Papa!" Firas whooped. "Papa, Papa!" Sami and Zayd ran forward into my arms. Tears ran down Souham's face, then mine. We held each other tight. The crowd swirled around us. We didn't care.

Our long, long family nightmare was over.

Life in America exceeded even our expectations, notwithstanding the precautions we've had to take to foil any attempt by Saddam at retribution. One thing we know: Saddam never gives up.

But after four years, we've begun to relax. If our sons are out late, we no longer worry that they have been picked up at a roadblock and disappeared into Saddam's jails. It is the American Dream we're living—free of fear, with unlimited opportunity for anybody who's willing to work.

All of our boys, in fact, have flourished, especially Firas. After everything he went through for me, he probably also deserves it the most. With a high-paying job as a computer consultant, a new car, apartment, and good friends, he couldn't be happier. But he never forgets the freedom he has, or his friends in Iraq. My other sons are following closely in his footsteps.

My wife yearns for the sisters she left behind, but now can't imagine living anywhere else. Her roots in southern Iraq were modest; she entered into an arranged marriage; she lived the high life as the spouse of a palace intimate. Now she's a suburban American housewife who enjoys Oprah Winfrey (and Howard Stern, much to my amazement) and downloads foreign recipes from the Internet. She's seen it all.

Many others we knew in Baghdad have taken far different paths.

The original envoys Saddam sent to inveigle me into designing a bomb in 1971 are both out of the program now. Moyesser al-Mallah, the voluble head of the nuclear program, retired comfortably in 1990. Husham Sharif, his glib, scheming deputy, is now chief architect for the presidential palaces that Saddam has built on the backs of the suffering Iraqi people.

Jaffar Dhia Jaffar, the fascinating aristocrat who never quite managed to enrich uranium despite Saddam's billions and the lash of the jailers, has stayed on in Baghdad, a prisoner in a gilded cage. After U.N. inspectors destroyed his magnetic enrichment plants, Saddam shelved him in a back room at the Ministry of Industry and Military Industrialization. With nothing to do, he asked for a personal computer and began spending his days playing games. The word from Baghdad today is that he's being treated for severe depression.

General Amir al-Saadi, the genial brains behind Saddam's weapons programs, remains a presidential confidant and adviser. A loyal, first-rate technocrat, he is busy at work planning the future of Iraq's military industries, particularly in chemical warfare and missiles.

Meanwhile, I have lost track of many dear friends. My friend Muafaq reportedly is still hiding out in Turkey.

Atomic Energy has been through several changes since Desert Storm. Its last chief, the oleaginous Humam al-Ghafour, became Saddam's minister of information and thus one of the mustachioed regulars on Baghdad TV.

Today, AE is a shell of what it was in the gold rush days of the 1980s, but its new chairman is typical of the party loyalists who stand ready to do Saddam's bidding. I have little doubt that Fadhil Al-Janaby, a Baathist civil engineer, would not hesitate to arm the bomb when Saddam has sufficient fuel and gives the green light. None of the old hands who might have reservations remains.

And then there is the horrifying fate of my old boss, Hussein Kamel. The world was astonished when Kamel decided to return to Baghdad five months after defecting to Jordan in 1996—and was, of course, promptly murdered. Live by the sword, die by the sword, goes the timeless adage, and nowhere does it go more swiftly than in Iraq. Perhaps I am one of the few who can understand the seductive power of Saddam's pledge to Kamel that "all would be forgiven" if he returned to the fold. After all, that was the message that Firas brought from Saddam to me in Libya. Unlike Kamel, however, I wasn't suffering from the removal of a brain tumor. My judgment of Saddam was, and remains, unclouded: He never forgives; he never forgets.

What to do about Saddam?

We've failed miserably in removing him, and containment hasn't been especially effective. A decade after Desert Storm, Saddam seems as strongly entrenched as ever, patiently rebuilding his stocks of chemical and biological weapons, and waiting for the chance to deploy a nuclear bomb. Washington, in fact, seems ambivalent about removing him, fearing what might fill the vacuum.

In the meantime, I have a modest proposal, based on my own personal experience: The CIA can, and must, make it easier for scientists like myself to get out of Iraq. Stripped of his brain trust, Saddam would no longer be able to build and maintain his arsenal of weapons of mass destruction.

If the United States cannot—or wishes not to—get rid of Saddam, and if it is playing a losing hand at international arms inspections, there's only one alternative left, which is to induce the escape of his experts. Deserted by his scientists, Saddam would still be a loathsome tyrant, but his threat to the rest of the world would be severely diminished. Moreover, since the West has repeatedly failed to overthrow him and shows no promise of doing it soon, it's the only policy that makes sense.

This is not a new idea, but a proposal to reinvigorate a tactic that worked so well during the cold war. For forty years the United States actively encouraged defections from the Soviet Union and its communist allies. The CIA stood ready to help them. Defectors were quickly paroled into the States and resettled with financial assistance and new jobs. They were invaluable in keeping the West informed about the Soviet weapons programs.

The Soviet Union is long gone, but new threats have arisen, not just from Iraq, but from an array of states with clandestine programs to acquire weapons of mass destruction—Iran, North Korea, Pakistan, and India. Penetrating the secrecy surrounding these programs has proved extremely difficult, as the CIA's apparent surprise at India's nuclear tests and North Korea's ballistic missile firings have shown.

Had the CIA approached me with an offer of safe haven during one of my nuclear shopping trips abroad in the 1980s, I would have jumped into its arms. But they not only ignored me, they rebuffed and even ridiculed my pleas for help in 1994. One can only imagine how differently things would have turned out had the CIA listened when I first picked up the phone.

What's past is past. My torturous journey had a happy ending. But I left behind scores of unhappy Iraqi scientists. Our counterparts in other rogue states, meanwhile, are laboring away on their own weapons of mass destruction. Most of them, I am sure, would like to get out. It is the civilized world's urgent duty to help them.

APPENDIX

In 1971, on the orders of Saddam Hussein, we set out to build a nuclear bomb. Our goal was to construct a device roughly equivalent to the bomb the United States dropped on Hiroshima in 1945, that is to say, with the explosive power of twenty thousand tons of TNT. The first one would be a crude device, a sphere about four feet in diameter, too big and heavy for a missile warhead but suitable for a demonstration test or, as we discovered to our horror, Saddam's plan to drop one unannounced on Israel. As I have recounted in detail in the text, the crash program to build the first bomb came to an abrupt halt with the looming Allied campaign to take back Kuwait and invade Iraq. All the evidence indicates, however, that Saddam has not forsworn his goal to make Iraq a nuclear-armed power.

From the beginning, Saddam was ambitious. He set a production target of six bombs a year, which meant that Iraq would have surpassed China as a nuclear power by the end of the 1990s, and possibly sooner, had he not invaded Kuwait and triggered Desert Storm.

We had a vast number of people working in the clandestine nuclear effort. At its peak in 1993–1994, the bomb program employed more than two thousand engineers. The mechanical design team alone numbered more than two hundred engineers. We had at least three hundred employees holding Ph.D.s in such fields as physics, chemistry, biology, and chemical and nuclear engineering. More than eight hundred employees had master's degrees in the same fields. With the addition of thousands of technicians, the total workforce employed in making a bomb was in excess of twelve thousand people—twice the size of the Argonne National

Laboratory, a principal U.S. nuclear weapons center. In the last three years of the 1980s, expenditures on the bomb and bomb-related programs exceeded ten billion dollars.

How close did we get to perfecting a bomb? Very. We had a device capable of producing a nuclear explosion equivalent to a few kilotons of TNT. Without a test, we could not know exactly what the yield would have been. However, the engineering estimates and simulation exercises we conducted put our device in the range of from one to three kilotons.

What we lacked was a complete nuclear core. We had more than twenty-five kilograms of bomb-grade uranium fuel rescued from Osirak, the French reactor bombed by Israeli jets in 1981. Twelve kilograms were 93 percent–enriched uranium, and about fourteen kilograms were enriched to 80 percent. Additional uranium was available from the irradiated fuel of our Russian reactor (although it would have been too hot to handle). Altogether, this would have been more than sufficient to produce the eighteen to twenty kilograms needed for a bomb. The advent of Desert Storm, however, did not leave sufficient time for the uranium metal to be extracted from the fuel. Instead, Saddam ordered his Special Security Organization to take possession of the bomb components and hide them from outside inspectors.

We had adopted what's called a levitation design, which leaves a gap around the bomb core and surrounding components to create a bigger bang per kilogram than other designs we could have managed. After Desert Storm, Iraq denied that it had pursued such a design, but recent evidence suggests that it pursued levitation, experimenting with flying metal plates and materials such as plastic and foams that can be used to space the explosive gap. During my tenure as designer of the bomb, we obtained a hot isostatic press to shape these and other bomb components by gluing powders under high temperatures and pressures.

Iraq misled the inspectors in several other areas. It lied about the strength of the shaped charges, known as explosive lenses, that we had manufactured. Iraq admitted only to having RDX/TNT explosives. In fact, Iraq had imported three hundred tons of HMX, a more powerful kind of explosive, which was used to make lighter and more powerful lenses than those that were declared. In my time, we carried out several experiments using a combination of explosives that included HMX. In any case Iraq did not reveal even the lower-power lenses for inspection, nor the equipment used to manufacture them. They were hidden in military camps around the country.

Meanwhile, the bridge-wire explosive caps we manufactured to trigger the lens explosions were as good or better than those used in the Manhattan Project. The fast electronics we learned in Poland were used to supply electrical pulses to the caps. We achieved a "jitter," or total time consumed in the almost simultaneous explosions of all the caps, of 0.1 microseconds—well within the tolerances required for a successful nuclear detonation.

We also managed to cast our own uranium-metal sphere, required for the bomb core, at four inches in diameter. Iraq concealed this achievement as well from U.N. inspectors, declaring only that it had made one sphere and four hemispheres at a smaller diameter. At the same time, Iraqi officials refused to produce even these for inspection, thus masking the quality of our purified uranium metal and the precision of the casting process from our own furnace, which was also disassembled and hidden.

Because the weight and size of our device made it too big to be mounted on a missile, Iraqi scientists pursued the development of beryllium and graphite reflectors that would be many pounds lighter than the uranium metal reflectors we originally planned. This, too, was hidden from inspectors.

We were also able to manufacture our own neutron initiators from polonium produced from our Russian reactor. Because they are radioactive sources with a short shelf life, they have almost certainly expired by now, but Iraq could replace them with its own neutron generator or by buying polonium or plutonium on the international black market. Neutron generators can be manufactured by reverse engineering those used by oil companies to detect oil depths during exploration. The challenge is to turn them out on a smaller scale suitable for a deliverable bomb, which Iraq did admit was within its means. Another option for Iraq, however, would be to employ a gun-type bomb design of the kind that was used by South Africa and doesn't require a neutron initiator, but it would require more uranium for the bomb core.

Acquiring or producing bomb-grade uranium was always the biggest challenge to our program. Iraq at first maintained that it had failed to enrich uranium by the diffusion method, but after my 1994 defection, it conceded it had solved this problem. U.S. satellites could easily detect the building of full-scale diffusion plants, with four thousand stages. Therefore, Iraq would most likely pursue the short-cascade options I designed and which are more easily dispersed and hidden in a dozen or more units. Short cascades also can be combined with another enrichment method, electromagnetic isotope separation, or EMIS, to produce bomb-grade uranium. As with many other subjects, U.N. inspectors were surprised at how far along Iraq was in achieving this goal. Supposedly, the magnets manufactured for EMIS were destroyed, but more could easily be made using precision equipment that was never declared or turned over to the inspectors. Another possibility would be for Iraq to use the centrifuge technology supplied clandestinely by West German scientists in the late 1980s.

Ironically, the first lessons we got on enrichment methods came from the Manhattan Project's own reports, which were long ago declassified. I found stacks of them in the dusty archives of our own Atomic Energy Commission, on a shelf labeled "This is a gift of the U.S. Atomic Energy Commission." Apparently they were given to Iraq at the start of its peaceful energy program in 1956.

Another option for obtaining bomb-grade uranium, of course, is simply to buy it on the black market. The most likely sources are disenchanted, unemployed, underpaid, or simply corruptible officials in Russia or other nuclear-armed states. Another possible supplier is Serbia, which clandestinely aided Iraq's missile programs in the past and is now said to possess fifty kilograms of bomb-grade uranium.

The X Factor in Iraq's nuclear equation is the availability of foreign, and particularly Russian, brainpower to solve remaining technological bottlenecks, if any, and improve the state of production and manufacture of the bomb's key components. During my visit to the crumbling Soviet Union in 1990, scores of Russian nuclear scientists virtually begged me for jobs in Iraq, but the onset of Desert Storm postponed their recruitment. By the time I defected in 1994, however, some Russian scientists were at work in Iraq on chemical weapons and others were expected to join them in other programs.

If some are in fact in Iraq now, they would be capable of producing a more workable system or making more powerful, and a bigger number of, atomic weapons.

In any case, I have no doubt that Iraq is pursuing the nuclear option. For a while after the Gulf War, the presence of outside inspectors and the economic embargo slowed down the pace. But at this writing, U.N. inspectors have been barred for more than a year, while oil revenues have been steadily increasing. The unity of the coalition that kicked Saddam out of Kuwait, meanwhile, has been shattered. The flow of dual-use imports to Iraq has been allowed to increase, while Russia, China, and France are pushing for a complete lifting of the embargo. If they succeed, Saddam could easily cross the nuclear bomb finish line.

This is a frightening prospect. A nuclear-armed Saddam is not only a menace to the West on his own but also a trigger for a new arms race among all the countries of the Middle East. Israel already has a nuclear stockpile; Iran is in hot pursuit of its own. With Saddam's arrival as a nuclear power, it would not be out of the question for Egypt, Syria, and even Turkey to pursue the same path.

And that is a nightmare. Saddam must be kept in a box or, better still, removed.

INDEX

INDEX

army, Iraqi:
  deserters from, 247, 254
  officer corps of, 173–75
  Shiite conscripts in, 198
Atomic Energy Commission (AEC),
    Iraqi, 18
  biological weapons and, 326
  bombing of headquarters of,
    245–46
  Computer Center of, 259–60
  computer controversy at, 56, 60
  and exemptions from military serv-
    ice, 122, 153
  Group Number Four of, 259
  Hamza's investigation of, 187–88
  Hamza's work with, 21–23, 49,
    54–56, 117, 120–21, 123–24
  and International Center of Theoreti-
    cal Physics, 88–89
  Jaffar's return to, 137–38
  loss of engineers from, 132–34
  nuclear bomb program of, 65, 67,
    165, 167
  purchases of sensitive material by,
    159
  Research and Development Office
    and, 140–41
  Saddam's control of, 77–78
  Saddam's denouncement of leader-
    ship of, 130
  Saddam's meeting with, 90–93
  Saddam's visit to and arrests at,
    115–17
  security measures of, 89–90, 92,
    124–26, 143–50
Atomic Energy Commission, U.S.,
    69
Atoms for Peace program, 69
Attia, Ali, 54–55, 61
Austria, 221
Ayoub, Ghazi, 93
Ayoubi, Adnan, 262
Azawi, Dafir al-, 224, 259
Aziz, Tariq, 87, 264
  assassination attempt on, 107
  in Soviet Union, 232

Baath Party, 41, 44, 48, 54–55, 58–59,
    61, 149
  hostility of, to Israel, 63
Babylon, archaeological dig at, 163
Babylon Software, 259–60
Badr industrial center, 190

Baghdad, 53
  bombing of, 245, 249
  in Iran-Iraq war, 122–23
  Republican Palace in, 169
  Saddam's rebuilding of, 163–64
Baghdad Pact, 41, 43
Baghdad University, 41, 42, 163, 241
  Hamza's teaching at, 56, 243
Baker, James, 243
Bakr, Ahmad Hassan al-, 44, 55, 90
  Saddam and, 110–11
Balasan Valley, gas attack on, 200
ballistic missiles, 193
Barbouti, Anas, 292–93
Barbouti, Ihsan, 293–94
Barzani, Massoud, 280
Bawi, Ibrahim, 250, 261–62
Bazoft, Farzad, 238
BBC, Hamza's death reported on, 296
Begin, Menachem, 124, 127
Bhutto, Ali, 104
biological weapons, see chemical and
    biological weapons, Iraqi
black market, 27
  in Kurdish area, 280
  in plutonium, 217, 335
  in polonium, 335
  in uranium, 217, 336
  U.S. exposure of, 224–25
  in West Germany, 209–10, 211–12,
    216
Boston, Mass., Hamza's visit to,
    158–61
bribery, 27, 28
bridge-wire explosive caps, 335
Brown Boveri, 134
Bull, Gerald, 225
Bunnia, Mahmoud, 177–79
Bush, George:
  and Iraqi invasion of Kuwait, 236,
    285
  Shiite uprising and, 251

cameras, for testing explosive charges,
    210, 221
Canada, defections to, 264
cancer:
  among engineers and scientists, 246
  post–Gulf War increase in, 262–63
capacitors:
  black market operations in, 224–25
  Iraqi manufacture of, 226
Caramel fuel, 133

340

Nuclear Nonproliferation Treaty, 74,
116, 125
nuclear reactors:
bombing of, 128–31, 246
French, 80–81, 83, 103, 105,
109–10, 120
in Libya, 290
proliferation of, 74
Russian, 69, 74, 80, 105, 119, 246,
290, 334
sabotage of, in France, 109–10
Nuclear Research Center, Iraqi, 54, 55,
61, 78, 88, 119
nuclear tests, Indian, 331
nuclear trigger, 227
Numan, Ahmed, 263

Obeidi, Hadi al-, 94–97, 100, 187, 196
Observer, 238
oil:
Iraqi financial difficulties and, 236
Iraqi revenues from, 337
neutron generators for drilling for,
234
prices of, 75
oil wells, burning of, 250
Olympics Committee, Iraqi, 178
Omar (Iraqi in West Germany), 212–16,
220
Operation Provide Comforts, 23
opposition groups, Iraqi, *see* Iraqi exile
opposition groups
Osirak nuclear reactor, 120
bombing of, 130
uranium salvaged from, 237, 334
Osiris nuclear reactor, 82–83

Pakistan:
nuclear technology of, 74, 104
uranium enrichment method of,
130
Palestine Liberation Organization
(PLO), 50–52
commando training camp, 255–57,
258
Iraqi expulsion of, 159
Pan Am 103 bombing, 293
pan-Arabism, 42
passports, false, 281
Pelletron accelerator, 99
Peoples Democratic Party of Kurdistan
(PDK), 280
Peoples Democratic Union (PUK), 280

Persian Gulf states, loans to Iraq by,
236
Persian Gulf War, *see* Gulf War
Philippines, nuclear technology of, 74
plasma focus device, 225, 226
plasma physics, 225
PLO, *see* Palestine Liberation Organization
plutonium, 69, 70, 217, 335
from secret reactor, 120
poison gases, 201, 227, 294
poisons, experiments with, 199
Poland, Hamza's trip to, 225–26
polonium, 237, 335
prisoners:
biological and chemical weapons
experiments on, 188, 199
Shiite, 198–99
Project 182, 120
public executions, 189
public funds, Saddam's use of, 93

Qaisy, Basil al-, 246
Qaisy, Riyadh al-, 155
Qassim, Abdul Karim, 43, 44, 59

Rabah (Iraqi in Libya), 294, 300, 301
radiation sickness, 237
radiation weapons, 175
Ramadan, Taha Yasin, 113, 202
Rashid, Salman, 133–34, 150
Rassool, Abdul-Rahman Abdul, 134
RDX/TNT explosives, 334
Reagan administration:
Iran-Iraq war and, 153, 186
and missile sales to Iran, 235
refugee camps, 31
Republican Guards, Iraqi, 173, 252
Republican Palace, Baghdad, 169
Research and Development Office, Iraqi,
140–42, 167
Revolutionary Command Council, 194
Revolutionary Council, 48, 55
Ricks, Roy, 221–22
roads and highways, in Iraq, 24, 25
Rome, Hamza's visit to, 146–47, 148
Rumaila oil field, 228
Russia:
and embargo on Iraq, 337
Iraqi recruitment of nuclear scientists
from, 336–37
Kuwait invasion and, 242
see also Soviet Union